BECOMING AMERICAN

A Political Memoir

CARY D. LOWE

Black Rose Writing | Texas

©2020, 2023 by Cary D. Lowe
All rights reserved. No part of this book may be reproduced, stored in a retrieval system or transmitted in any form or by any means without the prior written permission of the publishers, except by a reviewer who may quote brief passages in a review to be printed in a newspaper, magazine or journal.

The author grants the final approval for this literary material.

Second Edition

The author has tried to recreate events, locales and conversations from his/her memories. In order to maintain anonymity in some instances, the author may have changed the names of individuals and places. The author may have changed some identifying characteristics and details such as physical properties, occupations and places of residence.

ISBN: 978-1-68433-462-9
PUBLISHED BY BLACK ROSE WRITING
www.blackrosewriting.com

Printed in the United States of America
Suggested Retail Price (SRP) $19.95

Becoming American is printed in Sabon

*As a planet-friendly publisher, Black Rose Writing does its best to eliminate unnecessary waste to reduce paper usage and energy costs, while never compromising the reading experience. As a result, the final word count vs. page count may not meet common expectations.

AUTHOR'S INTRODUCTION

Becoming American is a journey taken by millions of people, each in their own way, based on their individual and family experiences. My story is built on the foundation of my parents' stories—how one survived the Holocaust and the other escaped it, even as many of our relatives were killed by the Nazis.

Countless others influenced me on this journey and participated in shaping my story: the intelligence agents who were my father's colleagues in post-war Europe; my Austrian nanny Herma and her family; my teachers and classmates in Europe and the United States; my colleagues in a score of political organizations; editors at several newspapers; writing instructors at various universities; and friends and relatives who provided encouragement.

I began writing this book after a trip I took with my daughter in search of our family's roots in Eastern Europe and particularly a cemetery outside Prague where my paternal great-grandparents were buried. That trip stirred up the memories which became the heart of this book. My recall of people and events from my childhood astonished me. Memories of more recent events came back easily. I initially wrote a series of independent stories about important times in my life. It soon became apparent that these stories formed a thread with an increasingly important theme—the experience of becoming an American and the meaning of being an American.

During the time that I worked on the original version of this book, and now this revised version, I participated in the San Diego Professional Writers Group, whose members regularly reviewed and critiqued my writing. Mark Jackson, Heidi Langbein Allen, Margaret Lang, Tim Kane, Lee Polevoi, Jim Riffel, Jack Innis, and Bonnie Bracken provided me with invaluable input crucial in refining my story and preparing it for publication. I also want to acknowledge and thank the staff at Black Rose Writing for enabling me to share this book with the rest of you.

BECOMING AMERICAN

CONTENTS

FOREWORD	
CHAPTER 1 - THE SEARCH	1
CHAPTER 2 - IN HITLER'S SHADOW	25
CHAPTER 3 - THE ROAD TO VIENNA RUNS THROUGH MOSCOW	37
CHAPTER 4 - THE COUNTERINTELLIGENCE MEN	42
CHAPTER 5 - REAL AMERICANS	48
CHAPTER 6 - DIGNITY IN A DISPLACED PERSONS CAMP	59
CHAPTER 7 - MOVING ON	63
CHAPTER 8 - SURVIVAL AMID THE RUINS	68
CHAPTER 9 - TEACHERS, GAMBLERS, AND SPIES	73
CHAPTER 10 - DIFFERENT KINDS OF AMERICANS	80
CHAPTER 11 - THE RUSSIANS ARE COMING	85
CHAPTER 12 - ON THE ROAD	96
CHAPTER 13 - REDEMPTION	110
CHAPTER 14 - A NEGRO GENERAL?	115
CHAPTER 15 - WHAT WOULD JOHN WAYNE DO?	120
CHAPTER 16 – COMING TO AMERICA (BUT NOT QUITE LEAVING EUROPE)	128
CHAPTER 17 - REBELLION	137
CHAPTER 18 - IT'S MORE THAN ROCK AND ROLL	143
CHAPTER 19 - THE BOYS OF AUTUMN AND WINTER	147
CHAPTER 20 - BECOMING OFFICIALLY AMERICAN	151
CHAPTER 21 - BECOMING EDUCATED AND POLITICAL	155
CHAPTER 22 - ANCHORS AWEIGH	170
CHAPTER 23 - GETTING BACK TO THE WORLD	180
CHAPTER 24 - LAW AND DISORDER	186
CHAPTER 25 - A DIFFERENT KIND OF LAW	199
CHAPTER 26 - FOUR BIG MOMENTS	207
CHAPTER 27 - A FRESH START—TOM AND JANE AND CED	215
CHAPTER 28 - MAKING A BIGGER IMPACT	225
CHAPTER 29 - BACK TO THE FUTURE	235
CHAPTER 30 - UN-AMERICAN?	240
CHAPTER 31 - MEDIA STARDOM CALLS	252
CHAPTER 32 - THE AMERICAN DREAM	256
CHAPTER 33 – THE FIRST AMERICANS	278
CHAPTER 34 - END OF THE SEARCH	282
CHAPTER 35 - AMERICAN AS ...	287
ABOUT THE AUTHOR	

FOREWORD

I met Cary Lowe over dinner at the home of a mutual writer friend. Hearing him share details of his family's experience, I immediately saw parallels to what happened to my own family, as I described in my memoir *The Choice*. His mother survived the war in hiding in Slovakia, while most of her family perished in Nazi concentration camps. His father narrowly escaped from Vienna to the United States, returning after the war to work for the prosecution at the Nuremburg War Crimes Tribunal. He went on to a career with US intelligence agencies, beginning in occupied Austria shortly after the war.

Cary was born during that time, growing up there and in Germany. As a result of his father's work, he was increasingly exposed to Americans and to American culture. Even before his family immigrated to the US., Cary, in his early teens, became interested in John F. Kennedy's 1960 presidential campaign. Campaigning for Kennedy among classmates at a military school in Germany launched him into the excitement of American politics. What especially impressed me about Cary was how that early experience grew into a lifelong commitment to immerse himself in American culture and do all he could to sustain and improve it.

Cary became a US citizen at age seventeen. In college, he worked on Robert Kennedy's 1968 presidential campaign, inspired by its platform of altruism and public service. Following graduation, he served as an officer in the US Navy, something he had aspired to since childhood, but clashed with the military over the Vietnam War. His concern that the war was undermining American values and leadership led him to work for George McGovern's 1972 presidential campaign.

While attending law school and graduate school, and embarking on a legal career, Cary's interest in political activism grew more intense. He co-founded People's College of Law, a law school for political activists in Los Angeles. As a public interest lawyer, he represented successful efforts at reform in the political, financial and development worlds. He helped create the Campaign for Economic Democracy, a statewide political organization led by Tom Hayden. He then served as an adviser and consultant to California Governor Jerry Brown. Finally, he went on to teach at the University of Southern California and other major California universities, and to write columns for the *Los Angeles Times* and other leading newspapers. All of this enabled him to have an impact on American politics and society to which most immigrants can only aspire.

Cary's experiences—his clashes with authority and his successes in achieving reforms—made him a highly engaged citizen. Yet, as much as he loved the values and freedom of his adopted country, he couldn't forget the culture in which he was raised and which his family had left behind. Even as he became increasingly American, he yearned to remain tied to the people and places associated with his earlier years in Europe. That desire eventually led him to travel with his daughter to reconnect to those roots, and especially to embark on an adventure in search of the rural cemetery in the Czech Republic where his paternal grandparents were buried.

Most immigrants seek to retain connections to their original cultures while also embracing American culture. Even as we continue to favor our native foods, dress and customs, we become engaged in the social, economic and political dimensions of American life—sometimes more than native-born Americans, as Cary's own experience illustrates.

Virtually all Americans, if not immigrants themselves, are descendants of immigrants. But most have forgotten, or perhaps never knew, their own families' experiences in coming here and becoming Americanized. By contrast, Cary's memoir takes us from his childhood in post-war Europe through the entire arc of his Americanization, all while experiencing both the virtues and the failings of his new country.

The world today is awash with people seeking places of refuge—more than at any time since World War II. And the citizens of the countries in which they are finding refuge—particularly the United States—are wondering whether these immigrants can ever assimilate and are increasingly resistant to welcoming more of them. In such a time, we need stories that illustrate how much immigrants want to become part of the fabric of their adopted countries and how successfully they can make important contributions.

In this book, Cary provides just such a narrative. In relating his unique but truly American story, Cary also reflects the experience of millions of other immigrants, and makes that experience understandable, interesting and unthreatening to many more native-born Americans.

Cary Lowe emerged from his journey as a proud and involved American. But one who, like me and innumerable others, continues to feel a strong connection to his roots. This story illuminates the immigrant experience and should be read by anyone interested in the meaning of becoming an American.

Edith Eger, Ph.D.
La Jolla, California
Author of *The Choice*

CHAPTER 1
THE SEARCH

Growing up in postwar Austria, my greatest hope was someday to become an American. A real American, like the khaki-clad soldiers occupying the country or the cowboys in the westerns at the local cinema. My father, a refugee from Vienna who worked on the Nuremberg war crimes military tribunal, promised me that hope would be fulfilled one day. What I didn't realize then was that becoming American would cut me off from my roots. Many years later, after my parents and my brother had died, I resolved to restore that connection.

* * *

On a sunny autumn afternoon in 1997, I arrived with my nine-year-old daughter at the entrance of a long-closed Jewish cemetery near Strakonice in the countryside south of Prague. Thirty-five years after my family had left Europe for America, a search worthy of Indiana Jones had brought me and Coralea here from our home in Los Angeles. Inside, I hoped to find the graves of my paternal great-grandparents.

Stepping out of the car into a light breeze, I felt the momentary burst of elation of a marathon runner crossing the finish line. Then reality interrupted. Pursing my lips, I turned to Coralea.

"I just hope this is the right cemetery," I said. "Aunt Mimi told me only that it was near Strakonice, but she didn't remember anything more. It's been a long time since she was here."

"It has to be the right one," Coralea responded with the certainty of youth.

Six-foot stucco-encased walls and eight-foot wrought-iron gates blocked our way. If I could get in, would I find the graves? How would I read Hebrew inscriptions on the headstones?

Author at gate of Jewish Cemetery, Strakonice, 2005

I felt as nervous as when I stood before a federal judge to take my oath of United States citizenship at the age of seventeen. Clasping Coralea's left hand, I took a step toward the gates, then another and another, with her in tow, until the gates loomed over us like sentinels. An ancient-looking lock the size of my fist secured chains wrapped around the innermost bars. I searched for a sign with information on how to gain entry. A musty smell, a combination of rust and fallen leaves, momentarily caught my attention. Trembling, I reached out with my left hand, grasped the rough bars, and shook them. I knew I would not be entering through those gates.

"We've come so far," I said. "We've got to get in there." Yet, the graves beyond the gates seemed out of reach.

I thought of the stories of my father's narrow escape from Vienna on the eve of World War II, of my mother's years in hiding during the war and her harrowing escape, and of their improbable return to Europe for the Nuremberg trials. I recalled the similarly amazing stories of survival told by nearly everyone I knew in my childhood. As my father said, "If they didn't have an amazing story, they wouldn't be here to tell it."

Turning to Coralea, I said, "I wish my parents could be here with us."

"Especially grandma," she replied with a sigh. "She wanted to bring me back here so much."

Closing my eyes, I searched for an answer. My thoughts rushed back over the unlikely path that had led me to this time and place.

I recalled my childhood in Austria, just a few hours' drive away. The Iron Curtain had blocked us off from our roots for years just as the cemetery walls threatened to do now. Although the slaughter was over, the guns were silent, and the armies mostly had gone home, I lived amid the aftermath of the war—the bombed cities being rebuilt, the Hitler birthplace that cast a cloud over my hometown, my refugee nanny Herma, displaced persons in squatters' camps, and concentration camp survivors piecing their lives back together.

I remembered my first interactions with Americans—the military occupiers, the intelligence agents that gathered at our home and told wild tales, and my childhood friends in Austria and later in Germany. And the combination of excitement and apprehension I felt later, realizing I was becoming gradually Americanized. I marveled at how immigrating and becoming an American citizen had launched me into a life of political involvement in my adopted country.

Most of all, I thought about how much those experiences had changed my life. I had evolved from a German-speaking, Austrian-born child of war survivors into an English-speaking American, eagerly drawn into a new and exciting culture. What I experienced and witnessed in the years after the war had shaped how I viewed the world, how I interacted with people, and how I identified myself.

In becoming Americanized, however, I had lost much of my connection to those early years and to my family's places of origin. They had receded behind the more recent people and places of my American experience.

Opening my eyes brought me back to the present. The gates seemed even more ominous. Still holding my hand, Coralea looked up at me expectantly. I peered between the bars at the rows of headstones. The closest ones looked ancient, like those in the old Jewish cemetery in Prague, with weathered, barely legible Hebrew lettering. Behind them stood newer markers, taller and more ornate.

Weeds and grass had so overgrown much of the cemetery that I wondered when anyone had visited last and opened those gates. Whatever I might find inside, I could not imagine being denied after coming this far. I struggled to figure out our next step until Coralea interrupted my thoughts.

"You can do it, Dad," she said. "You found this place. You can find a way in."

***

Two weeks earlier, Coralea and I were at home in Los Angeles packing, preparing to leave for Europe, when my elderly aunt Mimi called from Louisiana. My late father's older sister, she had married and moved to the South soon after their family escaped from Vienna to New York in 1939 on the eve of the war.

"Please do one very important thing for me," Mimi pleaded in her still-strong Viennese accent. "Find the graves of your great-grandparents and see that they are alright. You will find them in the old Jewish cemetery near Strakonice. I haven't seen it since '39. It's in the next town from the one where they lived, the house in the photo you got from your father."

I knew the photo well. It showed a two-story, stucco home in the village of Volenice. My father took the picture in 1949, just before the Iron Curtain came down, the last time anyone in the family could visit there. Both siblings treasured it as their last connection to my father's birthplace and to a time before the Holocaust tore the family from its roots.

Loewy family home, Volenice, 1949

Mimi had recently turned eighty-five and did not expect to see her homeland again. She was the oldest living relative on my father's side of the family and suffered from diabetes and heart disease. My father had died ten years earlier. Her husband, Eugene, also was dead.

I hadn't seen Mimi since her last visit with my parents a dozen years before, but we talked occasionally by phone. We kept our conversations brief, just catching up on family news. This night, she wanted to talk more. She reminisced about her and my father's idyllic summers at their grandparents' farm, feeding the chickens and bringing sandwiches to workers in the field.

Then she grew serious again. She spoke slowly, her breathing heavy.

"I've lost so much. The good life we once had in Vienna. My parents, my brother, my husband, all gone. I don't know how much time I have left. I want to know that something of our family survived there."

"How will I find the cemetery?" I asked. "Does it have a name? Can you describe the location?"

After a long pause, she replied with a tone of resignation, "I can't remember. It's been too long. When you get there, just ask. I'm sure people will know."

"I'll try my best," I promised. Then we hung up.

I resumed helping Coralea pack. We planned to travel light for the two-week trip—just her pink backpack, my blue nylon shoulder bag, and a single carry-on suitcase.

This trip was a long time coming. With each loss of a family member, I thought more and more about how I wound up so far from where my family began and about the unpredictable path I had taken to become an American. Coralea's birth had triggered even greater interest on my part in rediscovering my family heritage—the places where I lived as a child, the key places in my parents' survival of the Holocaust, and places that figured further back in our family stories.

Coralea loved hearing those stories. We often hiked together on weekends, in wilderness parks near our previous home in Laguna Hills or in the Anza-Borrego desert, and we talked as we walked. The more I told her, the more memories surfaced. I recalled my first realization that I was not an American and my longing to become one. By the time I was her age, I had started on that journey. Now I wanted both of us to reconnect more deeply with the people and places I described to her.

I had no hesitation about taking Coralea to Europe. She had been traveling since she was an infant, visiting friends and family in Texas, Louisiana, and Colorado, and vacationing in Hawaii and Mexico.

I first broached the idea of a family trip back to Europe when Coralea was six. I wanted my mother, Valerie, to come with us, since she still spoke fluent German and Czech, and presumably could locate places from her past. She resisted at first. During my own youth, she avoided talking about her early years in Europe, especially about the loss of her family and her experiences hiding during the war, but that too changed after Coralea was born.

My mother lived near her only grandchild's elementary school. She often picked up Coralea after school, spending time with her until I stopped by on my way home from work. One day, after letting myself into her house, I smelled the familiar rich aroma of my mother's chicken soup and saw the two of them in the kitchen. As always, even when cooking, my mother dressed with style, this day in a silk blouse, gray wool skirt, and high heels. While she cooked, she told stories of her youth in Slovakia and her wartime experiences, while Coralea sat spellbound at the table.

"You would not believe what we had to do to survive," Mom said to her, looking down and shaking her neatly coifed head. "I'm so happy you don't have to go through anything like that."

I held back, not wanting to interrupt.

"My father thought the Slovaks wouldn't turn on us," she continued. "Thank goodness he made plans, just in case. He was friendly with the local police chief. When he told us the Germans were coming soon to round up Jews where we lived in Zilina, my father sent me and my sister Magda to hide in small towns. Our older sister Edith didn't want to go. She didn't want to leave her boyfriend.

"I lived with a baker and his family in a town called Poprad. Magda lived with a family in a town nearby. Both families were very religious people, Baptists. I pretended to be one of their relatives, even getting baptized to fit in. But the Nazi soldiers still almost caught me. So, we had to flee."

Author's mother as a baby with her mother and sisters, Zilina, 1922

Mom paused to stir the soup pot on the stove. She gazed into the distance for several seconds, then turned back to Coralea, who leaned forward, her chin resting on her hands.

"Magda and I heard about an uprising against the Germans on the other side of the mountains. It was the middle of winter and I was sick, but we decided to go there anyway. A friend drove us part of the way, then we walked for four days through the forest in the snow. Somehow, we made it and joined the partisans. We were free again. But then the Germans beat down the uprising, and we had to flee for our lives once more."

Looking over at Coralea, my mother saw me standing in the adjoining room. She drew back toward the stove.

"Mom, how come you never told me a lot of that?" I asked, spreading my arms, palms up, perplexed.

"I don't like to talk about it. Being here alone with Coralea made me start thinking about my early life and my family. But I need to stop now."

She turned back to Coralea.

"I'll tell you more some other time."

Sure enough, the next time I came to pick up Coralea, I found my mother reminiscing again. This time, I sat down next to Coralea at the kitchen table. Mom didn't object. She spoke with ease, pausing only briefly every few minutes to collect her thoughts.

"Some things that happened to us were very sad or very scary. When we were running from the Germans the second time, their planes flew over our trucks, so low we could see their guns. But they didn't shoot at us. I don't know why.

"I made it back to the baker's family in Poprad, but they couldn't take me in again. Too many local people had become suspicious. A bakery worker who had been my boyfriend took me to stay with a relative at a village in the mountains.

"Then the Russians came. We were scared of them too, but something funny happened. A Russian officer and his aide came into our house in the middle of the night. He sat down in the one good chair in the living room. He was dirty, sweaty, and needed a shave. We all froze. We had no idea what would happen. To our surprise, he demanded that someone give him a manicure and wash his uniform collar. I was the only one who knew how, so, in my nightgown, I sat and manicured his dirty hands and cracked nails. Another girl washed his collar. Afterward, he was happy. When the soldiers left the next day, they gave me a ride most of the way back to Zilina.

"I found out my parents had been sent to a concentration camp. No one knew what happened to my sister Edith. A neighbor told me Edith just disappeared one day, shortly before my parents were taken. No one saw her or heard from her again. I still wonder about what happened to her.

"A refugee organization helped me find Magda. She had married a Hungarian doctor, Thomas Hora. They had moved to Karlovy Vary, where he got a residency position at the city hospital. A family I didn't know had taken over our home in Zilina, so I joined Magda and Tom.

"Together, we all decided to come to America. Magda got in touch with one of our aunts, who lived in New Jersey. She agreed to sponsor us. It took us another year before we got papers and took a ship to New York."

With that, my mother stopped and sat down at the table with us. She turned to me.

"That's where I met your father. It almost didn't work out. After we dated a while, he asked me to marry him. But then he told me about his job offer to work on the Nuremburg trials and asked me to wait until he returned. I told him I would marry him, but I would not wait. It was now or never."

At that, Mom laughed, then continued. "He acted surprised. He didn't think I would want to go back to Europe. But it was fine. Soon after we got married, he left for Nuremburg and I followed him a little while later. You know the rest of the story."

She reached over and stroked Coralea's arm. Mom's face looked softer, her shoulders higher, as if she had unburdened herself of a great weight.

Despite that, I could tell from her story that she remained bothered by not knowing Edith's fate. At the time, we had no way of finding out. Then, twenty years later, after massive troves of Nazi files became available, a researcher at the U.S. Holocaust Memorial Museum in Washington, D.C., found records of what happened to my mother's family. As she had heard, her parents were indeed arrested, taken to the Terezin concentration camp, and killed there. But Edith was not apprehended until weeks later, in Poprad, the town where my mother had been hiding. Presumably, Edith was trying on desperation to reunite with her sisters. She, too, was sent to Terezin and killed.

Ernest and Valerie Lowe wedding, New York City, 1947

I wished Coralea could have heard my father's family experiences directly from him, too. She would have found interesting his experiences of growing up in the heart of Vienna, attending college to become an engineer, and then having everything taken away from him and his family. Soon after the Nazis took power in Germany, their first act of expansion was the annexation of Austria in late 1938, an event, sadly, supported by most Austrians at the time. Soon after that came Kristallnacht, the Night of Broken Glass—the government-sanctioned attack that shattered not only windows of Jewish homes, businesses, and temples throughout Germany and Austria, but also the illusion that Jews could be safe there any longer.

With my grandfather's businesses destroyed and my father forced to withdraw from school, the family left for America as soon as they could make the necessary arrangements. One cousin escaped through the *Kinderstransport*, a program that evacuated several thousand Jewish children from Nazi territories to England. Those relatives who remained behind, whether by hesitation or inability to flee, perished in the Holocaust.

***

Knowing how many of my relatives, along with countless others, perished because this country refused them a safe haven troubled me to no end. For most of American history, the nation had no limits on immigration. In the late 1800s, the first immigration laws were enacted to limit entry by Asian immigrants. Later, controls were imposed to bar "undesirable" immigrants from Eastern Europe, Ireland, and Italy.

Then the Immigration Act of 1924 set quotas based on national representation in the 1890 census. Economic conditions during the Great Depression reinforced anti-immigrant views. As a result, refugees fleeing Naziism or Fascism in the 1930s had no better chance of immigrating than someone from Switzerland or New Zealand. And antisemitic views among the American population made even progressive politicians, right up to President Franklin Roosevelt, reluctant to advocate for admission of Jewish refugees fleeing for their lives, even children.

***

My mother soon warmed to the idea of the trip to Europe. To my disappointment, she put it off in order to travel to Scandinavia with her new husband. Then, by the time we finally planned to go a year later, she lay dying of breast cancer. My wife, Joan, had severe, chronic back pain and couldn't handle extended travel anymore. In one of her last lucid conversations, my mother urged Coralea and me to go on our own.

"I'm sorry we waited," she whispered to me, "but you two should go as soon as you can, while Coralea remembers what I've told her."

Following my mother's advice, we laid out a route of travel that would take us to all the significant places in my family's history over the last three generations, from my father's family roots in Prague and my mother's hometown north of Bratislava to my own hometown near Salzburg.

In Prague, I particularly wanted us to see the tomb of our most illustrious ancestor, sixteenth century Rabbi Judah Loew ben Bezalel, famous in Jewish legend as a practitioner of Kabala and for creating the creature known as the Golem. Coralea and I pored over books at the local library and searched on-line for stories about the rabbi. I also showed her photos of the tomb taken by my father on a visit a few years earlier.

But that was a historical connection. I hadn't thought of finding something as personal as a lost gravesite of more immediate relatives. Mimi's last-minute request added a new motivation to our plans. This trip would be more than an exploration. It would be a search.

So, a month after my mother died, Coralea and I were on our way, with my parents' stories and my aunt's urgings fresh in our minds.

We made an interesting pair of traveling companions. Barely four feet tall but athletic, with shoulder-length light brown hair, Coralea could look as serious as a Buckingham Palace Queen's Guard one moment and break into a mischievous smile as broad as the Catalina Channel the next. I was more reserved than my daughter. A middle-aged lawyer with a military bearing and short black hair going gray, I displayed a bemused expression as she acted out her growing self-confidence.

We arrived at LAX early to check in for our flight to Prague. Coralea leapt from the taxi with her bulging backpack.

"There's our flight," Coralea said, pointing at an overhead monitor in the terminal lobby. With that, she marched up to a ticket agent.

"We're going to Europe," she announced. "Do you have our boarding passes?"

The thirtyish, blond woman behind the counter looked up bewildered, then peered down to see Coralea staring up at her. The agent struggled to keep a straight face.

"Why, yes," she declared. "We've been looking forward to having you travel with us."

Coralea's face softened into an infectious smile. The agent smiled back as Coralea handed her our tickets.

Later that night, as we soared forty thousand feet over the North Atlantic, I pictured us standing before a pair of graves in a rural cemetery.

Reaching into my carry-on bag, I pulled out the faded black-and-white photograph of the house Mimi mentioned, the home of my father's paternal grandparents, Samuel and Julie Loewy. It was a common-looking house—boxy, with no front yard, a shingle roof, and no external ornamentation other than dark wood shutters bracketing the two front windows. At the time of the photo, the ground floor had been converted into a bank, with a sign above the front door.

I looked over at Coralea in her window seat, a blanket drawn up around her torso. She smiled and leaned over to give me a hug. Then, with the muted roar of the aircraft engines as a lullaby, we both drifted off to sleep.

***

We arrived in Prague early on a Saturday morning. The taxi ride from the airport to our hotel took us through miles of plain, Soviet-era, industrial suburbs. I felt apprehensive. I held great hopes from what I had read and heard about the city that people compared to Paris in the 1920s. As we approached the city center, the Prague Castle came into view on a ridge overlooking downtown and the Vltava River. Gray stone buildings decorated with sculptured busts and ornate doorways soon surrounded us, putting my concerns to rest.

We checked in to the Casa Marcello, romantically named after an Italian family who had converted it from a nunnery to a hotel in the late 1800s. It stood at the end of a cobblestone street, tucked behind a medieval church on Hastalske Square in the Old City. Our room provided a view over the rooftops of the surrounding buildings, many dating back to the fourteenth century.

The next morning, after a lavish breakfast of meats, cheeses, pastry, and coffee, we began exploring. Coralea never tired, always looking forward to a new discovery around the next corner.

We strolled cobblestone streets and narrow sidewalks to Josefov, the former Jewish quarter. Near the walled ancient cemetery, we passed the Kafka Café, housed in the birthplace of Franz Kafka. Aromas of coffee and pastry wafted out to the street. We wandered through the Gothic Old-New

Synagogue, where my father had his *bar mitzvah*. Its stone facade rose to a series of hooked points, like a pair of inverted saw blades. Nearby, we paused to admire the Spanish Synagogue, with its intricate Moorish artwork and stained-glass windows, and the gabled roof and Baroque design of the older Pinkas Synagogue.

"The Nazis spared all this during the war," I told Coralea. "They were going to turn it into a 'museum of an extinct race.' Now it's all a Jewish museum."

Ornate headstones and tombs dating back to the early fifteenth century filled the cemetery. For lack of land, the Jewish community for hundreds of years had buried their dead up to twelve deep. We soon found the crypt of Rabbi Judah Loew. After briefly standing silently before it, I reminded Coralea of the stories we had read of how the rabbi brought the Golem to life from inanimate matter by invoking the name of God, to protect the community from outside threats. One version of the story, I told her, supposedly inspired Mary Shelley over two hundred years later to create the famous literary character named Dr. Frankenstein.

"Why are there rocks on top of a lot of the gravestones?" Coralea asked.

"It's an ancient tradition," I explained. "They mark visits by relatives and friends. Sometimes people also leave notes."

Rabbi Loew's stone crypt, with tall, engraved tablets at both ends, was piled with pebbles. A few of them secured scraps of paper bearing messages.

Author at crypt of Rabbi Judah Loew, Old Jewish Cemetery, Prague, 2005

"I want to leave him a message," Coralea said solemnly.

I handed her a pen and tore a piece of paper from the corner of a city map. She wrote a personal message on it. We needed a stone heavy enough to hold the note in place, but we could not appropriate one left by another visitor. Hoping to find something suitable, I looked down. Where countless thousands of visitors had stepped before us and picked the earth bare of pebbles, I saw a yellowed fragment of pottery pressed into the soil inches from the end of the crypt. I dug it out of the moist, mossy ground with my fingernails.

"Do you think he knows we're here?" Coralea asked as we placed the note and its holder at the edge of the sloping roof of the crypt.

"I think so, Doll," I replied, calling her by her family nickname.

At that, she closed her eyes and stood motionless, breathing slowly, for a full minute. Then she opened her eyes and declared, "I'm sure he knows."

We noticed a guide nearby leading an English-speaking group, relating to them the saga of Rabbi Loew. Six feet six, dressed all in black, wearing a yarmulke, and talking intensely, he stood out from the crowd.

"I want to tell him we're related to Rabbi Loew," Coralea said.

I led her over to the young guide and introduced her to him as a direct descendent of the famed rabbi. He paused for a moment, then leaned way down, shook her hand, and said to her in a serious tone, "I'm very impressed to meet such an illustrious visitor!"

Coralea beamed, then waved at the guide as he led his party away.

We crossed the Vltava River on the Charles Bridge, lined with centuries-old statues of religious and historical figures. Along both sides, artists displayed paintings of Prague scenes and chatted with passersby. From there, we made our way uphill through the steep, cobblestone streets of the Hradcany neighborhood to the venerable Prague Castle. Later, we meandered down Wenceslas Square, amid market booths selling colorful embroidery, fine wool scarves, and nested wooden dolls, along with luscious fresh fruits and vegetables.

In the late afternoon, we walked round and round the Old Town Square, filled with people of all ages chattering in Czech, English, and German. By a corner of the New Town Hall stood a gray stone statue of Rabbi Loew. Nearby, on the hour, the massive Town Hall clock put on a show featuring chimes, music, and a parade of statues of the Apostles. We sat on the steps before the bronze Jan Huss memorial, the backdrop for so many scenes in the Czech Velvet Revolution, as a parade of visitors swirled past us.

While we drank coffee and people-watched in an outdoor café at the edge of the square, a young man in his late teens leaned over from the next table.

"I hear you speaking English," he said. "Are you American?"

"Yes," I replied, smiling.

"I want to go to America. I read about it and I see it on television. It must be wonderful."

"Prague is wonderful too, in a different way."

He shook his head. "I like Prague, but my friends and I, we want to be Americans," he continued. "Someday, I will move there."

"I hope you get your wish," I told him, feeling a little awkward at his effusive desire to go to the United States just as I was immersing myself in his country, but also with an inner glow of pride.

Coralea and I got up from our table, waved goodbye to the young man, and wandered back into the square. I remembered feeling just as he did, liking where I lived as a child, but wanting so badly to move to the United States, to become an American. Coralea would never know that exact feeling. She was born in Los Angeles and had lived her entire life in the United States. Mimicking Bruce Springsteen, she would sing, "I was born in West L.A." But I hoped this trip would show her a side of me she hadn't seen before, from long before she was born, from when I just was awakening to the possibility of becoming an American.

Back at our hotel, we had one important task—to arrange for a driver to take us on our search for my great-grandparent's graves.

"We need someone to drive us to Volenice and Strakonice," I told the hotel concierge. "He must speak English and know the countryside."

"I have someone for you," the young man replied. "His name is Ivo. He has driven for other American visitors."

When Ivo came to our hotel that evening to meet us, I wondered at first if he was our man. I imagined an older fellow, one who would be patient with our quest. Ivo looked thirtyish and intense, in need of a shave. He dressed in a flannel shirt and jeans, like someone just off work in a factory or garage. But he spoke fairly fluent English and also some German.

"We have come from California to find the graves of our relatives," I explained. "We want to start tomorrow, but it may take more than one day."

"I am sure we will find them," he responded, with an enthusiasm that gave me confidence.

Ivo picked us up promptly at eight the next morning in his middle-aged maroon Renault. Dents and scrapes decorated the sides and it needed a wash, but the engine sounded fine.

I felt anxious, as we could not find the small village of Volenice on any of our maps. Aunt Mimi was confused about its location after so many years away. In her childhood, the family traveled by wagon for hours on winding unpaved roads just to reach nearby Strakonice, so her sense of direction and distance was uncertain.

I got in front with Ivo while Coralea buckled up in the rear seat. Ivo grinned at me impishly and handed me a map book. I turned to a marked page and saw, circled in red, "Volenice." A great omen. I let out a breath and grinned back.

So, we were off for a day that soon would have us feeling like adventurers in search of a long-lost antiquity. But first, we had to make our way out of Prague through a maze of traffic-packed, one-way streets.

We emerged from the city on a divided highway carrying us west into the Bohemian countryside toward Plzen, the ancestral home of Czech brewing—Pilsen in German, hence Pilsner beer. We drove among rolling hills, with golden farm fields backed by green-black pine forests, probably little different from a century, or two, or three, earlier.

Ivo was chatty. He rarely had the opportunity to spend a whole day practicing his English. We talked about him. He came from a working-class family and had spent his whole life in Prague. At first, he worked in factories, but he liked being a driver better. After learning English in school, he now improved it by hanging out with young English-speaking tourists.

We talked to Ivo about ourselves. Coralea told him about Rabbi Judah Loew and the Golem. To our surprise, he had not heard that story before. I described our quest for my paternal roots there in the Czech Republic and the upcoming search on my maternal side in Slovakia. He soon got caught up in the romance of father and daughter coming eight thousand miles to find the graves of their last ancestors buried in their homeland.

After twenty-five miles, halfway to Plzen, we got off the main highway and headed south toward Pribram. The roads got tricky here, narrow and not well marked, and we repeatedly lost the route.

An hour later, we arrived in Strakonice, entering through the older part of the city filled with small, neat homes and big, leafy trees. Then we hit the newer areas, which looked like any city of light industry in Western Europe or the United States—manufacturing plants and trucks, lots of traffic, lots of people. Especially young people, most of them wearing American-style clothes. A teenage girl with long blond hair and tight jeans stood at a bus stop, her t-shirt redundantly declaring in English, "Sexy Young Thing."

"Now, how are we going to find the cemetery?" I asked Ivo. He stared back at me with a blank look.

"You have no address, no directions?" he asked, after a long pause.

This would be more difficult than I anticipated. Ivo suggested that we first go on to Volenice. I agreed.

The narrow road from Strakonice to Volenice wound through more fields and pastures. Several times it crossed a stream which seemed tame enough now, but the old bridges had statues of saints on them to protect travelers in crossing. After a sharp left turn in the road, I saw a sign marking the town limits. The town itself perched on a hilltop directly ahead. Fields of row crops spread out in all directions. I wondered which ones my great-grandparents had farmed.

No wonder Volenice wasn't on most maps. It consisted of fewer than a hundred houses on just four principal streets. They came together in a square around the town church, which seemed oversized for such a small community. I wondered how virtually every village in Europe found the resources to build a church with a two-hundred-foot steeple. The homes at the periphery of town all were connected like row houses. Their rear walls formed a defensible perimeter toward the outside world, dating back centuries, supplementing the protection provided by the hilltop location.

Coralea cocked her head, looking puzzled. "Why did Grandpa's family leave Prague and move way out here?" she asked.

"They had no choice," I explained. "Back in the 1800s, when this was part of Austria, Empress Maria Theresa ordered all Jews to leave Prague, so our family moved to this area and became farmers."

"But you said your dad grew up in Vienna."

"It's a complicated story. His grandfather, the one whose grave we're hoping to find, left here and came to the US in the 1870s, I think. He went west all the way to the Arizona Territory. He lived there for a couple of years, selling goods from a wagon to ranchers, small towns, and Indian reservations. Can you imagine how different that was from this place? I heard a rumor in the family that he had a romance, maybe even kids, with an Indian woman, so maybe we have some distant Navajo cousins."

That drew an incredulous look from Coralea.

"Anyway," I continued, "he might have thought about staying in the US, but he came back and married a distant cousin, and they moved into the house in Volenice. My dad's father, my grandfather, left here and moved to Vienna when he grew up. He worked in different businesses there. Once he established himself in Vienna, he got married. Aunt Mimi was born there. The family moved back here to the farm for a while during World War I, when food became scarce in the cities. My dad was born here during that time. When the war ended, they returned to Vienna, and my dad grew up there. He was studying at the Technical University in Vienna when things became bad for Jews. That's when his family decided to leave for the US."

Coralea nodded, taking all this in, just as with my mother's stories.

I knew where to look for our family home, but I pulled out my father's photograph to refresh my memory. Sure enough, we found the house on a corner across from the main entrance to the church. The two-story building had been restored to use as a residence, but black lettering from the former bank sign still peeked through a thin layer of gray paint. Despite its proximity to the church, with the bell tower looming above it, the house had been the center of activity for the small Jewish community in the area. I recalled my aunt's stories of weddings, *bar mitzvahs*, and other celebrations in the trellised garden.

Through an open door, we saw an elderly woman puttering about, placing flowers in a vase. Ivo knocked at the door. The old woman, wearing a faded cotton dress, hobbled to the door. In a pattern we would repeat throughout the day, I fed Ivo questions as he translated back and forth.

"Did you know any people who lived here before you, people named Loewy?" he asked.

"No, I have only been here a few years. I don't know that name."

We knocked at two other houses along the street. People were friendly but had no information. At the house next door, once occupied by other relatives, a smiling, middle-aged man in a colorful sweater appeared.

"Have you lived here long?" Ivo asked.

"My family has lived in this town for generations."

"Do you remember the Loewy family, from before the war?"

"I think I remember the name. I'm not sure. My father probably knew them, but he is dead."

We thanked him and walked back toward the car. Coralea curled up on a weathered wood bench at the side of the house, settling for at least a short while in the shadow of her great-great-grandparents. She was uncharacteristically quiet, staring intently at the entire scene. We took each other's pictures, and Ivo snapped one of both of us in front of the house.

With nothing left to see, we headed back toward Strakonice. On the way out of town, I stopped to take a picture of the sign announcing the town limits. It made for a sparse image, surrounded by vegetable fields and a bit of the town visible in the background. Just a way of saying goodbye, maybe for good.

During the thirty-minute drive back to Strakonice, Ivo spoke little but glanced at me frequently. "I need to stop and eat," he suddenly blurted out as we entered the town.

With that, he jerked the steering wheel to the left and pulled across the road into the gravel parking lot of a restaurant with a sign announcing only "Cafe." The car screeched to a halt.

"Maybe someone in the restaurant can help us find the cemetery," he suggested as he exited the car.

Inside, other diners, all speaking Czech, sat at a dozen square wood tables. A man carrying a tray of dishes waved to us to seat ourselves. We picked a table by a window looking out at the road through faded curtains. I felt confused, wondering if our search was nearing a dead end.

Our server, a young woman wearing blue jeans, a colorful shirt, and a white apron, approached us. In a quiet voice, Ivo explained to her who we were.

"Do you know where there is a Jewish cemetery in Strakonice?" he asked.

She looked puzzled. "No, I don't know of a Jewish cemetery," she said, shaking her head. "But that man," she continued, pointing to an older, bearded, heavyset man sitting alone at a table against the far wall, "he has lived here his whole life. I will ask him."

Not exactly ask. She called out to him in a voice loud enough to be heard in the parking lot. I could make out only the words for "California" and "Jewish," but I saw Ivo turn ashen. So that was what he had been nervous about, needing to ask strangers for directions relating to something Jewish. I felt apprehensive too, knowing virtually no Jews remained in the area after the war and that old prejudices lingered. I caught Coralea's eye. She shook her head and shrugged, as if confused by what was happening.

The bearded man wiped his mouth with his napkin and stood up. In a booming voice too loud for the room, he yelled to Ivo the directions to the only cemetery in town, where, as far as he knew, Jews and Gentiles alike were buried. To make sure, the server then looked around the restaurant and yelled to the patrons at the other tables. Most had now picked up on our conversation. But no, none of them were aware of a strictly Jewish cemetery either.

Armed with this new information, we paid our check and left. Ivo acted calmer now. His inquiries had linked him publicly to this search for dead Jews and no one reacted badly or said anything racist or insulting. Instead, they seemed intrigued and tried to help. I doubted the directions we received would lead to our goal, but I, too, felt more at ease.

His anxiety gone, Ivo became chatty again. Gripping the steering wheel, he sped into the center of town, then right, past some industrial plants, and up a long hill into a neighborhood of small, uniform, well-kept houses. It reminded me of an older tract development back home. On the left was the town cemetery described by the old man in the restaurant, with a low stone wall running parallel to the street frontage. Ivo pulled into the mostly empty parking lot, bounded out of the car, and knocked on the door of a single-story, wooden house containing the manager's office. No one answered. The manager would return in two hours, a note stuck in the door advised.

We wandered into the cemetery, determined to find clues. The grounds, roughly a hundred yards square, sloped down a grassy hillside. A dozen people stood about quietly, some placing flowers at graves. The dates on headstones indicated this was a fairly new cemetery. We noted just a few bearing stars of David.

Ivo inquired with several other visitors, but none knew of a separate Jewish cemetery. Someone pointed out the oldest part of the cemetery, down the hill, beside an abandoned stone house. Now Coralea became eager. She ran ahead of us to see. A few graves there went back to the turn of the century, but all the headstones bore crosses.

Then one of the other visitors called to us and pointed out an old man tending some graves.

"He has worked here many years. Maybe he knows about other cemeteries in the area."

The cemetery worker stood up as we approached, wiped his hands on his overalls and laid down his shovel. Ivo explained our situation. The old man scrunched up his lined face, ran a sweaty palm through his thinning gray hair, and thought hard.

"There are few Jewish graves in the cemetery," he finally said, "because few Jews remained here after the war."

"They must have been buried somewhere here before that," we suggested. "We've come so far, we have to find it."

"I wish I could help," he said, shaking his head and stroking his chin.

Then he smiled, as if suddenly remembering something he hadn't thought about for a long time.

"There was a Jewish cemetery," he said. "Not in the town, but not far away. It was there for many years. It went out of use before the war. I was never inside it, but I remember seeing the entrance from the road."

His voice grew higher and louder. He had no idea what we would find. He didn't know if anyone went there anymore, but he recalled the way and described it to Ivo.

We dashed back to the car, now with a sense of purpose. Back down the hill we went to the center of town, this time taking a sharp left a block before the main highway. Down that narrow, winding road, as the old man had described, we crossed under a wooden railroad trestle and passed the front of a military installation. Soldiers looked up at us speeding by, the only car in sight.

At the far end of the base, an even narrower road wound uphill to the left. Then, finally, a cracked concrete driveway veered off to the right for a hundred yards. Once, it would have been a country road leading to the only Jewish cemetery in the region.

The driveway ran between two plain, stucco farm houses surrounded by gardens. Just beyond them stood a set of iron gates secured by a rusty lock and flanked by whitish, crumbling-stucco-covered walls too high to see over. A white sign bearing black Hebrew lettering arched above the gates.

I trembled as I climbed out of the car, approached the gates and peered through the bars at rows of headstones. Looking left and right, I searched for a means to get inside the cemetery. I hoped for a sign giving information about gaining entry but saw nothing. The gates and walls seemed impenetrable.

Coralea stood beside me. I reached out and clutched her hand. I shook my head in frustration. Thoughts flooded my mind. Was it possible that we really were blocked from even finding out if our search had been successful?

I turned to Coralea and Ivo. With all the determination I could muster, I told them, "We're not stopping here. I'm going to climb over the wall!"

CHAPTER 2
IN HITLER'S SHADOW

At the age of five, I often walked with my mother around the town square of Braunau am Inn, then south through the gateway beneath the Torturm, the ancient stone tower that once formed part of the town walls. Just beyond that, on the east side of the street, at **Salzburger Vorstadt 15**, stood a tan, two-story building of stone and stucco with ornate window frames. I noticed that my mother grew silent and made a point of keeping to the other side of the street whenever we approached that house. My nanny, Herma, and others did the same or at least averted their eyes.

"What is that house?" I asked Herma one day as we made our way to a friend's home.

"Ask your *Mutti*," she replied. I did.

My mother frowned and looked down. "A very bad man lived there," she said. "He killed my family and many others."

In the early 1950s, a heavy cloud hung over Braunau. It emanated from that house. The structure was unmarked, but everyone knew the *Hitlerhaus*, the birthplace and childhood home of Adolf Hitler. People rarely mentioned it in conversation. They didn't need to. I sensed early on, and as long as we lived in Braunau, that the *Hitlerhaus* was a symbol of something so evil that no one could bring themselves to acknowledge it.

***

My parents moved to Braunau in early 1948. My father had just finished working as an investigator and translator at the Nuremberg war crimes military tribunal, the proceedings that followed the international trial of the major war criminals.

His presence here resulted from a series of unusual circumstances. After fleeing Vienna with his family in 1939 and immigrating to the United States, he was drafted into the Army and served with a field artillery unit in General George Patton's Third Army. He received a shrapnel wound in the Battle of the Bulge. At the end of the war, the military recruited him to work at the Nuremberg trials, based on his Eastern European background and his fluency in several languages. For much the same reasons, when that work ended, the US Army Counterintelligence Corps recruited him and stationed him in Braunau.

Shortly before moving there, my parents took a vacation trip to Czechoslovakia. They visited my father's birthplace in Volenice, where he took the photograph of his grandparents' house that I carried back there nearly fifty years later. My mother chose not to visit her hometown of Zilina. The following year, the Iron Curtain came down, cutting them off from their birthplaces for the next several decades.

Six months after my parents' arrival in Braunau, I was born in the American military hospital in nearby Linz. That marked the start of my lifelong connection to Braunau, a connection that would engage me in ways I couldn't have imagined during my childhood.

A small town north of Salzburg, separated from Germany by the Inn River, Braunau had no military significance. The only reason for maintaining an American military presence seemed to be that it was Hitler's hometown.

Braunau appeared to be recovering, having survived the war without significant physical damage. That, I later learned from my father, was by a stroke of luck. In the waning days of the war, US Army troops massed across the river and threatened to launch an artillery barrage unless the German garrison in Braunau surrendered. Despite orders to hold out, the garrison commander gave in just in time to avoid destruction of the town.

My family lived well on an American government salary, with free housing and with access to the American military exchange and commissary stores an hour away in Salzburg. The Army even provided us with a car and driver, as no private autos were available. But what made our lives especially pleasant during that time was Herma, our nanny and housekeeper.

Herma had joined us when I was just a few months old, in early 1949. She heard from friends in our small town that my parents were looking for help. Jobs remained scarce in postwar Austria. With some experience caring for children, she convinced my mother that she would be a good fit for our family. Although the position lasted only a few years, it turned into a lifelong friendship.

At nineteen, Herma was what people used to call "solidly built"—average height, a little heavy, but muscular. Brown, wavy hair framed her broad, smiling face. She had large, strong hands, as if from working in the fields.

Herma came to our home to interview for the job, as did several other local women. She dressed plainly in a print dress, single-color cardigan, and brown lace-up shoes. My father liked her immediately. My mother wasn't so sure. Herma had walked a considerable distance to our home on the day after a rain, so her shoes were muddy.

My mother took my father aside and expressed concern. "This woman comes here with dirty shoes," she said. "What kind of housekeeper would she be?"

In the midst of this, I started crying, but stopped as soon as Herma took me from my mother and held me close against her chest. This impressed my mother, but she still selected another woman for the job. Within days, for reasons I never knew, that choice proved to be a mistake. My father reminded my mother of how I had taken to Herma the day of the interviews.

"My goodness," my mother declared, "you're right. Cary liked her immediately. Let's see if she is still available."

She was. Herma quickly bonded with our family. At first, she declined to discuss her past, especially her wartime experiences, but later she opened up a bit. She came from a small town in eastern Austria, south of Vienna. Like my parents, she'd had a tough time.

"Many of my relatives died or disappeared in the war," she told them. "I fled to work with the Red Cross at a refugee camp outside Vienna. When the Russians came, my sister and I decided to leave. A truck driver took us to Braunau. I didn't know anyone here, but it felt safe, so I stayed." My mother saw something of her own story in Herma's experience.

Once my parents decided to keep Herma on, they moved her in with us. We had just two bedrooms, so my room became Herma's, as well.

Our home comprised half of a well-kept, white-stucco duplex that we shared with the family of one of my father's colleagues. Plain and rectangular, with a steeply sloped, red tile roof, the house looked solid enough to weather any storm. My room occupied a corner of the second floor. A sunny garden filled with flowers filled the yard behind the house.

A small town then, Braunau had fewer than ten thousand residents. Our house sat in the neighborhood of Ranshofen, along the road toward Salzburg and separated in those days by forest from the main part of town. Originally founded by the emperor Charlemagne in the 9th Century, modern Ranshofen was developed in the 1930s with a mix of single-family homes and duplexes to house employees of a nearby aluminum plant.

No one in the community spoke English, except at my father's workplace. My parents and Herma taught me German as my first language.

I related to Herma like a second mother. Even as an infant, I went with her as often as with my mother to the market, to the town square, or down to the river. Herma wheeled me about the neighborhood in a fancy baby carriage, and later a stroller, introducing me to the locals. My first views of Braunau were looking up from that carriage. From my perspective, the town must have looked as if it were all upper-story windows, gables, and rooftops. Every other day or so, while my father worked, our driver took my mother, Herma, me, and the carriage to the center of town. While one of them shopped or socialized, the other rolled my carriage around the town square.

The townspeople found the carriage to be quite a curiosity. My mother's sister had shipped it to us from New York City. It was entirely white, with elliptical sides, a curving sunscreen, and shiny, stainless-steel trim. Very post-modern, and unlike anything else in Braunau or maybe anywhere else in Austria at the time.

Herma, with author in baby carriage, Braunau, ca 1949

By the time I turned three, I accompanied Herma on regular walks about town. Dressed in fashionable American clothes and always smiling, I drew frequent attention from locals as we meandered across the cobblestoned town square, popping into the grocery or pharmacy for some shopping or conversation. Doting storekeepers treated me to a bit of candy, fruit, or sausage. Whether they genuinely liked me or they were simply currying favor with the American occupiers, I enjoyed the attention.

Standing on the ramparts overlooking the Inn, we could see the German town of Simbach. Retreating German troops had blown up the bridge across the river near the end of the war. Its steel frame lay collapsed in the river like the skeleton of a gargantuan beast. US Army engineers constructed a pontoon bridge nearby, enabling American troops to cross the river and occupy the town in 1945. Ten years later, near the end of the post-war occupation, the government built a new steel bridge.

Braunau Town Square from Cathedral Spire

From the river, we walked around the medieval town square. Herma always laughed when we passed the town hall and looked up at the relief sculpture of Hans Staininger, a sixteenth century mayor who was known for a beard that reached to his feet. He died when he tripped on his beard, fell down a flight of stairs, and broke his neck.

The real highlight of the square, however, was St. Stephan's Church, with its spire towering nearly three hundred feet above the town, built when Braunau was a prosperous trading center in the 1400s. Herma was not openly religious, but sometimes walked me into the church for a moment of quiet devotion. From my first visit, I found myself awed by the Gothic architecture—soaring granite walls held up by unusual interior flying buttresses and lined with personal chapels the size of large closets; pillars decorated with angels and apostles, rising fifty feet to the sloping ceiling; an altar encrusted with gilded images of saints; and one of Europe's finest pipe organs, commanding attention when hymns erupted from its loft at the rear of the church. I watched Herma stand in the multi-colored light from a stained-glass window, head down, crossing herself, speaking in a voice too low for me to hear, maybe remembering her lost loved ones.

Outside, street life abounded in and around the square. The end of the war gave people permission to return to normal day-to-day activity, much more readily than in towns that had suffered significant wartime damage. Shoppers shuttled in and out of businesses, not buying much but enjoying the experience. Horse-drawn wagons and small trucks made deliveries. Grocers stocked their outdoor displays with cabbages, root vegetables, and whatever fruit they could find, though much of the produce from farms in the surrounding countryside went to larger cities where people paid more. Children in neatly pressed outfits trotted through on their way to and from school. Occasional visitors arrived at the Post Hotel, operated by friends of my parents. And a handful of locals, mostly elderly, chatted and sipped weak chicory coffee in an outdoor cafe.

And then there was the *Hitlerhaus*. Later, after the occupation ended, neo-Nazis gathered there each year on Hitler's birthday. Aghast, the community in 1989 placed a three-foot-high granite block from the Mauthausen concentration camp quarry in front of the house, inscribed with a dedication to the memory of the victims of the Holocaust and an appeal for the end of fascism.

No apparent Jewish religious or cultural presence existed in Braunau anymore. Ranshofen had been home to a wealthy Jewish family whose estate the Nazis seized. Any pre-war Jewish residents likely perished at Mauthausen or Dachau.

More recently, in 2006, the town participated in the *Stolpersteine* (Stumbling Stone) project, in which over 75,000 brass plates have been installed throughout Europe at the last known addresses of individuals killed by the Nazis for religious, ethnic, or political reasons. Like the monument before the *Hitlerhaus,* this helped ease Braunau's burdensome association with Hitler.

Hitlerhaus and Memorial to Holocaust Victims, Braunau

In the postwar period, however, when Hitler still cast a longer shadow, people sought escapes. In occupied Austria, my father's American government salary went far. My mother especially seemed determined to make up for her wartime losses by enjoying this time as much as possible.

The birth of my brother accelerated that. Shortly before I turned three, he was born at the US Army hospital in Salzburg. Our parents named him Dean after Secretary of State Dean Acheson, whom my mother thought looked distinguished. They had named me after the actor Cary Grant because my mother had a crush on him. Mom took on motherhood reluctantly, but she committed herself to it. She wouldn't talk then about her lost family and her wartime experiences, except to say it was important that our family continue.

With two children in the family, we started getting out more. A favorite day trip consisted of a short train ride to the mineral baths at Bad Schallerbach. For the Austrians, this offered an affordable diversion in a time of considerable privation. But one experience there shocked me. Amid the crowd lounging near one of the pools, I spied a heavyset, middle-aged man with inch-deep furrows in the flesh across his back and shoulders, as if sliced by a knife but never properly healed. I could only imagine what agonizing torture he must have undergone at the hands of some Nazi sadist during the war.

On long weekends, we drove to at an inn in the Tyrolean Alps, near Innsbruck. Haus Koch, named after the family that operated it, was a classic Tyrolean *Gasthaus*, a three-story, brown wood structure with a steep slate roof to shed the winter snows. Geranium-filled flower boxes hung from balconies and window sills. We walked the hills, sunbathed on a deck facing the mountains, and breathed cool air scented with wildflowers. There, we forgot for a while the war and its aftermath.

When we needed to shop beyond what was available in Braunau, we drove south to Salzburg or north to the Danube town of Passau, where German border guards had nearly detained my father on his way out of Europe a dozen years earlier. Salzburg provided more of a treat, because a visit there included an opportunity to climb the hill to the old castle overlooking the city or to ride a train into the ancient salt mines outside town.

My father especially loved visits to Bad Ischl. Once the summer home of Austrian royalty, it still boasted one of the finest pastry shops in a country famous for them—the Konditorei-Kaffee Zauner, long an official pastry purveyor to the royal court. Now, even amid postwar shortages, the proprietor managed to scrounge the ingredients to produce at least limited quantities of layer cakes covered in chocolate butter frosting, puff pastries bursting with whipped cream, custard tarts topped with fresh berries, and flaky strudels filled with sweetened apples or poppy seeds. Seated in the mirrored dining room, my father rarely looked as happy as when feasting on a plate of pastries from Zauner's glass display cases. That became the favorite habit I acquired from him.

Our route to Bad Ischl or Salzburg often took us through the village of Oberndorf, home of the classic Christmas carol *Stille Nacht* or *Silent*

Night. The memorial chapel, on the site of the original town church, appeared tiny and plain—a round, white-washed, single-story building that would fit many times over inside St. Stephan's Church in Braunau. It perched on a slight rise along the country road passing through town, with only a small sign drawing attention to it.

My first visit there, on a gray afternoon in early December, was a cultural revelation. A dusting of snow covered the village. On this day, we had the chapel to ourselves. A hidden phonograph played a scratchy rendition of *Stille Nacht* as we entered. I heard it performed during Christmastime festivities in Braunau, so I knew the melody and some of the German lyrics.

I stood fascinated as my father read to me the story of how, on Christmas Eve in 1818, choirmaster Franz Gruber set to music a poem written by a young priest, Joseph Mohr, and then performed *Stille Nacht* during Christmas services the next day. The song meant nothing to me personally. It had no connection to my roots or culture. Yet, the lyrics and melody washed over me like a warm wave in the cool winter air. It was my first realization that important cultural contributions sometimes flow from obscure sources, like great rivers beginning in small mountain springs.

While my parents moved toward the altar, Herma stayed back. On an impulse, I walked toward her. She smiled and closed her eyes. Then, in a low voice, she began to sing to herself, "*Stille Nacht, Heilige Nacht.*" Tears rolled from her eyes, but she smiled even more broadly. Perhaps, for the first time since the war ended, she had found a moment of true peace.

***

In 1954, we moved from Braunau to Linz, an industrial city on the Danube, a two-hour drive to the east. Herma moved with us, which seemed only natural. But this plan had a wrinkle. Back in Braunau, Herma had acquired a boyfriend, Loisel, the son of the local police chief. I never realized there could be anyone else in her life, so I reacted with astonishment when she informed us a few months later that she soon would move back to Braunau and get married.

We still saw her frequently after that, and Dean and I always looked forward to those visits. The bonds grew even stronger when Herma's daughter was born and she named the child Karin, after me. The following year, however, the postwar occupation of Austria ended and we moved to central Germany, too far away for casual visits.

We never lost contact, though, and my relationship with Herma stayed strong through letters and holiday cards. When we saw her from time to time, I felt as if nothing had changed. In 1961, we left Europe and moved to the United States. On the rare occasions when any of us visited Europe after that, we made a special trip to Braunau.

I last saw Herma in 1997, when I brought Coralea for her first visit, after we finished our explorations in the Czech Republic and Slovakia. Herma and Karin doted on her in a way that made me slightly jealous. Five years later, Herma died of a heart attack. Her family buried her in the local cemetery in Braunau. When Loisel died a few years later, he was buried next to his wife. Karin continues to live in Braunau, and I visit every few years.

**

In the postwar period in an occupied country, accomplishing the simplest tasks—buying groceries, finding a doctor, getting to the nearest train station—could be extraordinarily difficult for local people. Yet, remarkable things could happen if someone with even a little power or access wanted them to happen.

Herma's sister, Anna, with whom she had arrived in Braunau, suddenly became very ill. Small-town doctors in Braunau couldn't help. She needed a transfusion of a rare blood type, and even the hospitals in Linz and Salzburg were not equipped to deal with it.

Herma prevailed on my father to help. He found a supply of the needed blood at a hospital in Vienna. He then called a colleague at the Army airfield in Salzburg and asked for a favor—the use of an airplane and pilot for a few hours, to fly to Vienna and bring back a medical package. Things were looser then. Without paperwork, without approval through official channels, and based on nothing more than a phoned request, this could be done. A two-seater, single-engine plane would be on its way within the hour. One obstacle remained: Braunau had no airport.

So it was that local residents were treated to an unusual sight later that day. A brown aircraft emblazoned with US Army insignia came in low over the woods south of town, circled back toward Ranshofen, and touched down on the narrow highway near our home. As quickly as the plane rolled to a stop and the pilot cut the engine, a local health worker reached in and retrieved the packet of blood. The engine roared again, and the plane lifted off. Presumably, the pilot returned to base and recorded the day as nothing more than a routine training flight.

Two weeks later, Anna had recovered from her illness. When word of her recovery spread, my father briefly became a local hero.

The mere possibility of such a small miracle produced hope, a commodity still in short supply at that time. With life or death hanging in the balance, someone had chosen life and made it happen. It wasn't the magnitude of the effort or the risk involved, but that someone made the effort at all. And so, with that realization, if only briefly, the shadow of Hitler lifted from the community.

CHAPTER 3
THE ROAD TO VIENNA RUNS THROUGH MOSCOW

Throughout my childhood, my parents loved visiting Vienna. Although it had been less than a dozen years since his family fled as refugees, my father had wonderful memories of growing up there. For my mother, it was as close as she could get to her former home in Slovakia once the Iron Curtain dropped.

During the early years, this trip was complicated. The Allies had divided Austria into four zones. Vienna, though governed jointly, lay deep in the Russian zone. Traveling from our home in Braunau and later from Linz, both in the American zone to the west, meant traversing a narrow highway corridor in which the Russians allowed vehicle crossing.

I saw real physical impacts of the war for the first time in Vienna. Bombing and artillery had damaged or destroyed thousands of buildings, and craters pockmarked large parts of the city.

Few cars appeared in the streets, as gasoline and tires were scarce and expensive. Groups of men, most of them either young or elderly, pulled carts loaded with construction materials. The war had taken many of the working-age men. A few boys and a noticeable number of women filled out their ranks. Using whatever they could salvage from the rubble of destroyed structures, they repaired ornate buildings from the previous century. Scaffolding covered the soaring tile roof of the Stephansdom cathedral, as an army of masons risked life and limb to restore Vienna's iconic church.

Most workers wore shirts and trousers, not laborers' outfits. They otherwise would have been working in offices, shops, or classrooms. Those jobs were still as scarce as black market gasoline, so they gratefully took whatever work they could find. Their thin faces and sunken eyes followed us as we passed.

We saw other signs of the war's aftermath. Bulletin boards in public squares displayed notes from people seeking information about missing relatives and friends. Men in long coats or standing by pushcarts offered black market goods, especially food items that were strictly rationed, while keeping a wary eye out for police or occupation troops.

We often drove or walked past the two-story stone apartment building where my father's family had lived. It stood in a middle-class neighborhood west of the Prater, the park with the giant Riesenrad Ferris wheel, and east of the Ring, the tree-lined boulevard surrounding the old central city. The first few times, my father stood outside and looked up at the second-story windows.

"Look, boys," he said to me and Dean. "That was my home when I was your age." I had difficulty imagining my father being that young.

I never saw the inside of the building, but I liked knowing my father had lived there. Later on, he just drove by, giving the building a quick glance, as if to assure himself it was still there.

Author's father, Ernest Lowe, Vienna, 1935

On one of our later visits, we stopped before the Technische Hochschule, the prestigious engineering and technology college where my father had been a student in the late 1930s. He got out of the car and stared for a long time at the imperial architecture of the granite buildings. Then, he motioned for me to join him at the curb.

"I studied so hard to succeed here," he said, looking down. "My family was so proud. And then the Nazis and their supporters took it away from me. They harassed me and other Jewish students for months, stole our books, pushed us around in the halls. They finally made us all leave the school. Soon after that, my family left Vienna."

He turned and looked at me.

"You will go to college someday," he continued. "You won't have to experience anything like that, thank goodness."

I had never before seen him so wistful, or heard him talk so sadly about his experience as a young man.

But we had mainly pleasurable experiences in our visits. Though the economy in Vienna, like the rest of the country, was still emerging from the war, shopping opportunities were better there than in closer-by cities like Salzburg and Linz. And the signature feature of Vienna, its coffeehouses and pastry shops, had sprung back to life.

My father favored Demel, a two-hundred-year-old pastry shop in the heart of the old city, where we indulged in any available chocolaty and creamy delights. He recalled half a dozen coffee houses from his university days, places where one could sit for hours sipping strong coffee, with milk or whipped cream if desired, while reading, conversing, or just watching the pedestrian parade outside.

Experiencing Vienna meant first enduring several hours on the road in the car provided by the Army. A dark brown sedan with American markings on the door, it stood out as a military vehicle.

Most of the drive took us through the Russian zone, where the authorities prohibited stopping. The Berlin blockade had occurred only a few years earlier, and the Cold War was in full swing. We had to take care of any vehicle or personal needs before entering that corridor. Usually, the drive was a little tense but uneventful. Not always.

On an autumn morning in 1954, we set out from Linz for Vienna. Dean remained at home with Herma. After heading eastward for an hour or so, we stopped at a roadside café for a snack and to use the toilet.

Shortly after that, we came to the guard post at the border of the Russian zone. A young soldier in a gray wool uniform asked in halting German for our passports. My father responded in Russian, but the fellow showed no interest in a conversation. After inspecting our papers, he motioned to another soldier, who raised the crossing arm and allowed us to pass.

We drove on a two-lane road through rolling countryside, mostly forest with occasional small towns surrounded by farms. My parents and the driver chatted while I stared out at the scenery. It seemed strange that we were in a kind of enemy territory, as the farms, the towns, even the occasional people looked just like the ones in the area where we lived.

Then, from under the car, came a "thump, thump, thump," signaling a flat tire. The driver pulled over to the right shoulder just before a curve in the road. Seeing no other people or vehicles, we all got out of the car. The driver removed a toolbox from the rear, and he and my father prepared to change the tire.

Before they even jacked up the car, another vehicle appeared around the bend, an open military truck carrying a dozen Russian soldiers. My father and the driver glanced at each other, then back at the road. The truck pulled over to the shoulder opposite us. A tall, boyish-looking officer stepped out from the passenger side of the cab, put on his hat, and strode toward us.

"We're in trouble," whispered our driver. His comment startled me.

My father approached the Russian officer and they began to talk. I didn't speak any Russian but, from the tone of their voices and their gestures, I was pretty sure I knew what they were saying.

"You are not allowed to stop here!" the officer exclaimed, waving his arms for emphasis.

"We just need to fix our flat tire and we'll be on our way," my father responded in a soothing voice.

Then he asked the Russian something. After exchanging a few more remarks, the tone of their discussion became friendlier, until the officer laughed out loud. At that, he ordered several soldiers out of the truck. I tensed up as they approached us, but then relaxed when the soldiers took over changing the flat tire.

While the soldiers worked, the officer and my father strolled over to our car. My father introduced the officer to us and explained their conversation. He had recognized an insignia on the officer's uniform. It turned out to be from the same Russian unit that my father's US Army unit had met up with near the end of the war somewhere in Germany. My father was just a sergeant at the time but, because he spoke decent Russian, he accompanied his commanding general to a dinner with the Russian commander. The same general still commanded that Russian unit.

Hearing this at the roadside, the young officer was skeptical at first, until he asked my father what he remembered most about the Russian general from that dinner.

"He was a big drinker," my father recalled. "He passed out before the dinner ended." That apparently rang true with the officer and brought on his loud laugh.

Soon, the soldiers finished changing the tire. My father thanked them and shook their hands. One soldier smiled at me and patted me on the back. My father offered them American cigarettes, another scarce commodity, which they all took and pocketed. With the incident over, we were off again for an uneventful rest of our journey.

I didn't know why Americans and Russians were no longer friends, but I was impressed with how a simple flat tire on an empty road in a foreign country could give people a reason to be the best of enemies.

CHAPTER 4
THE COUNTERINTELLIGENCE MEN

My earliest real-life heroes were the dozen men of the US Army Counterintelligence Corps unit in Braunau. The evenings I spent listening to them tell stories thrilled me more than anything I could have found in books or movies.

Like my father, most were thirtyish and had grown up in Eastern or Central Europe before the war. All spoke fluent German, English, and at least one Eastern European language. Most had fled Europe as refugees at the onset of the war and were recruited to return afterwards. While none were born or raised in the United States, and some had just become US citizens, here they were, engaged in the first line of defense of American interests in the next round of international conflict.

Other than my parents and Herma, my father's colleagues stood out as the most memorable adults of my early childhood. These men seemed like warriors in a new crusade, while the local Austrians looked beaten down from the recent war.

However, unlike my father, who had just come from working on the staff at the Nuremberg war crimes tribunal, most of the others had been employed at ordinary office jobs when the military recruited them. Some were recent refugees.

With the Cold War getting chillier by the day, the western Allies, especially the US military and intelligence agencies, wanted to know about events in Eastern Europe as relations with the Russians deteriorated. They also wanted to thwart Soviet espionage operations.

With no extensive spy networks in place yet, the best opportunity to gain intelligence information lay in the refugees who steadily streamed westward, getting out of Eastern Europe while that was still possible. After screening by staff at the embassies and military posts where they applied for entry papers, the ones who seemed like promising information sources or had the potential to become agents were referred to the Braunau group or others like it. The refugees found themselves interned there under military custody. Not exactly as prisoners; more like temporary, involuntary guests.

The refugees comprised an alphabet soup of names, nationalities, backgrounds, and experiences. Everything from ordinary citizens who had witnessed something of interest or patriots who wanted to help their home countries, to Nazi collaborators trying to bargain for a second chance in exchange for useful information. They stayed in Braunau only as long as it took to interrogate them and determine their possible usefulness. Most then moved on to new lives in whatever nation would have them. A few succeeded in immigrating to the United States.

The real prizes were the ones willing to return to their home countries as counterspies, gathering more information and potentially misleading espionage efforts aimed at the West. I knew when that happened, as my father would come home in an upbeat mood and announce, "We had a real breakthrough today," or "We found a really good one willing to go back."

Braunau provided an ideal location for this enterprise—a small town bounded by a river on one side and miles of fields and forests in all other directions. Belying its illustrious history, it now was just a quiet place far from the post-war action, practically a model for a future CIA safe house.

My father and his colleagues worked in an unmarked office complex buried in the pine forest south of town, off the road to Salzburg. The single men lived in a hotel in Braunau. Those with families, like us, lived in the enclave of two-story duplexes in Ranshofen.

The group often gathered at our home after work. My mother and Herma both were excellent cooks, and my parents liked to entertain. For the single men, especially, this provided a welcome respite from the isolation of the town. Food and drink remained in short supply for Austrians, but the military commissary in Salzburg provided us with enough meat, sausages, cheese, and produce to fill our pantry and a small refrigerator.

The men took off their suit jackets, loosened their ties, and lounged on sofas and easy chairs in our living room. Any wives in attendance helped my mother in the kitchen. Once refreshments were served, the women settled in next to their husbands.

As the men got acquainted, they talked a lot about their experiences before and during the war.

"Let me tell you how close I came to getting caught as I was leaving Berlin," one led off. When he finished, others told their stories of similar close calls. Nervous laughter followed each story as they recalled how narrowly they had cheated death and the Nazis.

Once, when a new man, Karl, joined the group, someone called out, "Ernie, tell him about your amazing escape!" I had heard my father tell this story before. He nodded, smiled, and began.

"I was traveling by train from Vienna to Bremen, to catch a ship to New York. My sister had gone ahead of me. I heard Jews were being stopped so of course I felt nervous. I bought a ticket in a first-class car, even though I couldn't afford it. I hoped no one would bother me there.

"The train had just started for Munich. An older man, very well dressed, sitting across from me, asked if I played chess. I replied I loved chess. He stood and pulled an ivory chess set from his bag in the rack above his seat. So, we started playing, all the way across Austria. We were in the middle of a game when the train pulled into Passau, at the border.

"Suddenly, German policemen rushed through the train. Two of them, both very young, threw open the door of our compartment and demanded to see our papers. I pulled my passport and travel permit from my jacket pocket and handed them to the nearer policeman. He looked at them, looked back at me, and then said loudly, 'You are Jewish. You must leave the train.'

"I stood up, trembling. Then, to my astonishment, my chess partner pulled out his own papers and held them up to the policeman. I could see a Nazi official seal. He motioned to me to sit back down and barked at the policeman, 'Leave him alone, we have a game to finish!' That was it. The policemen apologized, backed out of the compartment, and closed the door. Then the train started moving again.

"The other fellow said to me, 'Come, let's continue our game.' I was so shaken up I could barely concentrate. Of course, I lost the game. But I made it to my ship with no more trouble."

When he finished, all the men shook their heads in amazement, even those who had heard this before. All had interesting stories, but his was unique, real life outdoing fiction.

Over time, the men talked more and more about the stories they encountered in their daily work. Those tales especially fascinated me. I felt like a fly on the wall at a spy conclave. Although I didn't fully understand the significance of what they were doing or why, I felt like the adults were letting me in on something special and secret.

Usually, I was the only youngster present. I kept in the background, but made myself useful serving food and drink to the adults. Then I found an unobtrusive perch from which I could watch and listen. They had no apparent reticence about talking in front of me. When Karl, in one of his first visits, questioned the wisdom of this, someone responded, "He's Ernie's boy, there's no problem."

As an evening progressed and the men drank more, their stories became more detailed and vivid.

"I talked to someone today who claimed he saw Russian tanks being moved into a new base outside Prague," one began. Others nodded, then joined in with similar information gleaned from other interrogations.

"A guy showed me photos of a new factory being built in his town, with heavy security, maybe for military production," someone tossed out. That opening led to another man launching a larger discussion of industrial conditions in the Eastern Bloc.

Sometimes individuals being interrogated were identified as war criminals using fake identities. More often, they identified others wanted by the authorities. Eventually, inevitably, someone would drop a bombshell.

"I don't know whether to believe this," one man said in a lowered voice, "but a former SS officer told me today he saw one of the commanders of the Treblinka concentration camp just weeks ago, dressed as a refugee, with fake papers, being processed for emigration at an office in Vienna. What do I do with that?"

I came to understand these cases were problematic. Great resentment had developed, especially in Germany, over the war crimes trials and the subsequent military tribunals. Now, the occupying powers were more concerned with building Cold War support among the civilian population than in pursuing every last war criminal. They even allowed ex-Nazis and others who had committed atrocities to serve in government, military, or police positions. So, when the Braunau group uncovered information that no longer interested the authorities, the typical comment was, "If we can't use it, send it to Simon."

I later learned they meant Simon Wiesenthal, who became the most renowned hunter of Nazi war criminals. He had recently opened his documentation center in nearby Linz.

I understood what I overheard was not to be shared. When I asked my playmates, the children of some of my father's colleagues, if they had heard interesting stories when the adults gathered at their homes, they had no idea what I meant. Knowing that made me feel even more included and privileged, as if I had been granted a unique level of trust.

I don't remember many of the men clearly. Like most people involved in the world of espionage, they had no remarkable traits. They certainly didn't fit the media image—no James Bond types. They dressed plainly, in light-colored suits and white shirts, like accountants or engineers, which many had been before accepting this assignment. A few, though, were indelible characters.

Paul was a chubby, balding, vivacious fellow from Germany. Apart from his work, he had assembled a collection of war widows around Europe whom he visited on a regular rotation. After each weekend sortie, he returned to regale the gatherings in Braunau with his exploits.

"What a great time I had," he would declare. "Those Bavarian [or Dutch or Italian] women really know how to treat a man!"

The adults always laughed uproariously at his exploits. I laughed along with them, but I could only guess at what he meant. He remained lifelong friends with my parents, though I remember my mother commenting, after each of his visits, "It's a little immoral, what he's doing." My father always agreed, though not convincingly.

Peter, a young, handsome Hungarian, said very little about himself, but asked endless questions of the others. Some in the group commented on his secretiveness.

"Why does he take so many days off, and where does he go?" they wondered. No one knew, but many didn't trust him. Within a few months, he suddenly disappeared.

After five years in Braunau, the group moved to the US Army base in Linz. They operated there for two more years, until the end of the Austrian military occupation.

Thirty years later, I was visiting my parents in Seattle when their old friend Paul from Braunau stopped in. Hearing him and my parents talk and laugh about events in that distant past took me back to those gatherings at our home in Ranshofen. It felt like listening to aging former gunfighters recalling their exploits in their Wild West days.

With the evening winding down, they talked about what had become of people in the Braunau group.

"What about Peter?" my father asked. "I always wondered if he was really an agent spying on us for the other side."

"Yes," Paul interjected. "He was a spy! Our people caught him years later, still spying for the Hungarian intelligence agency."

"Really," my father said, sounding not surprised. "What happened to him?"

"They shot him!" Paul blurted out.

The two gave each other a knowing look and simultaneously burst out laughing. That ended the evening, closing the book on an era that few people remembered and far fewer experienced.

CHAPTER 5
REAL AMERICANS

I took my first big step toward becoming an American after we left Braunau in 1954, when my father's counterintelligence group relocated to Linz. We moved into a pre-war apartment complex taken over by the Army, in the Bindermichl neighborhood on the south side of the city. They called it Old Bindermichl to distinguish it from a new apartment complex built nearby after the war, which naturally they called New Bindermichl.

Old Bindermichl consisted of three stories of apartments, about a hundred units, built around two large courtyards, each containing a playground and auto parking. Archways and driveways pierced the buildings on opposite sides of the courtyards. My family occupied an apartment on the second floor, next to one archway.

Old Bindermichl apartments, Linz, 1955

Ash-gray stucco covered the buildings, while lighter-gray concrete lined the fifteen-feet-high arches. Small balconies and window shutters on the upper floors somewhat relieved the drabness. Residents hung wooden flower boxes filled with geraniums or petunias from some window frames.

Herma moved with us to Linz, but returned frequently to Braunau on weekends to see her boyfriend. She soon married and remained in Braunau for good. I occasionally stayed with her and Loisel for a few days. Although I missed her and Braunau, I was becoming more of a city boy.

Where Braunau had been a small, intimate village, Linz felt like a real city. I had visited bigger cities, but living in Linz meant daily noise, traffic, and bustle. I loved driving around town with my family in our newly acquired Opel Taunus.

Linz's downtown centered around a square dating back to the Middle Ages—similar to Braunau's square, but much larger. It had typical cobblestone paving; centuries-old buildings three or four stories high with sandstone facades and copper roofs; apartments with bay windows overlooking the square; and a fifty-feet-high column topped with a golden cross and sunburst, in memory of the many who died in long-ago plague epidemics. Also like Braunau's square, this one sat close to the river, the original reason for the city's location. But this river was the Danube, the quarter-mile-wide main artery of Central and Eastern Europe.

Where Braunau had one manufacturing plant, Linz was an industrial center with factories ringing the city and railroads connecting it to the rest of Europe. After heavy bombing during the war, plants and rail yards were just resuming operation. Neighborhoods of apartments for the city's workers stood between downtown and the factories. Those outer areas especially, like the nearby plants, showed heavy wartime damage—rubble-filled craters where buildings once stood, and parts of buildings still standing like gravestones marking the recent slaughter.

Even neighborhoods that remained intact looked grim compared with Bindermichl. We saw building facades with cracked walls and fading paint; few cars on the road; children walking to school, book bags on their backs, dressed in neat but drab and threadbare outfits; tight-lipped grownups, eyes downcast, carrying a few groceries home or searching for work.

The biggest change from Braunau, though, was not the place itself, but the people. So many Americans! Mostly Army personnel and their dependents, though also civilians like my father, working for the military. While we saw few soldiers back in Braunau, here I saw American soldiers in uniform everywhere. I started learning the meaning of various insignia—ranks, military units, and decorations.

In Braunau, I learned English at an early age, but spoke it only with my own family and the other families from the Army Counterintelligence unit. Now I had to speak English as the primary language of my daily life, on the playground, with neighbors, at the military stores, and soon at school. Naturally I didn't speak it as fluently as the kids born and raised in the United States.

"Where are you from?" served as a common conversation starter on the playground or at school among kids whose families came from all over the country. In my case, the question seemed more pointed, as if to ask, "Where are you from that's obviously not in America?"

The people around me in Braunau, if not Austrian, came mostly from other parts of Central or Eastern Europe. I had thought of the United States as one place. Now, from the descriptions I heard from my new friends in Linz, I realized America had many parts, all different.

In Braunau, if people spoke English with an accent, that accent typically was German or Czech. In Linz, I heard English spoken with a half dozen accents, most of them American regional ones—midwestern, New England, New York, and especially southern. That Americans didn't all sound the same came as a revelation.

Or look the same. I had seen a few Black soldiers on the street in Salzburg, but here I lived among whole families of Black people, most with accents similar to the White southerners.

I noticed a few families who looked White but had names like Lopez and Ramirez. They also spoke with multiple accents, but different in some cases from any of the others.

We all mixed easily on the playground. I didn't know what was going on among the adults, but the kids paid little attention to differences in color, birthplace, way of talking, or father's military rank. That easy acceptance changed as we got older.

What we now call a convenience store occupied one corner of our quadrangle of Old Bindermichl. It shared space with a counter dispensing sodas, hot dogs, hamburgers, and the basic three American flavors of ice cream—vanilla, strawberry, and chocolate. Kids with a little money in their pockets could find everything they needed to get through the day without ever leaving the housing complex.

The store gave change in American coins, the first I saw. In Braunau, we only used Austrian shillings. But the coins were the only American money we handled here. The occupation authorities outlawed US paper currency to avoid black market trading in it. Instead, they issued paper scrip in the same denominations as regular US currency, but usable only at stores on military bases. That practice prevailed throughout post-war Europe. I didn't see actual American currency until a visit to the United States years later. The other American kids joked about this new experience, calling the scrip Monopoly money.

The other center of activity for us was the nearby US Army base, Camp McCauley, in the community of Hörsching just west of Linz. Unlike the new facilities I saw later in Germany, this base had been converted from a German *Luftwaffe* airfield. The US Army took it over and hung a banner across the entrance announcing the base's new name. It contained offices, a medical clinic, a commissary selling food, a small base exchange selling anything else available, and a movie theater, all in boxy, somewhat dilapidated buildings. At the end of the occupation, the base would become Linz's commercial airport. For now, it served as an alternative to the playground for me and my friends and as a workplace for our fathers.

On Saturday mornings, we packed into Army buses for the ride from Bindermichl to Camp McCauley, where we trooped into the small auditorium that doubled as a theater. I came to know those Saturday movies as a ritual at every military base. Most films were screwball comedies or westerns, all in black-and-white. Westerns fascinated me. Roy Rogers, Gene Autry, Randolph Scott, and John Wayne all became vivid features in my life. Cowboys, Indians, outlaws, and ranchers all were new to me. The scenery too. The familiar backdrops in so many westerns, places I later knew to be Monument Valley in Arizona or Vazquez Rocks near Los Angeles, made me think about how much more of the world I had to see.

That thought resonated with me early. Playing outside our apartment one day, listening to kids chattering about their hometowns in Alabama, Nebraska, or California, I thought, "I'm six years old, and I've lived nowhere but Austria."

My parents had taken me for a brief visit to New York at the age of six months to show me off to my dad's parents and other relatives. My mother told me years later that I must have enjoyed the ocean voyage on a military transport, the USAT *General Maurice Rose*, as I slept and giggled my way through North Atlantic storms that had most of the adults seasick for days.

Soon after we moved to Linz, my father received news that his mother had died at her home in New York. With no time or way to plan a family trip, he left as quickly as he could get on a military flight from Munich.

During his return trip a week later, our family's life as we knew it nearly ended. As my dad drove the Opel from Munich back to Linz, a large truck driven by a drunk Austrian hit his car head-on at high speed.

He spent what seemed to me like an eternity in a hospital in Munich. I knew about all the family we had lost during the war, but had not previously experienced the prospect of death up close. While my mother held in her fear and grief, I worried openly day and night. I couldn't imagine how we would go on if my father didn't recover.

The truck driver had the misfortune of not only wrecking his vehicle but, far worse, seriously injuring a member of the military occupation forces. I heard he went to prison for a long time.

Once my father returned, with no lasting injuries, he ordered a larger car, a Ford four-door sedan. When it arrived a few weeks later, courtesy of the Military Sea Transport Service, I stood in awe. Compared to the clunky Opel, this looked like my idea of a spaceship—two-tone, light blue with a white roof; big head and tail lights; a windshield as wide as the road; and a huge, shiny hood ornament. Compared to the Opel, or the Army staff car before that, the new Ford felt like a royal coach. It drew the envy of the block until a neighbor bought something newer and even bigger.

With the new car, we drove about town more. I viewed going to the central square as a treat. Once my mother finished her shopping and errands, and provided Dean and I had behaved, she would take us to a café or pastry shop. And then, time permitting, we would stand at the rail by the river, which was so much wider than the Inn in Braunau, watching ferries and barges pass by en route to Germany upriver or Czechoslovakia and Hungary downriver.

Although the Danube fascinated us and appeared scenic, we soon learned it also could be treacherous. Our first spring there, rapid melting of winter snow combined with heavy rains upriver caused the Danube to jump its banks and inundate the downtown area. The indoor swim school where I took lessons flooded, giving me a respite from the unheated pool for a few weeks.

In Linz, we continued our frequent weekend trips into the countryside and to nearby points of interest., but with one notable exception. We never visited the site of the Mauthausen concentration camp, located ten miles southeast of Linz. I heard friends mention going there, so I asked by father about it. He was non-committal.

"Some of my family died there," he told me. "I don't think I want to go there. It would just make me sad. Maybe you'll go there when you're older."

I did go fifty years later, stopping there on a drive from Vienna to Braunau. Walking through the fortress-like gateway, viewing the quarry where inmates labored to produce granite for Nazi public works, and staring into the gas chamber, I understood my father's reticence. I didn't regret being there, but the experience certainly left me sad, imagining relatives being worked to death in the quarry or being killed in the gas chamber.

Camp McCauley had no dental clinic, so, when I needed a tooth filled, my mother took me to a dentist in a dark building just off the downtown square. That day, I had my first experience with a dental drill. The doctor didn't believe in painless dentistry or he skimped on the anesthetic. As soon as he started drilling, pain tore through my jaw. I screamed and bit down on his thumb, at which he let out a scream much louder than mine. He would not work on me further, he informed my mother angrily, and he would sue her for his injury. She pulled out her wallet and handed him a few shillings. That payoff quickly eased his pain and allowed us to make a getaway.

But I had a price to pay. Striding back to the car, my mother glared at me and curtly informed me, "You get no pastry today!"

Family excursions soon became less frequent. The year we arrived in Linz, I started my formal education. The school for military dependents contained all the grades, one through twelve. Located too far from Bindermichl to walk, we traveled there and back by school buses, on which I would spend countless hours of my youth.

Just one indelible memory remains from that first year. The school hired Austrian musicians to teach those interested in playing various instruments. Along with several other elementary students, I opted for the recorder. An earnest young man who dressed in three-piece suits and combed his hair back from his forehead, our instructor spoke passable English and seemed excited about being there. From the first session, however, things went badly. Some students acted oblivious to the instructor. They focused instead on taking apart their instruments, which they then struggled to reassemble.

"Austrian children would not behave this way," the instructor admonished them, but that meant nothing. The more frustrated he became, the more they delighted in his anguish. One day, he didn't show up for class. He never reappeared. The school principal told us the fellow had given a very emotional notice and could not be enticed to return to the classroom.

When I told my mother, she expressed sympathy for him. "There are no other jobs now for a young musician," she said. "He will probably have to work as a clerk in an office or a store and will be very unhappy."

My friends and I, on the other hand, remained very happy, especially back on the playground in Bindermichl. All being Army brats in one form or another, we delighted in playing war games. The older boys organized the games, picked sides, and led the opposing forces as we mowed each other down amid the playground equipment in our concept of combat.

Those of us with unusual names had a special experience. Tommy, one of the organizers, declared to me and a few others, "You need real American names if you're going to be in the Army. You're Joe [or Bill, or Jack]." We understood. I already knew I wasn't yet a real American. I just wished they didn't make such a big deal of it, announcing it in front of everyone on the playground. Besides, some of our fathers who had fought in the actual recent war had names that didn't sound so "American" either.

Still, I felt on my way to becoming an American. Someday, I thought, I would get to live in America and see the places my friends called their home states.

***

During this time, I realized what a large role food played in our family. The farther we moved geographically from our roots, the more important food became as a tangible link to our past. I loved hanging around the kitchen, watching my mother and Herma cooking and baking all the dishes that kept the house smelling so much better than the homes of most of my friends.

Rich, hearty dishes. No steamed broccoli or low-calorie salad dressings here.

"What could be healthier than a nice pot roast with gravy and dumplings?" my mother often said with conviction.

In Austria, dumplings played a starring role on any menu. They came in all varieties, like pasta in Italy. Huge dumplings almost the size of a football, studded with pieces of dense bread, boiled in a soup pot, then sliced and served under meat and gravy. Golf ball-size liver dumplings cooked in chicken broth or vegetable soup. Tiny dumplings spooned into boiling water and served as an accompaniment to Wiener schnitzel and red cabbage. My all-time favorite, though, was plum dumplings—not plum-flavored dumplings, but whole plums encased in potato dough. They could be a snack, a dessert, or an entire meal.

Back in Braunau, Herma and my mother began by boiling several potatoes on our ancient-looking gas stove. They peeled the potatoes and shredded them onto a large wooden cutting board, adding beaten eggs, melted butter, and finely sifted flour.

While the dough rested, the cooks pitted two dozen or so plums—small, oval plums with dusty, bluish-purple skins, known to Americans as Italian prunes. They inserted a teaspoon of sugar into each gaping plum, and set a fresh pot of water to boil.

Next, they spread a dusting of flour on the cutting board and placed the mound of dough in the middle. With a wooden rolling pin, they spread the dough out into a sheet a half-inch thick and sprinkled it liberally with more flour. One of them worked the dough in her hands while the other kept adding flour until the dough reached the magical perfect consistency.

The cooperative effort continued as methodically as surgeons at an operating table. Each of them tore off a piece of dough, spread it between her palms, laid a plum in the center, wrapped the dough around the plum, and carefully smoothed the dough to form a round dumpling. They repeated this until they had consumed all the plums. Each dumpling had to fully surround the plum, with no seams or leaks.

They carefully eased one dumpling at a time from a large spoon into the waiting boiling water. The dumplings initially sank to the bottom, but then, after a few minutes, rose to the surface, indicating that they were done.

While the dumplings boiled, the cooks melted butter in a cast iron frying pan on an adjacent burner, added cracker meal, and stirred the combination until it browned. Once the dumplings floated, the cooks lifted them out with a slotted spoon and rolled them into the frying pan.

By then, the rest of the family had gathered and seated themselves at the dining table. A green salad, made earlier in the day, already sat on the table, along with glasses of white wine for the adults and something less exotic for the children. Also, a small bowl containing a mixture of sugar and poppy seeds, to be sprinkled on the dumplings.

The cooks spooned two or three dumplings onto each plate, which I excitedly carried to the table. Cutting open a dumpling released a puff of steam, filling the room with a sweet aroma from the plums. Conversation stopped. Every bite became a treat—a combination of the sweet, silky plums, the smooth potato dough, and the slight crunch of the poppy seeds. As quickly as anyone finished their first portion, they returned to the kitchen for more.

After Herma returned to Braunau, I stepped in to help my mother prepare this dish. Before I eventually moved out, I made sure I had her recipe. When I visited Herma years later in Braunau, she made plum dumplings for me, as if to reaffirm the bond between us. I still make them at least once a year for my family and for select friends. Every time, with every bite, I am transported back to the kitchen in Braunau, to some of the happiest moments of my childhood.

Over time, I discovered many of my friends similarly had special dishes, cooked in their families for generations. It could be an Italian pasta sauce, a Russian cabbage dish, or an Indian curry. No matter how American they were or had become, those dishes were important to their identity and to remembering their family history. When people immigrated and became Americanized, those foods all became part of the American cultural fabric. But I always felt like few other foods could compete with our contribution.

"Plum dumplings," I told Coralea years later, "are the last thing I want to eat before I die."

CHAPTER 6
DIGNITY IN A REFUGEE CAMP

Apart from the American kids in our housing complex, I had other friends in Linz—kids from the squatters' camp across the street from our apartment complex. The camp was a transient community of war refugees, some of them concentration camp survivors. They lived in a collage of shacks and huts built from whatever materials they could find, scattered about what looked to have been a farm field.

In the first years after the war, Bindermichl hosted a formal camp for displaced persons (DPs), one of dozens of temporary way stations for war victims with no idea where to go or no means of getting where they wanted to go. This one housed solely Jewish survivors. It consisted of small houses for families and barracks for single adults, with community washrooms and toilets. Also, a school, a medical clinic and a chapel. The Jewish ORT relief organization provided services to camp residents and prepared thousands for eventual emigration to Palestine. Although such movement was highly restricted during those years, establishment of the state of Israel in 1948 opened wide that path for remaining refugees. The Bindermichl camp closed soon after that.

Few of the refugees in camps like this could emigrate to the United States. Just as before the war, American public opinion overall remained opposed to large-scale Jewish immigration, even of Holocaust survivors. And returning to their previous homes was unthinkable for most survivors. Not only would it dredge up memories of all the horrors and losses they had had suffered, but most had heard about survivors being beaten or even killed when they returned and tried to reclaim their onetime homes and businesses.

The informal encampment across the street had none of the amenities of the organized DP camps. It looked as Spartan as I could imagine. Just a collection of shacks with outhouses and a common water well. I saw the encampment from our apartment window soon after we arrived in Linz and asked my parents about it.

"They are people just like us," my mother said. "If relatives hadn't helped us, we could have wound up in a camp like that."

People just like us. With what sounded like my mother's endorsement, I wandered across the street and into the camp. A few people stared, as my clothes, shoes, and haircut all marked me as an outsider.

I soon encountered two boys about my age kicking a soccer ball in front of a wooden hut with a corrugated metal roof. An adult couple sat on a homemade bench outside the front door. The ball rolled in my direction. That seemed like an invitation so I dribbled the ball toward the boys and then passed it to the older one. He smiled, approached me, and introduced himself as David and the other boy as his brother, Henrik. The couple on the bench were their parents. The father had watched as I walked over from the apartments across the street, the first time he had seen anyone come over to the camp.

Pulling a knife from his belt, he sliced off a piece of a roasted sunflower sitting on the bench next to him and handed it to me. Then I noticed the huge sunflowers—golden heads surrounded by dark green collars, on stalk standing taller than me—in the garden beside the hut. The sunflower was crunchy on the outside, moist on the inside, with a consistency like dense bread and a flavor that reminded me of corn cooked over a fire. I played a while longer with David and his brother until time for me to go home.

"Come back whenever you want to play with my boys," the father said.

At home, I told my mother about the encounter in the DP camp. She seemed pleased. She didn't care for a lot of the brash American kids in the playground.

Over the next several months, I crossed the street often to see David and Henrik. After I started school in the fall, those visits became less frequent. Still, both boys always seemed glad to see me. I brought Dean with me a few times early on, but he felt uncomfortable there.

When I invited them to come over to the playground in the apartments, their parents were reluctant. The boys had wandered over there once on their own and had been yelled at and chased away by a bunch of American kids. The boys didn't understand what the Americans said, but they knew locals were not welcome.

These people's day-to-day lives were so different from my family's. The parents both were concentration camp survivors from somewhere else in Austria who had met in another encampment right after the war. None of their relatives survived, and they had no connections anywhere else. They didn't want to go to Israel. So they, and now their two sons, languished in the makeshift camp, waiting until one of the refugee agencies resettled them somewhere. They had spent time briefly in one of the formal DP camps, but preferred the less regulated conditions here. The father did odd jobs, and the mother grew vegetables and flowers in their small garden plot.

I wanted my parents to meet my new friends. My mother's refusal surprised me. It would make her too sad, she said. It would bring back too many memories. My father came over with me once and had a friendly chat with the parents.

"I wish I could do something for them," he told me afterwards, but there was nothing. This situation was different from the one in Braunau, where the more remote location and lack of oversight allowed him and his colleagues to operate under the radar. The best he could do was occasionally send over some scarcer food items with me.

A year later, David and his family remained there. Many other refugees had come and gone and the camp gradually emptied.

Then, everything changed. Some American boys had been playing a silly but seemingly harmless game that involved sneaking up behind an unsuspecting playmate and kicking them in the butt. One day, as David, Henrik, Dean, and I walked along the sidewalk on our side of the street, several of the American kids came out through the archway and followed us. Two of them ran up behind the Austrian boys and kicked at them. Then Tommy, the leader of war games on the playground, yelled for me to join in. I felt embarrassed not to, so I also took a couple of reluctant kicks at my Austrian friends. Stunned, they backed away. Henrik began to cry. Then they both ran across the street, back into the safe confines of their camp.

I knew I had done something wrong, but didn't know what to do next. After a sleepless night, I went over to the camp, to David's home. His father answered the door. I was no longer welcome, he told me. I had disappointed him terribly, mistreating and embarrassing his boys just like the other Americans had done. He would not kick a dog, so he could not imagine kicking another person without provocation. He and his family were poor and lucky to be alive, but they still had their dignity and no one would ever treat them like that again.

I tried to apologize, but the events of the previous day had broken the trust among us. I saw David and Henrik a few more times from our apartment window. Then, one day, a truck loaded the meager belongings from their hut and the family rode away.

Weeks later, I worked up the courage to tell my father about the incident. We talked about how easy it is to follow a group, even in doing bad things, like the things done to our own family before and during the war.

"What you did was wrong," he said. "But you can learn a lesson from this. The next time you see someone being mistreated, you'll know it's wrong. Instead of going along with it, I hope you'll try to stop it."

Soon enough, I would have my chance to live up to his hopes. But not until I learned some more lessons.

CHAPTER 7
MOVING ON

In early 1955, my parents announced we would move soon. With the end of the Austrian military occupation, my father had taken a new position in the intelligence branch at US Air Force Europe Headquarters in Wiesbaden, Germany.

This made no sense to me and my friends. We won the war. Why did we have to move? Why couldn't we stay there in Austria as long as we wanted? Of course, we knew nothing about the political machinations that had gone on for years after the war. While we engaged in playground war games, massive troop movements almost led to another actual war, this time with the Russians. Then, after lengthy diplomatic battles over the composition of the Austrian government, the western Allies and the Russians suddenly agreed to withdraw from Austria and turn it into a neutral country.

Compared to Linz, Wiesbaden looked like a garden city. For centuries, going back to Roman times, it was a spa resort. The name even means baths in the meadow. Despite having grown to a city of 200,000, the architecture and ambience of the city still reflected that.

Once we settled in, we began to take family walks around the Warmer Damm, an expanse of lawn and gardens covering in the center of town. Some days, we continued on to the great public buildings nearby—the opera house, theater, spa, casino, and 17th-Century City Hall. Even as a child, I found inspiration in the great stone colonnades, glittering fountains, building facades covered in sculptured flourishes, and broad cobblestone squares. Beyond those buildings lay the moss-covered stone ruins of the old Roman settlement.

South of the park, a broad, lush, grassy mall stretched several more blocks to the railroad station, an imposing structure of red stone and glass. Whenever we passed near the station, I asked my father to stop and let us look close-up at the huge steam locomotives pulling passenger trains in and out.

Wilhelmstrasse, alongside the Warmer Damm and at the edge of the shopping district, became my favorite street. Once our parents finished their errands, they rewarded me and Dean for our patience with a visit to one of the pastry shops there. We sat outdoors at elegant wrought-iron tables with linen tablecloths, facing the park and eating apple strudel or fruit tarts.

An even greater attraction for us was the world's largest cuckoo clock, outside a souvenir shop on Wilhelmstrasse. This monument of woodwork stood twelve feet tall, with a hand-carved face flanked by a pair of hunter's trophies—a rabbit and a pheasant. Above the clock face, two doors opened on the hour, making way for a mechanical cuckoo to emerge and squawk at the crowd that assembled on the sidewalk for this show. And crowning the whole thing was a life-size, carved stag's head with a set of actual antlers. While other viewers came and went, Dean and I stood and stared at the clock for long periods, regardless of whether the cuckoo was about to perform.

From downtown, we saw the rounded tops of the Taunus Mountains. For a special treat, we rode a funicular up to the Neroberg for a view out over the entire city, all the way to the Rhine River and the city of Mainz on the other side.

Wiesbaden had escaped the war with far less damage than other German cities. Frankfurt, an industrial and railroad center twenty miles away, was bombed repeatedly. In Wiesbaden, it appeared as if bombs or artillery shells had occasionally landed there by accident. As a result, the damaged or collapsed buildings stood out all the more, like raw sores on an otherwise lovely face.

By this time, ten years after the war, residents had largely recovered from the trauma and destruction, but lots of people still did marginal work, selling roasted chestnuts or grilled sausages from little charcoal braziers or moving goods about in small hand-drawn wagons. Although we often saw beggars, some of them missing limbs, most people looked well-dressed and went about normal daily business. Construction crews demolished buildings damaged in the war and replaced them with new, modern structures. Cars and buses again filled the streets.

Our first home in Wiesbaden was the lower floor of a two-story, turn-of-the-century house on Biebricheralle, a cobblestone boulevard lined with mature chestnut trees, running from the railroad station to the community of Biebrich on the north bank of the Rhine. An Air Force officer, his wife, and two sons occupied the upper floor. The surrounding neighbors mostly were older Germans, so we played in the backyard, enclosed by a wrought iron fence tall enough to keep us in and strangers out. A small paradise, it contained cherry, apple, and plum trees, berry bushes, and flower gardens. Throughout that spring and summer, sweet, lingering aromas filled the yard.

A German gardener tended the landscaping, appearing at irregular intervals and working silently. He stored his tools in a room under the back stairs of our apartment. When he opened the door, we saw masses of cobwebs. Charley, the older of the upstairs boys, claimed to have peeked into the unlocked room and seen an enormous spider in a far recess.

"I dare you to go in there," he challenged the rest of us.

The most curious of the group, I took the dare. Opening the door, I entered in slow, tiny steps. A mat of cobwebs hung across the room at the level of my chest. Then I saw the spider moving across the mat toward me. At that moment, I knew I had discovered the biggest, fastest spider in the world. The others, peering through the doorway behind me, saw it too. Before I could retreat, one of them slammed the door shut, leaving me in total darkness with the monster spider coming at me.

With my heart feeling like it would explode and my lungs heaving, I spun around and pushed on the door. Someone tried to hold it shut, but my adrenaline overcame them. I flung the door open, jumped out, slammed the door behind me, and dropped on the ground to recover from my first true moment of terror.

I looked up and saw Charley laughing.

"You bastard!" I yelled, certain that he was the one who held the door shut. He smiled and shrugged. The important thing, though, was that I took the dare and won. From that day on, no one else ventured into the storeroom.

With supervision, we could wander out of our yard. My parents liked to walk and often took me and Dean along on strolls through the neighborhood. Just a block north, across the boulevard, lay the Henkel winery, an estate surrounded by vineyards and gardens. It specialized in sparkling wines known as *sekt*, the German equivalent of champagne. When my parents entertained and served Henkel wines, they joked that we had a pipeline from the winery straight into our kitchen.

The increased distance from Braunau made us miss Herma even more. My mother went through a series of German housekeepers referred through a military agency that vetted them to work in American households. Local women sought this kind of work. Many were war widows or had never married due to the shortage of young men. All of them, however, suffered in our eyes from comparison with Herma.

The best of the German housekeepers was a young woman named Kristel who lived in nearby Biebrich. Cheery and hardworking, she seemed grateful for the opportunity. But she had elderly parents whom she supported, and had to leave early on certain days to help them. On those days, an older woman, Frau Schneider, came in to help.

That arrangement worked fine until the day a piece of my mother's jewelry disappeared. A gold ring with a sapphire stone, it had been a gift from my father. My mother confronted Kristel. The young woman vehemently denied taking the ring. Knowing how vulnerable her situation was, she pleaded with my mother to search further.

"I am an honest woman," she cried. "I would not steal from you!"

But my mother wouldn't give in. I hadn't seen her that adamant before. I had a feeling she wouldn't believe anything a German told her. She fired Kristel, who stormed out, still protesting her innocence.

Soon after that, Frau Schneider gave notice and did not return. Her disappearance got my mother thinking. She realized she had first missed the ring in the evening of a day when the older woman had been there. Now Mom strongly suspected that Frau Schneider took the ring. My father was more certain. He recalled seeing Frau Schneider wandering about the apartment, looking into areas where she had no business. He also remembered other little things disappearing after some of her visits. He inquired with the housekeeper referral office about Kristel, but found she no longer was listed with them. He wanted to make amends and give her another chance, but there was no opportunity.

My parents didn't talk about this incident further, but I thought about it a lot. I liked Kristel, and I wished my mother hadn't fired her. More important, I saw how much damage a hasty action could do to someone in a position without power, how it could literally change someone's life. This outcome was the opposite of what I had seen in Braunau, when my father used his power to save a life.

Soon after that, we moved again, this time to an apartment in the large military housing area known as Hainerberg on a hill overlooking downtown. If Linz was my introduction to living around a lot of Americans, Hainerberg would be full immersion.

CHAPTER 8
SURVIVAL AMID THE RUINS

In Wiesbaden, we attended Jewish services for the first time, at the nondenominational chapel in Hainerberg. Braunau had no Jewish community, and I didn't recall entering a temple or attending services in Linz.

My father had a religious streak in him, stemming from his family's long line of rabbis, though that had ended generations earlier. He wasn't terribly serious about it and we didn't attend services on a regular basis. Once in a while, though, he came home from work early on a Friday and announced we were going to Sabbath services that evening.

Wiesbaden once had a large synagogue, destroyed during the same Kristallnacht riots in 1938 that propelled my father's family to leave Vienna. We went to services as part of the small international Jewish community in Wiesbaden associated with the military occupation. The much larger Catholic and Protestant congregations used the chapel most of the time, so they outfitted it with all the fixtures and symbols needed for their services, from confession booths to a large Christ on the cross. When it came our turn, we brought out the ark containing the Torah scrolls and a different set of prayer books.

I found the services a bit long and tedious at first, but I soon learned particular prayers and songs that I liked and looked forward to. The rituals fascinated me, especially since we didn't practice them at home. Prayers associated with lighting Sabbath candles. Blowing the ram's horn to welcome the new year on Rosh Hashanah. Fasting and atoning on Yom Kippur.

The chaplain was an Air Force colonel, a kindly, older man, especially welcoming to families with children. He impressed me by remembering my name each time he saw me, even though we were not regulars. The rabbi delighted in telling us the Old Testament stories that underlay the important holidays. My favorite, no matter how many times I heard it, was the Purim story of Queen Esther, the Jewish woman who married a Persian king and then foiled a plot by his treacherous advisor to annihilate her people.

The best part of going to Sabbath services was the tradition of having wine and pastries afterwards. The congregation women piled the social hall table with food. Once services concluded and the crowd filed into the hall, we kids began circling the table and eyeing the pastries—miniature strudel, folded pastries stuffed with plum jam or poppy seeds, and cookies of every size and shape. Since there was far more food than needed, we had no limit on how much we could devour before our parents signaled the end of the evening.

The after-services social hour also featured trays of small glasses, like large shot glasses, filled with sweet red wine. After the rabbi led the blessing of the wine, the adults all took a drink. Focused on their ceremony, they rarely observed kids quietly making our way to the remaining glasses of wine. As with the food, there was more than enough wine, so no one noticed as I downed three or four glasses. We occasionally drank table wine with dinner at home, but I preferred this sweet wine.

The wine sampling almost came to an abrupt end one evening during our first summer in Wiesbaden. The rabbi had invited our whole family, along with some other couples, to dinner at his apartment to welcome us to the community. Dean and I were the only kids present. During dinner, the adults allowed us to have small glasses of wine to share in the ceremonies.

After dinner, the adults moved to the living room, leaving Dean and me to entertain ourselves. Seeing that several of the adults had left wine in their glasses, we set about finishing it for them. Mom calling us interrupted our drinking spree. I had a bit of a buzz, but Dean had an absolutely glazed look as he followed me into the living room. I stopped at the side of the sofa where our parents were sitting, but he kept walking right into the far wall. Before anyone could respond, he bounced back, groaned, and collapsed on the floor.

"Oh, my goodness!" yelled my mother as she ran over to him. He was fine, just a little stunned. Our parents apologized to the rabbi and the other guests, and made a quick, embarrassed exit.

"No more unsupervised wine drinking," my father commanded. That edict lasted until the next Sabbath service.

We also experienced a serious side of being part of the congregation. In Wiesbaden, as in most German cities, there lived concentration camp survivors and other Jews who had suffered horribly during the war. Many were ill or elderly and having a difficult time recovering. The congregation made an organized effort to reach out to these victims through social aid organizations. My parents, because of their own wartime experiences, were frequent participants. Our family regularly visited survivors in hospitals, in nursing facilities, or in their own homes. They were immensely grateful to receive the still hard-to-get food items we brought, and even more just to have some attention and interaction.

I met many people like that, but I remember most vividly one couple, the Bergmans. They were in their sixties, but seemed older. Both stood barely over five feet, partly from being stooped. They looked fragile and moved slowly, as if they might break if they fell or bumped into something.

The Bergmans had been prosperous before the war. She came from a well-to-do family, and he had a successful accounting practice in Frankfurt. Their two children lived nearby. The Nazis had scooped up the children and their families early in the war and sent them to a concentration camp. From which none returned. The Bergmans themselves had the good fortune to be taken in by longtime friends in a small town. Near the end of the war, they were found out and also sent to a concentration camp. Amazingly, despite their age, they both survived those final months. Then, along with thousands of others ostensibly liberated, they found themselves detained for several more months by

American forces, behind the same barbed wire and fences erected by the Nazis. Ironically, this happened on the orders of General Patton, under whom my father had served during the war.

Once truly liberated, they emigrated to Argentina, where Mr. Bergman reestablished his accounting business. But, after a dozen years there, his health failed in the South American climate. He developed a pulmonary condition, and his doctor told him he needed to return to the climate of his homeland. Back in Germany, he could no longer find work at his age. His wife's family had lost everything in the war. They now subsisted on small reparation payments from the German government.

I met the Bergmans in their apartment. Such as it was. They lived on the third level of one of the downtown buildings that had been bombed, a few blocks from the railroad station. It looked like a giant knife had cut the building in half. Part of it had collapsed, while the rest remained standing, still occupied.

It once had been a luxury building with large apartments. The Bergmans had a small part of one of those apartments, just a bedroom, a bathroom, and a combination kitchenette and dining area. Their furniture overflowed the small rooms. Younger German families occupied the rest of the floor in units similarly carved from one of the original apartments.

On one of our first visits, I went out exploring. A single ceiling fixture dimly lit the hallway outside the Bergmans' apartment. I smelled smoke and sweat. A cold breeze blew through a thin curtain at the end of the corridor. I peeked around the edge of the curtain and jumped back, seeing nothing but air on the other side, three stories up. The rest of the building that once stood there lay in a heap of rubble below. A crude barricade of two wood crossbars blocked the lower part of the opening. Just a few feet away, children played unsupervised in the hallway.

My parents grew very fond of this couple. The Bergmans, in turn, lit up whenever we visited. They had no one else, other than the occasional social worker. Mrs. Bergman patted my head and put her arm around my shoulder, as she must have done with her own children and grandchildren years earlier.

"It is very nice to have children in the house," she sighed. "I miss this so much."

Talking with my parents about the better times before the war, they grew animated. They even seemed larger and less fragile.

Whenever I saw the Bergmans, they dressed immaculately, he in a dark suit and tie, she in a dress with lace decoration. Our visits were the closest they came to the social life they once enjoyed.

They had so little, yet they always served us cake and coffee. Probably the only time each month they could afford such indulgence.

"Have some more cake," Mrs. Bergman always urged me. Even in their desperate circumstances, they clung to a dignity that was all they had left. Like the family in the squatters' camp in Linz.

My mother always kept to herself as we walked down the stairs and back to our car at the end of these visits. After one of the first visits, my father put his arms around Dean and me, and said, "These are good, kind people. No one deserves what happened to them. Remember that."

CHAPTER 9
TEACHERS, GAMBLERS, AND SPIES

Moving to Wiesbaden launched my love affair with school. It also exposed one deficiency that plagued me throughout my academic career—my indecipherable handwriting. In the Army school in Linz, we hadn't started learning cursive writing. On arriving in Wiesbaden, my parents learned that this was a common problem, since the Air Force schools started teaching cursive in the first grade. I would have to learn basic handwriting over the summer before starting second grade.

Like Abraham Lincoln in the stories, teaching himself to write with a piece of charcoal before the open hearth, I labored for weeks at the kitchen table in the house on Biebricherallee with my first lined notepad and a handful of pencils. By September, I produced what I considered passable script. I felt mortified when my second-grade teacher looked at my first writing assignment and blurted out, "Who wrote this? I can't read a word of this!"

I didn't need to see the page to know it was mine. And it got no better through twenty more years of school. Whenever a teacher peered at me over a handwritten assignment and started out, "Cary, for such a good student...," I knew the rest of the line that would follow. When I took the California bar exam many years later, I typed it to make sure the scorers could read my essays.

Otherwise, I liked Vandenberg Elementary School. Unlike my first school in Linz, here I walked to class. The school fronted on Texasstrasse (Texas Street in German) in the middle of the Hainerberg housing area, where all the streets were named after states. We lived two blocks away, on Coloradostrasse, in one of eighty identical three-story, eighteen-unit apartment buildings, all with earth tone exteriors and reddish roofs.

Hainerberg apartments, Wiesbaden, 1960

The school felt enormous. Two stories high, running the length of a block, it was all white brick separated by long banks of windows. The eastern end of the building housed the junior high classrooms. Across the street stood Arnold High School, an even larger edifice of brick and glass that the administration barred us from entering unless accompanied by an adult or by an older sibling enrolled there.

It was so different from the German elementary school near downtown that I visited with my father one day when he had business with an administrator there. That school looked like a stone fortress, with small windows, poor lighting, and little color. Where we were animated in class and boisterous in the halls, the German kids remained quiet and orderly. I felt lucky to be attending my school.

A giant gravel playground filled the rest of the block behind our school. Before class in the morning, during recess breaks, and after lunch, hundreds of kids engaged in games of tag, dodge ball, red rover, and marbles.

No walls or fences surrounded the school grounds or any other part of Hainerberg. Apparently, no one had concerns about threats from the outside world.

After school, we continued our games among the apartment buildings. Playgrounds with swings, monkey bars, slides, and carousels, along with ballfields, filled the space behind each row of buildings. The playgrounds here were more democratic than the one in Linz, without a handful of older kinds dominating the rest of us.

Despite my continuing challenge with handwriting, everything fell into place when I started third grade and had the good fortune to wind up in Mr. Foster's class. A tall, thin Midwesterner who favored vests and plaid shirts, he made it clear he had taken this job because he wanted to see the world. I felt in awe of him. In return, he provided the support and attention that made me want to read and learn as much as I could.

Mr. Foster sometimes took me bicycling on weekends. He rode an English racing bike with multiple gears. I struggled to keep up on my single-gear kid's bike and resolved to get one like his as soon as possible. We didn't stray far from Hainerberg, sticking to the small roads radiating out into the countryside. As we rode along, he talked to me, about nothing in particular, just whatever was on his mind. That made me feel very grown up and motivated me to strive even harder in school.

In Mr. Foster's class, I had my first crush, a slim, blonde girl named Dianne who frequently wore a brown-and-white checked dress that I found alluring. I talked to her every chance I had. She acted friendly, but didn't seem as interested in me as I was in her. One day on the playground, I decided to find out. While she chatted with some girlfriends, I walked up to her from the side and planted a firm kiss on her cheek. Dianne pulled back, her jaw dropped, and she wiped away the vestige of my kiss. Then she ran off. My friends who saw the whole thing laughed. A few minutes later, Mr. Foster appeared and took me aside.

"You can't just kiss girls," he told me in a firm but sympathetic-sounding tone, "no matter how much you like them or how pretty they are. Promise you won't do that again?"

I blushed and nodded. I felt bad that Dianne didn't like being kissed, at least not by me. Still, I was glad I did it, just as I had seen older guys do in the movies.

Down the hill, toward the center of town, I encountered my first American-style shopping center, with an Air Force Exchange the size of a Wal-Mart Supercenter, a snack bar, a barber shop, and a movie theater. And this theater, which linked us most directly to American culture, was cavernous compared with the one at Camp McCauley in Linz. When the Saturday matinee featured something especially popular, hundreds of kids filled the seats, huddled in the aisles, and even flowed onto the stage. Lying on the hard, wooden stage, staring up at the forty-foot screen, was how Dean and I viewed the new Davy Crockett film.

Hainerberg sat at the edge of the city. Across the street from our rear yard lay farm fields filled with rows of root crops. A few older German women dressed in simple cotton dresses and head kerchiefs worked the fields. They ignored the passing traffic and the houses across the street. I occasionally walked over and struck up a conversation. I wondered what they were growing and when the crops would be ready to pick. They always brightened, took a short break, and offered me a sample of carrots, kohlrabi. or whatever crop they were tending.

Wiesbaden Air Base sat just two miles to the southeast. We could catch a bus from Hainerberg to the Air Base to go to another movie theater, watch the occasional plane land, or just get a change of scene. In the other direction, north across the city, was Lindsay Air Station, containing an office complex for Air Force Headquarters Europe. It included my father's office, in a gray concrete building facing the parade ground with its impressive, tall flagpole.

Downtown lay just minutes away by bus or bicycle. By age ten, I roamed about without supervision. It was a more innocent time, and the Germans knew better than to mess with American kids. I quickly learned my way around town on the buses. For the equivalent of about ten cents, I could ride from Hainerberg, through downtown, out to one of the surrounding villages, and back again. The buses were crowded and smelled of sweat. I stood out on the buses by my American clothing. Other riders smiled, but few spoke to me. The only other young people were German kids riding with a parent. I tried once to strike up a conversation with a German boy about my age, but his mother held him back and he just looked at the floor and didn't respond.

My friends' parents rarely allowed their kids to leave Hainerberg with me. It surprised me how many of the Americans stayed cloistered in the military bases and housing areas. A lot of them came from small-town or rural backgrounds and seemed intimidated by the foreign culture and language. The bases offered so much in the way of American-style diversions that many families never felt the need to look outside. When I told my friends about my adventures, they sighed and told me they wished they could go with me.

The military provided lots of entertainment opportunities for those who preferred to stick with an American experience. The bases featured the usual officers' clubs and service clubs. Downtown, the Air Force converted a Georgian mansion into the Eagle Club, a kind of community center for Americans.

My parents joined the Civilian Club, in a villa at the top of the Neroberg, overlooking downtown. To get there, we drove up a winding street through one of Wiesbaden's best neighborhoods. Mature oaks and elms overhung the street, and grand houses belonging to doctors and lawyers lined the way. At the top of the hill, a driveway led into a cobblestone court in front of the club. Granite pillars flanked the entry. Once inside, red carpeting, crystal chandeliers, and dark wood paneling created an elegant atmosphere.

Our family enjoyed going there for Sunday brunch, something distinctly American but new and different for us. At a single sitting, we started with eggs and French toast, worked our way through salads and meats, and finished off with pastries. Plus, champagne.

However, for me and Dean, the best feature of our visits to the Civilian Club was not in the dining room. While our parents socialized and waited for a table, the two of us headed for the bank of slot machines on one side of the lobby—shiny metal machines the size of a television, just within our reach. We loved the ritual of dropping coins in the slot, pulling the lever, watching the spinning wheels bearing cherry clusters, bars, and the rest of the standard symbols, and then waiting to see if coins would come tumbling down the winner's chute.

We couldn't enter the casino room, and kids weren't supposed to gamble at the slots either, but the manager was friendly with my father and left us alone. Then, one Sunday, Dean hit a jackpot and a flood of coins poured out. That drew unwelcome attention from all the adults. While we scooped up Dean's winnings and shoveled the handfuls of coins into our pockets, the manager made a show of telling us we were underage and not permitted to gamble. Somehow, he forgot that rule by our next visit.

As much fun as we had about town, I found two activities at home just as interesting. My father had been an avid stamp collector since childhood and introduced me and Dean to this hobby. What attracted me to it most was learning history and geography by researching the nations that originated the stamps and the historical figures that appeared on many of the stamps. My father's other hobby was building and radios, something he had done on a factory assembly line upon first immigrating to the US. He involved me in assembling short-wave radios and then tuning in stations scattered about the globe, particularly ones in the US. As with stamp collecting, it expanded my awareness of how much more of the world there was to see and experience.

Even at that age, we sensed the pressure of the Cold War brewing to the east of us, as the adults around us talked about preparations for a possible conflict with the Russians. This situation particularly disturbed my parents. They wished they could venture into Czechoslovakia to visit favorite places they missed or to search for lost relatives. The border had closed several years earlier and would not open again for a long time.

One of my classmates, a skinny blonde girl named Nicolette, had a Russian-sounding last name. My friend Jeff decided that she and her family must be Russian spies. One day, we confronted the poor girl on her way home from school. She denied being a spy. I thought she sounded pretty sincere, but we weren't about to back off.

"Let's throw the spy into the rosebush," Jeff urged, pointing at the thorny plant behind her. She tried to fight us off, but to no avail. Into the bush she went. Her school books flew into the air. Thorns dug into her arms and legs and tore at her blouse. She bled and cried as she disentangled herself, while we ran off. We repeated this cruel ritual a few more times before she learned to avoid us. I wondered why no one ever came to her rescue. Maybe, I thought, her parents feared saying anything because they really were spies. Then her family moved away, so we never found out.

I told my parents the whole story, thinking they ought to know about our suspicions. To my initial surprise, they were horrified.

"What were you thinking?" my father asked, shaking his head. "Don't you see how badly you treated that girl, for no reason? If you're going to grow up to be a good American, you need to have better values than that."

I had no answer. I realized what we did to Nicolette was almost as bad as the incident with the boys from the refugee encampment in Linz. I didn't bully anyone ever again, and I resolved I would make up for this very disappointing behavior.

CHAPTER 10
DIFFERENT KINDS OF AMERICANS

In early 1956, my parents announced we would take a vacation trip to the United States that coming summer. This news excited me, as my only previous visit had been when I was less than a year old. Dean had never been. I finally would see something of the homeland of most of my friends.

On our departure date, we drove to what was then Rhein/Main Air Base, now Frankfurt International Airport. We lugged our bags into the single-story passenger terminal, where we found several other families already waiting. Through the window, I saw the stubby control tower topped by a glass box from which the air traffic controllers viewed the web of concrete runways and taxiways.

Our plane was one of several shiny C-54s outside with markings of the Military Air Transport Service. The four-engine propeller plane had been a mainstay of the Berlin Airlift a few years earlier. Its civilian counterpart, the DC-4, was in wide civilian use in the US.

On boarding, it surprised me to find the inside of the plane was nothing like what I had seen in photographs of commercial airliners. Exposed wiring and tubing lined the interior walls. Just a thin layer of padding covered the seats. A pile of parachutes just inside the door got my attention like a flashing warning sign.

I was equally surprised to learn that the four engines, large and powerful as they looked to me, couldn't carry the plane and its fifty passengers across the Atlantic non-stop.

"The first leg of our flight will be to an air base in Prestwick, Scotland," the pilot informed us over the intercom. "We'll refuel there. Then we'll proceed on the longest leg, to Gander, Newfoundland. We'll arrive there at night and stop for a rest. The next morning, we'll fly on to our final destination, McGuire Air Force Base in New Jersey."

We settled into a row of seats near the rear of the plane, with Dean and me on one side of the aisle and our parents on the other. I grabbed the window seat. Within minutes, the engines sputtered to life and the propellers began their windup. Soon the engines hummed like giant swarms of bees, and the plane lurched forward. We heard the tower over the intercom, clearing the pilot for takeoff. The nearby hangars raced by as we accelerated. With engines now roaring, we lifted off into a cloudless sky for what I knew would be a great adventure.

From Germany to Scotland, our first flight experience kept me and Dean mesmerized enough that we behaved ourselves. We stared out the windows, awed by views of the German, French, and English countryside from that great height.

Flying for hours over the North Atlantic, having no other kids to play with, we soon got bored and turned to our imaginations. We pictured ourselves as crew members in the warplanes we had seen in movies, waist gunners in a B-17. Gripping imaginary machine guns and crouching on the pile of parachutes, we simulated loud gunfire as we shot at swarming German fighter planes, eventually knocking them all out of the sky. Of course, after dispatching the first group, we imagined another and another. Our antics at first amused nearby passengers, but that soon wore off and they began to stare grimly at us and at our parents. My father got the message and stopped our drama.

A cold darkness greeted us in Newfoundland. We spent the rest of the night there, getting a few hours' sleep on cots in a room made swelteringly hot by steam radiators. The following morning, we departed for New Jersey. It took us thirty hours in all to cross the Atlantic.

We spent two weeks in New York. Mostly, we visited relatives, beginning with my mother's sister, Magda, and her husband. Then came an endless stream of aunts, uncles, and cousins of various degrees of relation. Also, friends of my parents from their time in New York before going back to Europe, and a few of my father's Army buddies.

New York City was a revelation, a huge metropolis compared even to Vienna and other European cities I had seen. More people, cars, and noise than I expected. Scores of buildings taller than anything I had imagined. Gigantic Central Park, with endless pathways, lakes, bridges, and gardens. So many kinds of people, speaking in so many different ways with so many different accents. Yet, all of them Americans. I thought I might fit in here.

Uncle Tom had established himself as a psychiatrist in Manhattan. He and Magda had an apartment in a high-rise building across from Central Park. From their balcony on the tenth floor, I could see up and down the island.

We stayed at a hotel near them. Our parents allowed Dean and me out on the streets by ourselves, as long as we had a destination and directions. Here, too, it was a more innocent time. The Natural History Museum, a few blocks down Central Park West, became our favorite destination. The stone lions at the head of the broad staircase seemed to roar a welcome. We spent hours in the museum, staring at animal dioramas, dinosaur skeletons, and display cases filled with exotic insects. In Europe, we often visited art museums, but nothing like this.

The emotional highlight of our visit was a ferry ride to the Statue of Liberty. I had seen pictures of the towering green copper colossus in schoolbooks and on postage stamps, but viewing it for real as the boat approached Liberty Island made me catch my breath and fight back tears. Climbing the winding staircase inside the statue, up to the viewing windows in the lady's brow, added to my excitement. Then, on the ferry's return to the foot of Manhattan, we passed Ellis Island. The buildings lay in disrepair in those days, not open to the public, but I saw my parents hug tightly and grow wistful at the sight. As for millions of others, that had been their Plymouth Rock, their first stepping stone to new lives in America. Years later, when New Yorkers established a foundation to restore Ellis Island and turn it into a museum honoring immigrants and their contributions to America, I proudly donated to the cause in my parents' names.

Then we were off to Monroe, Louisiana, to see my dad's sister, Mimi, her husband, Eugene, and my cousin, Steve. My father had spent time in the South during wartime basic training at Camp McCain, Mississippi. For the rest of us, it was an entirely new experience.

We flew out of New York's LaGuardia Airport in a twin-engine DC-3, the smallest commercial airliner of the time. Over the Smoky Mountains, the updrafts bounced us around like a ping-pong ball. By the time we landed in Memphis to change planes, I had become nauseous. I threw up in the middle of the only doorway leading into the passenger terminal. My parents apologized and airline staff rushed to clean it up, but anyone in a hurry had to walk through it or leap over it.

If New York had been an awakening, northern Louisiana was culture shock. Nearly everyone in Monroe spoke with a certain accent I had heard in several of my schoolmates. People lived in single-family homes, most with wood shingle exteriors. The wealthier neighborhoods featured brick homes. Expanses of lawn studded with magnolia trees surrounded every home. Downtown buildings were plain and no more than three stories tall. Compared to New York, or even Wiesbaden, it didn't seem like a city at all.

I met lots of relatives for the first time here, too, all from my father's side. The highlight was meeting Pearl Binder and her family, who drove over from Greenville, Mississippi. Her mother, Sophie Frank, had been instrumental in helping my father's family get out of Europe just before the outbreak of the war. She not only sponsored them, but used her influence with a member of Congress to get them visas in a hurry, bypassing a waiting list that had grown to hundreds of thousands due to tight immigration quotas.

We saw a lot of Black people, far more than anywhere before. They all seemed to be maids, clerks, or handymen, and acted subservient to any White people, even children. My aunt's maid entered the house through the back door. Restaurants and movie theaters had separate sections for Black patrons, and banks and stores made them wait until White patrons all had been served. Public water fountains had signs marked "White" and "Colored." I had seen nothing like this on the military bases overseas.

"What's going on?" I asked my father, as we sat in my aunt's living room. "Why do they have to stay separated like that?"

"This is how it is in the South," he said in a low voice, looking around to see if his sister or anyone else was in earshot. "It isn't right. I hope it changes someday."

After a moment of reflection, he continued. "It isn't so easy for Jewish people here, either," he said. "They are accepted, as long as they don't stand out and don't cause any trouble. But there are places they can't go."

That came as even more of a revelation. I knew about my family's experiences before and during the war, but I personally had not experienced discrimination in Europe on account of being Jewish. Now I learned that I would more likely encounter it here in the US.

After two weeks there, I looked forward to going home. We followed the same route of travel, in reverse. The visit had been a genuine cultural awakening. I lived around and went to school with Americans from many parts of the United States. Now, for the first time, I had seen some of those locales and experienced the culture of those places on their home turf.

On the flight home, I talked with my parents about everything that we experienced.

"I liked a lot of it," I told them, "but there were some things I really didn't like." I thought especially of the way I saw Black people treated in Louisiana.

"That's fine," my father responded. "America is big, with lots of different kinds of places and people. Someday you'll see a lot more. It's good that you got a taste of it. This is how you become an American."

Becoming an American, I thought. I guess so.

After returning home, I did feel different. Now, when I heard American kids speak with different accents or talk about their different home states, I understood better that there were lots of ways to be a real American, and I was starting to find my own way.

CHAPTER 11
THE RUSSIANS ARE COMING

In the fall of 1957, my father came home from work one day and informed us that we soon would move again. He sounded dead serious, not at all excited.

The Cold War had been ratcheting up. A few months earlier, the Russians brutally put down a revolt in Hungary that overthrew the Moscow-aligned government there. Pictures of troops occupying Budapest and of bodies in the streets shocked us. Meanwhile, the Russian-controlled regime in East Germany closed off movement between East and West Berlin and began construction of what became the Berlin Wall.

We all had heard stories of the Berlin Airlift that broke the siege of West Berlin when the Russians cut off land access ten years earlier. Now, our parents and teachers talked about a new, maybe bigger crisis. So great a crisis that USAFE Headquarters was moving from Wiesbaden to the smaller air base at Ramstein, fifty miles west, close to the French border.

Hundreds of families received notice to prepare for evacuation. Our relocation was necessary, my father explained, on account of a land feature called the Fulda Gap, a valley cutting through the mountains to the east, pointing directly at Wiesbaden and providing a route of attack from East Germany for Russian armored units.

Our parents seemed panicked at this news. We kids, on the other hand, initially grew excited. I had seen World War II tank battles in the movies. I pictured the Russians storming westward only to be ambushed and driven back by American armor. This imaginary confrontation quickly dominated our games. Playground equipment and toy wagons stood in for tanks and armored cars. On any day, some of us played the sneaky Russians and others the valiant Americans. The next day, we switched roles. It didn't matter. The outcome was predetermined. The Americans always won.

In school, we practiced nuclear war drills. At the sound of a siren, we dropped to our knees and huddled under our desks. This, too, became a game for us. As much as the adults treated these exercises with great seriousness, we joked among ourselves about the unlikelihood of our wooden desks protecting us from a nuclear attack.

Packing for the move interrupted our games. This time, unlike the previous moves to Linz and then to Wiesbaden, our parents involved me and Dean in the preparations. We had to make quick decisions about what to leave behind. Time to abandon stuffed animals and children's board games. I hated having to make the decisions, but being included made me feel grown up.

Then I had a profound realization. As I talked to my friends, I discovered not everyone was moving, just those families directly connected with USAFE Headquarters. Many others would remain in Wiesbaden. Would my friends who remained behind have to fight the Russians? I might never see them again. Or they might wind up heroes.

We said goodbye to friends and classmates. We all had experienced moves before as a regular part of life in the military world, but this one felt different. I noticed our parents' tight, grim expressions. The seriousness of it sank in.

Movers packed up our household goods and loaded them onto military transport trucks. After spending our last night in Wiesbaden at a hotel run by the Air Force, we left by car for Ramstein the next morning.

On arrival, we parked the Ford in front of the office where my father had to check in. While he was inside, I realized that we had arrived at the new base in time for lunch. I had imagined a long trek, putting a safe distance between us and the looming Russian invaders. I was no military strategist, but this short distance didn't strike me as much protection.

When my father returned, I asked him about it. He shook his head and smiled.

"If the Russians attack," he explained, "our troops should stop them before they get to Wiesbaden and Frankfurt. Even if they break through, it will take them hours to get here. In the meantime, our leaders will figure out a way to stop them."

He sounded so confident. That should have been good enough for me, but I couldn't stop thinking about those Russian tanks ready to plunge through the Fulda Gap. To get that off my mind, I focused on exploring our new surroundings.

Our apartment building in the housing area at Ramstein looked virtually identical to the one we had just left in Wiesbaden. The resemblance ended there. The base sat at the edge of a forest, far from any real city. Trees still filled the interiors of the blocks of pastel-colored, three-story apartment buildings. Fifty-foot evergreens loomed over the playgrounds where crowds of school-age kids played on swings, hung from monkey bars, and coasted down slides.

The apartment buildings marched right up to the school campus. I started fourth grade there. My class met in one of the dozen prefabricated classrooms of steel and glass that the Air Force placed behind the original school buildings to accommodate the sudden arrival of so many new students.

The street along the front of the main school building led to the working part of the base. Ramstein operated as a NATO base, with troops from several countries. In front of the four-story, white stucco headquarters building stood a row of flagpoles displaying the flags of the United States, France, England, and Canada.

My friends and I often rode our bikes there at dusk to watch the evening retreat ceremonies. A US Air Force color guard wearing starched blue uniforms marched four abreast in tight formation to the pole flying the American flag. The outer two carried rifles, with the butt secure in their right palm and the barrel resting on their right shoulder. They halted when they reached the flagpole. As the inner two soldiers stepped forward, a bugle sounded "To the Colors" from a hidden loudspeaker, followed by the national anthem. One soldier untied the halyard and lowered the flag, while the other caught the flag before it could touch the ground. In a well-practiced ritual, they folded the flag into a neat triangle and stepped back into formation. All four then returned to their starting point. The other three color guards repeated the ceremony with their respective flags.

I loved the pageantry of all the color guards, but I found myself increasingly stirred by the American flag ceremony. The bugle call, the soldiers, the flag, all combined to bring a tear to my eye and give me a feeling of belonging. I could see that the emotions hit me much harder than my American-born friends, who treated this as mere entertainment.

On one of my first days in school at Ramstein, the roar of jet engines drowned out the classroom lesson. Out the window, I saw a cluster of fighter planes carving an arc through the clear blue sky above the base. I wondered where they came from. That evening, I asked my father. From Landstuhl, he informed me, the other base, right across the highway.

Another base? The next weekend, I collected a few friends to go exploring. We followed the road past the headquarters building to a bridge over the autobahn. Sure enough, on the other side we saw a sprawling airfield.

Fences and gates secured this base, unlike the Ramstein side. We rode up to the guard post in the middle of the entry road.

"We want to see the airplanes," I told the sentry. He smiled, pointed behind him, and waved us through. Such lax security at a military base seems unimaginable today. Even then, security tightened after a sentry apprehended a purported Russian spy seeking to enter the base.

We headed straight for the flight line. In front of a series of cavernous hangars, we found rows of jet fighters. Most were older, stubby-nosed F-86s, the kind we saw in newsreels from the Korean War. Also, a few of the sleek, new F-100s, which looked faster and more dangerous. We also noticed propeller-driven cargo planes off to the side, including C-54s like the one in which I crossed the Atlantic the previous year. While some planes landed and took off, airmen moved others in or out of hangars. We saw constant action. From that day on, for the two years we lived at Ramstein, this was our favorite hangout.

Once a year, on Armed Forces Day, the flight line hosted a massive air show. All the NATO air forces sent planes and crews. Scores of the latest fighters, bombers, transports, and helicopters crowded the concrete apron in front of the hangars. The aircraft were open for us to explore. I loved clambering into the cockpits of the fighters and roaming the cargo bays of the transports. Aerial demonstration teams, usually including the US Air Force Thunderbirds, streaked overhead, sometimes so low that we could feel the thrust of their engines. The Army Golden Knights parachute demonstration team bailed out of a transport plane high above us, performed an acrobatic show on the way down, and landed on the nearby runway.

Troops from the various NATO forces staged colorful parades. My favorite was the Scottish unit, led by a bagpipe band in plaid kilts and black bearskin hats. A drum major marched in front, twirling a lance as if it were a mere baton, then flinging it high in the air and catching it in full stride. A dozen pipers followed, starting off with a rousing rendition of "Scotland the Brave." Flanking them marched half a dozen drummers pounding on their bass drums and twirling their tasseled white drumsticks over their heads.

I felt pride in being around all these skilled professionals. Different nationalities, races, and languages, we all were in this together. And the Americans obviously the leaders.

The pilots seemed invincible. We couldn't imagine how the Russians hoped to defeat us, with men like these in our front lines. But that invincibility was punctured one day as we played outside the school during morning recess. We heard the roar of jet engines daily, even aircraft breaking the sound barrier on occasion. This time was different. After the plane passed overhead, the engine sound grew lower and closer. Everyone stopped and stared in the direction the plane had gone. Then the engine sound ended in an explosion that shook the playground and echoed off the school buildings. One of the fighter jets from Landstuhl had gone down. The pilot stayed with the plane, we learned later, steered it away from the base, and died in the crash.

The next day, down at the flight line, we saw ten-ton trucks hauling the shattered remains of the plane. I felt confused over how this could happen. Then fear and apprehension set in. The pilots were human after all, and their planes could break down. Maybe we weren't so certain to beat the Russians.

Those concerns passed as we returned to our adventures around the base. Our second favorite place to hang out was the firing range. At a far corner of the base, against a dirt hill, troops trained with rifles and pistols. No one minded, so we stood and watched from behind the shade structures from which they fired. The low boom of .45 caliber pistols contrasted with the higher pitch of .30 caliber carbines. Once the shooting stopped, we dashed out to the targets to dig bullets out of the dirt. Impact mashed most of the lead slugs, but we found lots of intact copper-jacketed bullets. We collected them and traded them. The range staff smiled and wondered aloud why we found this so fascinating.

Inspired by our visits to the flight line and the firing range, we played war games, just as we had in Linz and Wiesbaden. Despite the tensions surrounding the move to Ramstein, our games were more about recreating World War II battles with the Germans than about fighting the Russians. On the hillside by our apartment building, my friends and I carried out mock shootouts and ambushes. I fought and died a hundred times on that hillside. We even rated one another on how convincing our performances were, as if we had any real idea.

At this isolated base, the Air Force tried their best to keep us entertained. One outlet was the Boy Scouts. I had already joined a troop in Wiesbaden and continued my involvement here. We went for day hikes in the German countryside and sometimes camped overnight on weekends. I remember a campsite in a meadow by a trout stream, with the stone ruins of a medieval castle looking down on us from a nearby hilltop. At night, the Milky Way flooded the sky, and the glow of fireflies lit the surrounding meadow. Out there, we forgot about the threat of war with the Russians.

The schools and the Air Force organized field trips for us, sometimes for our whole families. On any given weekend, we might visit the Roman ruins at Trier, the gem mines at Idar Oberstein, or Martin Luther's church at Worms.

Sometimes we joined in tours or hikes with local German scout troops. These activities did not always go well. Despite our common interests, some American scout leaders, all military men, acted contemptuous of the Germans. On one occasion, when a German troop's bus broke down, the American scout leaders refused to transport the German boys and their leaders home. The German scoutmaster, for whom I had been translating, asked me to prevail on his American counterpart.

"They're scouts, just like us," I said to my scoutmaster. He just stared at me.

"There's American Girl Scouts on that base with us," he finally replied. "I'm not letting any of those German boys near them!" Embarrassed at having to deliver that news, I left out the part about the Girl Scouts and said there simply wasn't room on the bus.

It wasn't just Germans who were at the receiving end of bigotry. In Ramstein, I witnessed real racism by Americans toward other Americans for the first time in the military world.

Walking home from school with classmates one afternoon, I saw two younger Black kids ahead of us. One of the boys with me yelled a racial slur at them. They turned and stared for a moment, then crossed the street without saying a word. The first boy yelled at them again, more loudly. The Black kids looked down and quickly walked up a side street.

I was stunned. No one I knew had previously talked that way. I didn't know those other kids, but I felt badly for them.

"Why did you do that?" I asked.

"I hate those niggers," he replied. "My dad told me what they're like."

I knew his father. an Air Force sergeant with a strong southern accent and a mean temper. Kids in the neighborhood stayed out of his way.

After that, I noticed those kinds of comments more. I didn't understand why this kind of behavior suddenly appeared. Or maybe I just hadn't paid close enough attention. I thought about my experiences a year earlier during our family visit to Louisiana. Somehow, it seemed explainable there. But here? I couldn't figure it out. We were all on the same side, all part of the military family.

I was paying closer attention when I got my first taste of antisemitism among the military community. My schoolmates often asked questions about one another's background, including religion. I never felt constrained about saying I was Jewish. Most of the time, the reaction was positive, sometimes comically so.

"My dad is Jewish," one classmate told me. "That's why he's so much smarter than my mom."

Then I went to a movie that opened my eyes to a different point of view. The film was *I Accuse*, based on Emile Zola's exposé of the antisemitic accusation of treason against a Jewish officer in the French Army, Captain Alfred Dreyfus, his banishment to Devil's Island, and his eventual exoneration. My parents saw it first and were happy that I expressed interest in it. Sitting by myself in the theater, I heard a few people make snide remarks about Jews. That shocked me. Why did they even come to this movie, I wondered.

Then a louder voice a few rows away said, "Dreyfus probably was guilty." In the dark, I couldn't see who was talking. I hoped none of them were my classmates or their parents, but I didn't know and I wondered. Again, I felt like this violated everything we were supposed to stand for, as Americans all in this together. I wondered how different, deep down inside, we really were from the Germans we had defeated in the war.

I forget about those kinds of concerns when I took drives with my parents on weekends. A favorite route was to cross the French border at Saarbrücken and drive to Metz or one of the smaller towns in between. My father's Army unit had fought in this area during the war, so he described feeling some nostalgia. My parents shopped for goods unavailable on the German side of the border. I had more interest in the food and pastries at the little cafés and bistros where we stopped for lunch.

For the Germans and French, crossing the border was tedious, involving waiting in line to have passports checked. Not so for us. I noticed we could go to the head of the line, show our US passports, and be waved through.

In Ramstein, I also got a first taste of official responsibility. Teachers at my school recommended boys to serve as safety patrols at street intersections around the school grounds. I was one of about twenty selected to be trained for what we understood was a position of great trust. Wearing white helmets and sashes, much like the Air Police officers who directed traffic, we acted as crossing guards to ensure the safety of kids walking to and from school. A few kids made fun of us, but they all followed our direction, pausing at the curb to allow traffic through and then crossing when we waved them on. To my surprise, even adults complied with our directions. My friends and classmates seemed impressed, treating me with newfound respect. I realized for the first time that accepting responsibility and exercising it properly was a major step toward growing up. And there was something distinctly American about this experience. I couldn't imagine German boys my age being given the same level of authority.

Meanwhile, conditions in Germany stabilized. The adults quit talking about the danger of war with the Russians. Then, as suddenly as we had heard about move to Ramstein, we received notice that we were moving back to Wiesbaden.

So, in the summer of 1959, we packed up again. On returning to Wiesbaden, we moved back into the Hainerberg housing area, this time to an apartment on Washingtonstrasse, a block from our previous home.

I felt happy to be back in Wiesbaden and looked forward to starting the sixth grade. T0-he two years in Ramstein had been eye-opening. I understood better how easy it was for people to think less of one another, based on things like race or religion. Yet, I felt stronger bonds than ever before with my friends and classmates. I was becoming a real American, like them.

As calm as things seemed on our return to Wiesbaden, tensions with the Russians still took a toll. The intense fear-mongering and red-baiting of the McCarthy era were only a few years behind us. Concerns about Soviet espionage created a paranoia visible to us all, especially in our positions so close to the frontier with Eastern Europe. One of my father's closest friends and colleagues, a Hungarian-born intelligence analyst now an American citizen, found his loyalty suddenly questioned. His name had been discovered on the membership list of a Hungarian labor union identified as a pre-war communist front group. That listing dated to his childhood, he explained, when his father had purchased a life insurance policy through the union and named the son as a beneficiary. Nothing more than that. Nonetheless, the investigating authorities refused to yield, and my father's colleague lost his job.

My father felt mortified at what happened to his good friend. He couldn't change the outcome, but he expressed his disappointment to us at home. I recall that as the only time I heard him question the fairness of the US government. It got me thinking too. Surely my father's friend was not the only person treated that way, despite his years of loyal service. How could I reconcile my pride at becoming an American with the possibility of such arbitrary action by my government? I soon put this thought aside, but it planted a seed that would germinate years later.

Returning to Wiesbaden also launched me into a deeper involvement with the Boy Scouts. The Air Force base sponsored the troop and made unusual resources available to us. An Air Force sergeant with long scouting experience served as the scoutmaster. Machinery shop at the base created ten-foot-tall, teepee-like tents from orange-and-white parachutes. Wherever we camped, we became known for those tents. When we took multi-day hikes or extended camping trips, Air Force personnel delivered supplies and water to us along the way. The Air Force even transported us as far as the English Channel when our troop traveled to England for an international scout gathering.

The highlight of my scouting experience in Europe was the celebration of the Boy Scouts of America fiftieth anniversary. Our troop and our

German counterparts held a ceremony at the downtown General Von Steuben Hotel. We placed a time capsule of memorabilia from that time in a marble monument to be opened another fifty years later. With the Cold War raging around us, this display of good will among former combatants in the last actual war gave us all a comforting feeling that transcended national pride.

CHAPTER 12
ON THE ROAD

We traveled around Europe a lot during my childhood. My parents believed traveling broadened one as a person, and they wanted to imbue Dean and me with that same feeling. They exposed us to new places, new cultures, new languages, new foods.

Each year, as winter approached, my father laid his collection of maps on the dining room table and invited us to gather around and talk about our travel plans for the coming year. He would suggest somewhere on the Mediterranean, and then we would talk about the merits of the south of France versus Italy. Or he would suggest the Alps, and we would discuss the relative attractions of Switzerland, Italy, and Austria.

Dean and I loved studying the road maps. Highway signage was poor in those days, so travelers found maps essential. I loved the sense of responsibility once my father let me serve as the navigator on our drives. We marked routes and waypoints on the maps, but I had to watch the distances and anticipate when we would approach a turn or landmark.

Every trip presented opportunities for adventure, especially unexpected, memorable interactions with people, both along the way and at our destinations. Those interactions made three summer trips particularly memorable and added to my Americanization.

**

Aunt Magda and Uncle Tom returned to Europe on vacation some years. They loved the mountains and particularly the resort town of Wengen in the Swiss Alps. Best known as a ski resort, it also was a popular summer destination. We met my aunt and uncle there twice for summer vacations. I remember best the summer of 1958.

My father wrote to our hotel well in advance. Within days, I began watching for a letter bearing Swiss stamps, confirming the reservations.

We didn't need airplane reservations. We drove our Ford sedan, even though the roads were still being rebuilt from war damage in many places. The distance was not great by today's standards, but we took our time, being careful not to damage tires or wheels in the frequent potholes. We also stopped for gasoline and to use restrooms whenever possible, as gas station locations were unpredictable and fuel remained in short supply. Roadside facilities were almost nonexistent, so missing a chance to use a restaurant restroom meant finding roadside foliage that afforded privacy from passing traffic.

After winding our way through southern Germany and into Switzerland, we stopped for the night in Zurich. In the morning, we drank cocoa and walked along the northernmost shore of the long, narrow lake before continuing on.

European nations all rigidly guarded their borders in that pre-EU time, but neutral Switzerland took extra precautions. Roads into the country often ran through steep-sided valleys or along mountainsides, with no way around the border checkpoints. Just inside the border, rows of flattened metal cones pierced the road surface in a narrow pass.

"See those?" my father asked as he pointed them out. "They're the tops of cylinders that can be raised to block the road against invading military vehicles. Somewhere nearby is a cave or bunker with controls for those obstacles and guns aimed at us right now. There are probably explosives buried in the mountainside to close off this pass." Sobering thoughts for a ten-year old.

Wengen was one of many mountain villages in the area known as the Bernese Overland. At a spot where the steep mountainside briefly leveled, it looked north across a glacier-cut valley toward a row of Alpine peaks. In the other direction, looming above the town, stood some of the most iconic mountains in Switzerland, including the Eiger, the Monch, and the

Jungfrau with its glacier-crowned tip second only in fame to the Matterhorn. The opportunity to walk for miles along the mountain paths and survey this spectacular scenery brought travelers. With them came hotels, restaurants, and shops. And eventually ski lifts.

Because of its remoteness, Wengen never lost its charm or became overly commercial. No roads went up the mountain. Only the winding path used by cattle herders, who fattened their dairy cows in the mountain pastures during the warm months and then walked them down into the valley for the winter.

Visitors relied on a cogwheel railroad. From the valley town of Lauterbrunnen, we rode the string of a half dozen wooden cars up what looked like an impossibly steep grade. We felt reassured by the clicking of the gear wheel locking into the ridged track between the rails. Snowy peaks soon came into sight. The air smelled as pure and fresh as the snow on the distant glaciers. Passengers oohed and sighed, smiling and snapping pictures.

Disembarking at the Wengen station, with its multi-lingual welcome sign, was like arriving at Shangri-La. The narrow streets contained no motor vehicles, only bicycles and small electric carts that delivered guests and luggage to the hotels. Even for fastidious Switzerland, it was remarkably clean and neat.

We stayed at the Park Hotel on a hillside overlooking the town. The owners had refurbished it since the war and again had an international clientele—Americans, Europeans of all nationalities, and the occasional visitor from Asia or Latin America. Guest rooms and outdoor terraces had long, unobstructed views of the surrounding peaks and valleys.

The hotel staff impressed me. All spoke better English than most of the Americans I knew, with perfect grammar and no use of slang or idioms. They dressed more formally than the guests and kept a military-like bearing as they moved quietly about. Their mission seemed to be to maintain a calm atmosphere in the hotel, especially in the dining room.

Dean could be rambunctious, especially with me. One evening, at the linen-covered dinner table, he persisted in kicking me under the table and otherwise provoking me. Of course, I responded in kind. With our parents becoming increasingly frustrated, the maître d' approached my mother, bent down, and in perfect Swiss understatement offered, "Madame, we would be pleased to serve the children in their room, if you would like." My mother rolled her eyes, we got the message, and the rest of dinner progressed more calmly.

A network of narrow trails connected Wengen to other villages. Pathways clung to the mountainsides or meandered across grassy, flower-filled meadows. My parents, especially my mother, never looked happier and more energetic than when the four of us, joined by Magda and Tom, took long walks on the mountain paths.

I had a small canvas rucksack in which we carried sandwiches and drinks purchased from a grocer near the train station. One day, we took a cable car up to the smaller village of Kleine Scheidegg, and then set out on one of the many trails. From an elevation of about 7,000 feet, the valley floor looked miles below us. Cows wandered about, announcing their approach with a dull clanging of large bells hanging on cords around their neck. Wildflowers dotted the meadows, but the real find was an occasional single edelweiss flower, the multi-pointed, velvety, white bloom that the Swiss treated as a national symbol. Everyone considered them good luck charms, like four-leaf clovers, and we picked a few to take home and press between the pages of a book.

Benches along the trails offered a chance to sit and appreciate the view. I loved these moments, eating a sandwich of Emmenthaler cheese and salami on rye, sipping on carbonated apple juice, staring out over the precipice at the opposing mountain range, I couldn't imagine anything more serene and satisfying. No wartime destruction, no noisy traffic, no school work.

The walks also provided a chance to get to know my aunt and uncle better. In those days, I only saw them on the occasional vacation visit. Tom fascinated me. He delved into every imaginable philosophy and religion, and he happily discussed it with anyone, even a ten-year-old. He underwent quite an evolution in his psychiatric approach, beginning as a Freudian, then an ardent Jungian, later studying Zen Buddhism and Christian Science, before formulating a method he called metapsychiatry.

"What do you think happens to us after we die?" he asked me, as we trailed behind the rest of the family. This struck me as a heavy question, something I hadn't previously considered. I gave him my off-the-cuff answer. He persevered.

"You know, Cary, different cultures and religions have different ideas about that. How do you think that came about?" I knew about different languages, but I didn't yet appreciate the vast differences among cultures. He piqued my curiosity and made me want to know more, which most likely was the point of his questions.

Later, my father asked me, "What were you and Uncle Tom talking about so seriously back there during our walk?"

"We talked about the meaning of life," I said, in what seemed to me a grown-up way of describing the conversation.

My father, always one to encourage learning, appeared happy with that.

"Keep talking to Tom," he urged. "He's a very smart man. You don't have to believe everything he tells you, but he'll make you think about things."

Fine with me. I looked forward to the next of many conversations I would have with my uncle.

Even in midsummer, the glaciers above us reflected sunshine like giant beacons, summoning us to come higher up the mountains. We rode the cogwheel train up, winding around steep ski runs and sharp drop-offs, to the foot of the Eiger glacier. From there, the track entered a series of tunnels cut through the face of the Monch and Eiger, in one of the most impressive engineering and construction accomplishments of the time. It eventually deposited us at the Jungfraujoch, at over 13,000 feet, the highest point to which one could travel by conveyance in Europe.

Stepping outside on the viewing platform, the entire world seemed made of ice, snow, and granite. Far below, we could make out small dots of buildings in a few villages. Otherwise, we saw only the mountains. I wouldn't reach a higher elevation until I climbed Mt. Whitney in California fifty years later.

As much as I enjoyed the family excursions, the best experience of the stay in Wengen happened back at the hotel. Children from many places congregated there, speaking many languages, like a mini-United Nations. We found common interest in the Monopoly board game, of which the hotel had several sets.

Walking through the lobby after breakfast on our first day there, I noticed half a dozen Monopoly boards laid out on a series of coffee tables along the wood-paneled wall opposite the registration desk. I watched from a distance at first, then edged closer. What I saw was a precursor to casinos I would visit years later, with players coming and going but the action never stopping. At any time, twenty or more youths, mostly boys between ten and fifteen, clustered around the boards, seated on upholstered benches. All intensely engaged in buying properties, placing houses and hotels, collecting rent, and hoping to pass "go" without landing on another player's property.

The games continued virtually non-stop, interrupted only by sleep. The rest of the time, players would join or leave as they wished, giving up their seat at the board when called for meals or to spend time with family. When any player departed, another youngster, waiting and observing, took the vacated seat and continued the play. One player, usually the oldest boy, took charge at each board. He picked replacements for players who left, acted as the banker, and settled minor disputes.

That first day, a tall, thin English boy named Edwin was in charge at the board I approached. Some seats remained vacant at that early hour. He looked up at me, smiled, and motioned toward an empty seat. "Come on," he said, "join in, we need another player here."

"Thanks," I replied, relieved at being invited in so easily.

"What's your name?"

"Cary."

"Sounds English, like Cary Grant."

"Yes, I was named after him."

He introduced me to the others around the board and showed me where my predecessor at that seat had left off. Then we resumed playing. I stayed until my parents called me away to go walking with the rest of the family. When we returned late that afternoon, I saw the games still in full swing. Edwin was gone but another of the boys I met in the morning had taken charge at that board.

"Do you want to play again?" he called to me.

"Yes."

"There's a free seat over there." He pointed to a seat at another board.

"Freddie," he called to a chubby, blonde boy running that one, "this is Cary. He played over here this morning. Let him join you."

"Yes, fine," said Freddie in a German accent. He motioned to me to sit and handed me the cards and money left by the previous player at that seat.

So it went. I joined the games at every opportunity. The hotel staff seemed amused and enthralled with this drama playing out in their lobby. Where dozens of children might otherwise be a disruption, we had found a perfect entertainment for ourselves. Waiters stood by, watching us roll dice and carry on our transactions. They brought us drinks and snacks, as well as the occasional message from our parents.

Most of the youngsters spoke two or more languages. When something needed to be said or translated, someone always could convey information in the needed language. Sometimes that meant one person translating from English to French, with another then translating that to Spanish or German.

Despite the intensity of the competition, virtually no conflict arose, and nothing that the leader at each board couldn't solve quickly. It all remained friendly and orderly. Even among kids from the US, England, France, Germany, and Italy, whose armies had just done ravaging each other. At the end of our stay, I wondered why all our respective home countries couldn't get along as well as we did.

***

The summer of 1959, just before my eleventh birthday, I first seriously noticed women's bodies.

I had traveled with my family to Lido di Jesolo, a beach town on the Adriatic coast, across the lagoon from Venice. We drove there via Munich and Innsbruck, then over the Brenner Pass on a two-lane road that snaked through the Alps. No autostradas and tunnels existed yet over or through the mountains.

Soon after crossing the crest, heading downhill into Italy, we discovered traffic blocked by a boulder that had fallen in the middle of the highway. The rocky mountainside dropped off sharply on the left and rose steeply on the right. No cell phones existed then, or even roadside call boxes. Someone had to drive back to the nearest town, find a phone, contact the highway authorities, and then hope they would send aid soon. Along with scores of other vehicles, we waited for hours.

Once it became clear we would be stalled for a while, people emerged from their cars and trucks. Kids rushed to inspect the troublesome boulder. Families shared sandwiches and drinks. Radios blared static-laced music. Eventually, a demolition crew arrived and blasted the rock into small pieces that they pushed down the hillside to reopen the road.

We checked into one of the new hotels in Jesolo built since the end of the war, a white stucco structure topped by a roof of orange tiles, with balconies and large windows facing the water. The hotel veranda opened onto the beach, a broad, mocha expanse sloping gently down to the calm, light-blue Adriatic. The water felt like a refreshing bath, shallow and comfortably warm.

For me, the hotel's most memorable feature was the huge dining room, where white-outfitted waiters bustled in and out, serving platters of an endless variety of pasta. Large manicotti tubes filled with meat or ricotta. Spaghetti covered in Bolognese sauce of ground beef and tomatoes or just squid ink. Flat fettuccine in creamy Alfredo sauce. Little shell-shaped conchiglie drizzled with olive oil and bits of anchovy. I loved it all.

The hotel had an international clientele, producing a cacophony of languages and cultures. Lots of families with children filled the public areas.

Most of the guests got along fine, except that everyone else disliked the older German tourists. In the early mornings, guests wandered down to the sand and staked out beach chairs of multi-colored cloth stretched on wood frames, leaving towels, shirts, or other personal items on the chairs. Returning after breakfast to begin a day of sun-worshipping, guests might find a middle-aged German couple occupying those same chairs, with our belongings tossed on the sand nearby. Some interlopers denied having moved our things. Others blustered that they had as much right to the chairs as anyone else.

"They sure are loud and pushy for people who just lost a war," my father declared the first time this happened. Others within earshot nodded or shrugged. Nothing changed.

While my parents and other adults reclined in their beach chairs, reading or chatting, we kids roamed the beach, splashed in the sea, and generally ran amuck.

A precocious child, I enjoyed adult attention. Adults told me I was a cute kid, especially stripped down to my bathing suit. They liked my being bilingual and talked to me more than to a lot of the other kids.

One morning, around the middle of our stay, I wandered off in search of a little quiet time. I stopped to watch the sand sculptors beginning work on that day's array of castles, animals, and abstract designs. Tides and wind had erased their work of the previous day.

Wading in the shallows, searching for interesting shells and following little fish darting around my feet, I heard someone call. I looked up and out to sea. Twenty yards off the beach, two women waved from a white paddleboat. Both looked twentyish. One was taller and blonde, the other brunette. Both slim but fit, their tanned bodies stood out against the boat.

"Hello," called one, in German. "Do you understand?"

"Yes," I yelled back.

"Do you want to come for a ride?"

I nodded.

"Swim out here. Get on the boat with us," she continued. I didn't hesitate. Parents did not yet routinely warn kids about responding to strangers.

Their boat consisted of a pair of benches on a platform astride two pontoons, like a small wooden catamaran with oars. I waded out to them and pulled myself up onto the platform.

It was only then that I noticed how skimpy their bathing suits were, and that one of them, the brunette, was topless. I can't remember her face or the color of her bathing suit. Just her long dark hair falling down onto pale breasts. Full breasts, though not voluptuous, and slightly pointed, not that I knew the difference. I couldn't take my eyes off them.

The other woman laughed. "What a cute boy. I think he likes you," she joked to her companion.

"Come sit by me," the topless woman invited, patting the wooden bench next to her. I complied with only slight hesitation. Then, in a quieter voice, she asked, "Do you like what you see? Here, give me your hand." She gently took my left arm, drew it across her and placed my palm over the nipple of her right breast, which stiffened to my touch.

"Go ahead," she urged, "Doesn't it feel good?" Did it ever! I squeezed and kept on squeezing, even after she removed her hand from mine. In the meantime, the other woman, sitting opposite us, rowed the boat further out from the beach.

Suddenly, a familiar voice called my name, like an alarm clock piercing a deep sleep. I dropped my hand and turned toward the shore. My mother, wearing a modest white, one-piece bathing suit and dark sunglasses, stood at the water's edge, waving.

"Cary, come here, we're going to lunch," she yelled across the water. I must have looked crestfallen. The women both laughed good-naturedly.

"Don't worry," said the one whom I'd been fondling. "You'll have other opportunities." She gave me a light kiss on the cheek and helped me down from the boat into chest-deep water. I waded to shore with an occasional glance back over my shoulder.

"Who were those girls?" my mother asked.

"Just two girls who let me ride on their boat," I replied as innocently 'as possible. I felt relieved she didn't ask more.

We stayed at the beach another week. Each day, as I wandered along the shore, played with other kids, or lay sunbathing, I looked for the two women from the boat, but I didn't see either of them again. I soon noticed other topless women on the beach. It seemed strange I hadn't paid attention to that before. I furtively stared at each of them. It didn't take me long to conclude, however, with my new expertise in these matters, that none of them had breasts as nice as the woman on the boat. Years later, what happened out there would probably be considered sexual abuse, but at that time it felt like a thrilling coming-of-age experience.

Then a shocking thought occurred to me. As friendly as the women had been, they were German, after all. Their families, our enemies in the recent war, might well have been killing people like my family just a few years earlier. I tried to put that thought aside, but it kept intruding, casting a pall over the rest of our stay.

* * *

In 1960, we visited England for the first time. We planned to drive our new Mercedes sedan from Wiesbaden to Calais, take a ferry across the English Channel, and then a train to London.

London had largely recovered from wartime damage. We saw all the tourist attractions. Like any youngster, I was impressed by the inscrutable Buckingham Palace guards, the opulent crown jewels in the Tower of London, the Nelson monument in Trafalgar Square, and the Big Ben clocktower looming over the Houses of Parliament.

I shouldn't have been surprised, but was, that everyone spoke English. Another version of English, however, different from that of any of my American friends back in Germany. Actually, more similar to the English spoken by the staff in Swiss hotels and shops.

Compared to Italy or Germany, I found the food bland and unremarkable. London had not yet become a hotbed of cooking from more exotic parts of the Commonwealth.

A highlight of our stay was a visit to Hamleys, which billed itself as the world's largest toy store, with six stories of every conceivable game, doll, and toy.

"How may I help you, young man?" asked a smiling sales clerk who saw me perusing a case of lead, hand-painted model soldiers. Using allowance money I had saved for the trip, I bought two sets—a group of Buckingham Palace guards and a quartet of lancers on horseback.

I moved on to the model airplane section. Assembling plastic models of contemporary military aircraft had become a hobby of mine. The store displayed hundreds of airplane model kits hanging from metal racks much taller than me. Reaching for a model on an upper level, I lost my balance, fell forward, and knocked over the entire rack, scattering models everywhere. My father rushed forward, apologized to the sales clerk, and began to help me pick up the sea of model kits. The clerk remained unperturbed, perhaps from dealing with such minor disasters regularly.

"It's quite alright," he assured us in a soothing tone. "Accidents will happen. I'll have someone take care of this. Is there anything else you would like to see?" He seemed so proper and civilized, forming for me an indelible impression of the English.

The most memorable interaction of that trip, however, occurred before we even reached England. We had planned to drive straight through to Calais, but started late. Then, despite our maps and my navigational efforts, we lost our way somewhere in northern France. My father decided to stop for the night and go on to Calais in the morning.

In the middle of a farming region, we didn't find a village with a hotel until mid-evening. By then, the town was dark, the town square empty, with a faint smell of horses and hay.

The solitary hotel occupied a plain, two-story building with a barely legible sign at the corner. Thankfully, lights still shone inside. A middle-aged man who turned out to be the proprietor stood at the open front door. We parked our car and entered the small lobby furnished only with two wooden chairs and a still life watercolor. In broken French, my father asked about rooms for the night and whether we could get dinner.

The proprietor looked us over, shrugged, and finally offered us rooms. But the dining room was closed until morning, he informed us curtly.

Tired and ready for bed, we saw no alternative. My father handed him our passports and prepared to sign in.

The proprietor, who had been checking his register and pulling keys from a drawer, glanced at the distinctive green-jacketed passports lying on the counter, with the American eagle emblem on the covers. He looked puzzled, stared up at my father, and paused for several seconds.

"American?" he asked.

"Yes," said my father. "Traveling to England."

The previously weary proprietor now moved at lightning speed. He leaped forward across the counter as if launched from a spring board and hugged my father.

"Marie," he yelled to his wife in the next room. "Open the kitchen, we have guests!"

He apologized profusely. Seeing us arrive in a Mercedes and not noticing our military license plates, he assumed we were Germans, like the ones who occupied the area so recently during the war. Instead, we were the first Americans he had encountered since the ones who liberated the village soon after D-Day.

The proprietor disappeared to take our bags up to our rooms. In the meantime, his wife emerged to escort us into the reopened dining room. She looked as weary as we felt, but the occasion was too good to miss. Once we sat down, she brought out plates of whatever foods she could quickly assemble and heat up for us. And local red wine for all of us, including Dean and me. Once her husband returned, he and my father made their best efforts to talk, in a mix of French and English, about their experiences during the war and since then.

When we were all too exhausted to continue, the man showed us to our rooms. Though sparsely furnished, they held large beds with down-filled pillows and comforters.

The owners doted over us again at breakfast. Then we had to be on our way.

We walked with our bags into the sunny morning. The square had come to life, with farmers carting produce, children walking to school, old people sitting in the sun. What caught our eyes, though, was the central feature of the square, something we missed in the dark at our arrival the previous evening. Most town squares held a monument, usually a stone obelisk or statue commemorating some local heroic figure or historical event. This town's monument was a Sherman tank, abandoned by US troops during the war and now standing on a low concrete platform.

The hotel proprietor must have been out that morning, spreading word of our visit. As we walked to our car, strangers waved to us. From a bench next to the tank, an old man smiled, nodded, and tipped his hat. I could only imagine what these people experienced during the Nazi occupation, but their obvious gratitude made me proud to be identified as an American.

CHAPTER 13
REDEMPTION

Behind our apartment building on Washingtonstrasse, beyond the chain-link fence marking the edge of the military housing area, lay an open, grassy field. My friends and I sometimes climbed the fence to play soccer or baseball out there. Otherwise, it stood vacant and unclaimed.

That emptiness changed one spring day, as new grass was sprouting on the field, when a caravan of horse-drawn wagons appeared. The drivers stationed them in a loose circle, erected a corral for their dozen horses and set up an impromptu encampment.

Roma (typically called Gypsies in those days, on the erroneous belief they originated in Egypt) were a subject of fear and intrigue. They were colorful characters who cultivated an air of mystery. However, when Roma were around, people complained about thefts and other petty crimes flaring up. And apocryphal tales abounded of abducted children and of adults lured into immoral situations. My parents told me all of that, but they also told me that Roma had long been persecuted and that the Nazis had killed many of them.

"Let's check it out," I called to some of my friends, pointing toward the wagons The intrigue far outweighed the fear. Over the fence we went toward the heart of the camp.

I had seen Roma caravans many times before, along roads in the countryside, but had not previously seen them in the city or so up close. What we found was beyond what I had imagined. Wooden wagons, like cabins on wheels, painted with exotic floral patterns in wild shades of crimson, gold, purple, green, and black. Women with long, black hair, dressed in flowing skirts colored as wildly as the wagons. Swarthy, muscular men in tight shirts, many wearing a single gold earring. And an unrestrained gaggle of children, looking like miniature versions of their parents.

Entering the camp, we heard people speaking rapid-fire in what sounded like an Eastern European language that I didn't understand. A tall, mustached man dressed all in black approached us, holding out his hands as if asking what we wanted.

I tried German, saying we lived in the nearby houses and were just curious. He smiled at that and waved us toward him as he stepped backward into the middle of the camp. His name, he said, was Karl or Karol. I held back at first. Then I smiled back and walked toward him. The other kids followed.

In broken German, he introduced us to various of his family and fellow travelers. They had just ridden from another city nearby where they had felt unwelcome, he explained. They were partway through an annual circuit that would take them back to somewhere in Yugoslavia later in the year. The field here in Wiesbaden provided one of the better stops, where no one bothered them or seemed bothered by them. They would stay a little while, seeking odd jobs and replenishing their wagons. Strangely, he made no mention of the kids' schooling, of medical care, or even of finding fresh water.

"We are here maybe one week," he declared at the end of the tour. "Come back when you want." I couldn't wait.

That evening, out my bedroom window, I saw a bonfire in the Roma camp. Guitars and accordions cracked the quiet night. I pictured Roma girls dancing around the fire, swirling their skirts and clapping tambourines.

The next morning, it being a Saturday, I went out early to the playground behind the next apartment house, expecting to find the usual bunch of kids playing on the slides and monkey bars, maybe tossing a ball. Instead, I found a commotion.

A boy from the Roma camp had wandered into the playground. He looked no older than ten, skinny, with longish black hair, dressed in mismatched shirt and pants. Five American boys had cornered him against a fence. One older boy, crewcut and muscular, was poking a finger into the Roma kid's chest and yelling at him as a dozen others watched.

"What are you doing here? You don't belong here!"

From within the adolescent mob, someone yelled, "Hit him, beat him up!" That made the older boy even more aggressive.

The pushing and yelling increased. Soon, the Roma boy began to break down, sobbing. I knew he spoke no English and had to be scared and confused. Even the German locals probably had never been this mean.

I knew the boy doing the bullying as the older brother of one of my sixth-grade classmates. He reminded me of the boy who led the war games on the playground in Linz, the one who instigated the attack on my friends from the refugee encampment.

"Bobby," I yelled, loud enough for him to hear me over his own yelling, and catching the attention of the entire group. I surprised even myself, but challenging him felt good.

"What are you doing? He hasn't done anything wrong!"

Bobby turned and gave me a surprised look. He backed off from the Roma boy and stalked toward me.

"This is none of your business," he barked at me. "We're going to teach him a lesson." The other American kids stepped back, leaving me to confront Bobby by myself.

"Wait," I pleaded. "Let me talk to him."

Bobby hesitated and looked down at the ground. In that moment, I jumped past him and started talking to the Roma boy in German. He told me he was curious, as my friends and I were when we went to the Roma camp the previous day. He swore he meant no trouble. Now he just wanted to go back to the camp.

I told the others what the boy said to me. "Let him go," I urged. "He didn't mean any harm."

I stood between the playground mob and the Roma boy. The other kids quieted down.

"Go!" I urged the boy. With a quick nod, he turned, jumped the playground fence, and ran off toward the camp.

That seemed to end it. Bobby glared at me, but said nothing. The other kids went back to playing. I tried to act nonchalant about what had just happened and joined a small group on the jungle gym for a while before returning to my apartment.

Near dinner time, my mother sent me out to fetch Dean from the playground. This time, I found an even bigger commotion. Several older Roma boys had come to the playground to confront the kids who earlier in the day had terrorized their younger companion. They stood in a line, yelling and pointing. A few had picked up rocks from the edge of the playground. Opposite them stood a group of American kids, also yelling but keeping a safe distance. Neither group could understand what the other was saying.

I saw Dean sobbing off to the side from the other American kids. I soon realized why.

The immediate object of the confrontation was Dean's bicycle, a blue racing bike that was a birthday present from our parents. One of the Roma teenagers held onto it while the American kids demanded he return it.

Dean ran to me. "Please," he cried, "make them give my bike back."

With my stomach tight and my breathing heavy, I walked slowly toward the line of Roma boys. "Please give the bicycle back," I asked in German, in as nice yet firm a tone as I could manage. "It belongs to my little brother. He hasn't done anything to you."

Initially, I got no response. Then a younger boy stepped out from behind the Roma line. It was the same boy I had helped earlier in the day. He whispered something to one of the older boys and pointed at me.

The older boy considered this for a moment, then turned to me. "We didn't know he was your brother," he said. "The boy you helped is my little brother. We just wanted to show your friends they can't push us around."

He grabbed the bike from the boy who had been holding it and held it out to me. Though shaking, I reached out and took the bike, turned, and gave it back to Dean.

"Thank you," I said to the two Roma brothers. I reached out my hand to the older brother. After a pause, he shook my hand, at which point we both smiled. Then everyone on both sides smiled, and the two lines broke up.

The Roma boys quickly moved toward the playground fence. Before leaping the fence, the older brother turned back to me and said, "No more trouble, yes?"

"Yes!" I replied, "and thank you again."

Then they were gone.

When we got home, I told my father everything that had happened. He gave me a big hug.

"I'm proud of you," he declared. "You did the right thing. I hope you see how that made a difference. Maybe your friends learned something from this too."

The next morning, I saw the Roma breaking camp, days sooner than originally planned. This time, their visit here had not been so welcoming.

I felt good about it all. No one on the playground mentioned it again, but that didn't matter. For me, it was my first personal lesson in justice. Also, my first experience with conflict mediation, something I would do professionally as an adult. I felt like I had redeemed myself from my previous blunders. I hoped the two brothers from the refugee encampment in Linz, and maybe Nicolette there in Wiesbaden, would be proud of me.

CHAPTER 14
A NEGRO GENERAL?

By the time I was in the sixth grade, my classmates had diversified a lot. I especially saw far more Black students. When there were just a few, most kids didn't pay attention to race. I heard an occasional racial slur, like the incident in Ramstein the previous year, but that remained rare.

Now in Wiesbaden, I noticed this changing. It began with cliques forming in every class. I was a floater, meaning I could hang out with the studious boys one day and the boisterous boys the next. Girls never formed part of the mix. They had their own cliques. But few of the groups, boys or girls, were racially integrated.

With all the kids returning from Ramstein, the schools became overcrowded. Several of the sixth-grade classes, including mine, met in schoolrooms built into the basements of nearby apartment buildings. Our classroom had its own outside entrance, down a flight of a dozen concrete steps. Inside, it looked like any of the classrooms in the main school building down the street, except for the small windows high on one wall letting in a little light through the building foundation. Maps and art projects lined the walls

Our teacher, Mr. Lenz, reminded me of Mr. Foster in the third grade—tall and thin, very serious, meticulously dressed, and very devoted to his students. And, as with Mr. Foster, I was his best student and the teacher's pet.

A grassy open space outside served as a playground that we shared with the class in the next building. Every morning before school and again during recess, we claimed parts of this yard for pick-up games of soccer and touch football.

One day during recess, as a group of us, all White, formed up for a quick game of football, a Black boy our age approached. I didn't recognize him. He might have come from the classroom across the yard. With his lean build and smiling expression, he was the sort of kid I would have picked to be on my team.

"Can I play with you?" he asked.

"No," exclaimed the boy holding the ball. "We've got enough players."

The new kid shrugged and walked off. I thought nothing of it. We played until the teacher called us back to class.

A couple of days later, the same thing happened. We were already playing when the same boy approached and asked to join us. Again, a boy in our group, a different one than the previous time, told him, "No!" The Black kid looked down. I thought for a moment he would cry but he just walked away.

When the Black kid was out of earshot, I asked, "Why did you do that? He looked like he might be a good player." Eddie, the boy who rejected him, exclaimed, "I don't want to play with niggers."

I flinched but said nothing. Neither did anyone else. We went back to playing, though everyone was quieter than usual for the rest of the game.

Mr. Lenz must have seen what happened. At the end of the school day, he asked me to stay. After everyone else filed out of the classroom, he turned to me, frowned, and asked, "What happened at recess today? It looked like you boys wouldn't let that one kid play ball with you."

I flushed., thinking I was in trouble.

"Nothing," I replied. Then I felt I had to say something more. "I guess some of the guys didn't like him."

"Is that all? Any particular reason?"

I didn't want to tell on my friends, so I hesitated.

After a long pause, he continued, "Did it have anything to do with his being Negro?"

"I guess so. That's what one of the guys said." I didn't want to name him.

Mr. Lenz frowned again.

"You know that's wrong, don't you?" he said. "He's your schoolmate, just like the boys you were playing with. Imagine yourself in his shoes."

I did and immediately felt ashamed. I should have said something out there when it happened, taking on Eddie the same way I challenged Bobby in the confrontation with the Roma boys.

"I'm sorry," I told Mr. Lenz. "I won't let it happen again. I promise."

He smiled. "OK," he said. "I know it's hard to stand up to your friends. But remember, we're all Americans and we need to treat each other with respect."

So Mr. Lenz saw me as an American. Just like him. And just like the Black kid on the playground.

While I didn't notice any other blatant racist incidents among my schoolmates and playmates, I sensed this becoming a bigger issue among the adults. By this time, the armed services were well on their way to being racially integrated, but that didn't set well with everyone. Southerners and midwesterners, many from rural or small-town backgrounds, still filled most senior officer and enlisted ranks. They had no choice about going along, but they made their displeasure known. In line at the base exchange, sitting in the movie theater, or riding the Air Force buses, I overheard conversations among adults complaining about these changes. They usually ignored me and other kids around them. Some were a little more discrete, lowering their voices if they noticed us staring up at them. When adults look around, as if to see who was within earshot, I could guess what kind of comments would follow.

As I became aware of these attitudes around me, I noticed the absence of any Black teachers or administrators in our schools. An almost total absence of any racial minorities, for that matter. While the military itself was becoming racially integrated, its support staff still needed to catch up.

At home, my parents started talking to me and Dean about racial integration and the growing civil rights movement in the United States.

When we visited Louisiana in 1957 and saw segregation up close, they weren't ready to engage us on it. Now they wanted us to understand the changes taking place.

"People have always discriminated against minorities," my father told us. "In America, it has been mostly Negroes, but also Chinese, American Indians, and others. Different groups have been targets at different times, especially recent immigrants. Here in Europe, it has been aimed more at Jews and other religious minorities.

"You need to understand this, When good people don't stand up to the racists and let them spread their poison, terrible things happen. That's how the Nazis came to power and killed so many, including our relatives."

Dean seemed a little bewildered by all this, but I understood perfectly. I thought about the incident in Ramstein, the more recent incident on the playground, and the things I had heard people say in between. My father's message was the same as Mr. Lenz's, only more emphatic, coming from direct experience.

My parents took great pride in the presence, first in Ramstein and then in Wiesbaden, of General Benjamin Davis, Jr. The son of the first Black general in US Army history, Davis himself led the famous all-Black Tuskegee Airmen during World War II. In Wiesbaden, he served as Deputy Chief of Staff at US Air Force Headquarters.

Not everyone appreciated Davis' presence. I heard adults make astonishingly racist comments about him and about his presumed unfitness to hold a command position.

During a dinner party at our home, my father remarked he was proud to be working with General Davis. A recently arrived officer who knew nothing about Davis asked what made this particular general so significant. When my father described Davis and his record, the new fellow's jaw dropped.

"A Negro general?" he blurted out in astonishment.

"Yes," replied my father. "And a great one. Better get used to the idea. There's going to be more."

My mother took even greater delight in observing people's reactions to General Davis. She particularly enjoyed recounting a conversation among a group of military wives about a recent social event at the Officers' Club. A southern belle married to a mid-level officer described her horror at being asked by General Davis to dance.

"I never touched a Nigrah man before," she moaned. "But what could I do?"

Each time my mother retold the story, she exaggerated the young woman's plight more and laughed harder at it. That might have seemed cruel, but Mom saw it as an opportunity to make people face up to their bigotry. She won my respect and taught me an important lesson.

CHAPTER 15
WHAT WOULD JOHN WAYNE DO?

The following year, as we began seventh grade, my classmates and I moved back into the main school building. My homeroom teacher informed our class that we would learn about civics by participating in the 1960 presidential election then underway in the US. She divided the class into Democrats and Republicans, and appointed me spokesperson for the Democrats. That suited me fine, as I knew my parents were Democrats. For my first assignment, I wrote a letter to the Democratic presidential candidate, Senator John F. Kennedy, requesting campaign literature. I tried to make my letter sound grown up, and didn't mention that this was for a junior high school project.

To my pleasant surprise, two weeks later, I received a large envelope filled with campaign materials—brochures, pins, bumper stickers—that I distributed among my classmates. The package also included a personal, signed letter from Senator Kennedy, thanking me for my interest in his campaign.

In mid-October, as we closed in on election day, I debated the spokesperson for the Nixon campaign, a tall, thin, dour girl. I read the campaign literature over and over, psyching myself up for this performance. My excitement at representing Kennedy overwhelmed my opponent's plodding representation of Nixon. When Kennedy narrowly won the election the following month, I felt as if my small contribution made a difference in some undefinable way. That represented a giant step forward in my identifying as an American.

A few of my classmates were of other nationalities. Since their fathers worked for the US military, the kids attended our school. I became friends with a boisterous Irish boy named Brendan and a more reserved English boy named Richard. Brendan took great pleasure in needling Richard at every opportunity, usually good-naturedly but sometimes with a sharpness that surprised me.

I asked Brendan why he acted so mean toward Richard at times. His response surprised me. The English, he explained, had occupied Ireland for centuries and had treated the Irish more harshly even than they treated people in their overseas colonies. Brendan's father told him stories of terrible suffering inflicted on his people, including the famines that killed hundreds of thousands and drove just as many to flee, mainly to the US. Brendan knew Richard wasn't responsible for those events, but his classmate presented the only available target for retribution.

That history was news to me. When my family moved to the US later, I found a large Irish American population in the Boston area. So Brendan's story made sense to me. Much later, when I traveled to Ireland and learned even more of its history, my understood became even clearer. For now, I wished my two friends could be better friends with each other, as well. After all, I reasoned, I didn't hold German kids my age responsible for what their parents might have done to Jewish people.

Just before the start of the school year, the Air Force moved my family out of the Hainerberg housing area and into a small apartment complex in the village of Bierstadt, two miles away, at the eastern edge of Wiesbaden. Once a separate community, Bierstadt had become part of the city, like Biebrich near our first home in Wiesbaden. Two large American housing areas built after the war replaced farms that once kept Bierstadt separate.

Still, Bierstadt had a character of its own. Narrow cobblestone lanes meandered through the village. Most of the community's several thousand residents lived in small, two-story, masonry row-houses fronting on narrow sidewalks. The village center, with the largest cluster of shops and businesses, lay close to the main road toward downtown.

Along with five other American families, we lived in a pair of new, three-story apartment buildings. They stood a few blocks from the village center, on long, straight Nauroder Strasse connecting to the highway nearby. Farm fields still occupied the area between our street and the highway.

Our landlord, Herr Müller, had a construction business and kept a yard full of building materials and equipment behind the apartments. That yard, became a playground for me and the other American kids. We clambered over the stacks of lumber and piles of gravel and cinderblocks, and played capture-the-flag on the large dirt mound at the rear of the yard.

During the colder months, we played tag and baseball in the fallow field across the street. And, if we felt like walking a little further and braving crossing the highway, we could find real playgrounds filled with other American kids in the Aukamm housing area.

Our day-to-day lives differed so much from those of the German kids in the village. On the street, we acted far more boisterous. We ran about the village on our own, while they remained at home studying when they weren't in school. They seemed much less happy than we were.

Herr Müller's eighteen-year-old son, Freddie, worked with him. Born during the war, he remembered nothing of it. Freddie became like a big brother to me. He loved American culture and used me to practice his English. The best thing about Freddie was his motorcycle. Unbeknownst to my parents, he gave me rides around the neighborhood. Sometimes on a Friday afternoon, once he was off work for the weekend, he placed me on the back of the bike and raced up the highway to his uncle's hilltop tavern. Since I was always the only American kid in the tavern and spoke German, the patrons chatted with me. I always got a small glass of beer from Freddie or his uncle. It tasted strong and bitter, but I sipped at it until I finished it.

Two of my classmates, twins Maureen and Mark, lived on the top floor of our building. Tom, who was a year older and played the French horn at all hours, lived in the unit above us. Being the oldest, Tom asserted himself as leader of the group. The twins acted more outgoing and aggressive than me, but followed Tom's lead. I was the quiet one. Any time the others teased me, which was frequently, I just thought about how I got to ride with Freddy and drink beer like a virtual grownup.

Each weekday morning, the four of us, along with my brother, walked down Nauroder Strasse into the center of the village, where we caught the school bus to Hainerberg. We made a point of stopping at the bakery near the bus stop. From two blocks away, we smelled the freshly baked loaves of dense rye bread and rolls of every variety—flaky golden crescents, poppy-seed-covered rounds, and plain crusty ones.

Short and chubby with a ruddy face, the baker always wore a white jacket. Flour dusted his trousers and shoes. Unless he had other customers in the shop, he took a few minutes to chat with me. On cold mornings, he let us wait for the bus inside the bakery.

Most of the other kids grew up on American white bread and didn't care for the crusty German breads. Not me. For just ten pfennigs, less than three cents, I could buy a roll so fresh and tasty that I wouldn't have traded it for a dozen candy bars. If the baker was in a particularly good mood, he didn't charge me anything. Either way, I devoured the roll before the bus arrived.

In the afternoon, the bus returned us to a nearby corner in the middle of the village. Five streets came together there in a blind intersection that was created in an era of horse-drawn wagons but now spawned regular auto accidents.

After getting off the bus, I often led my friends on a small shopping spree through the village, stopping at the butcher, the baker, and the grocer to see if my mother had left orders I needed to pick up. This routine was one time when the others followed my lead. In my twelve-year-old's mind, it felt grown up, like I was in control and doing important things. Being in control seemed synonymous with being an adult. The scariest thing for me at that age was the possibility of finding myself not in control at all, like at the start of the showdown with the Roma kids back in Hainerberg earlier that year.

One memorable autumn afternoon, we burst from the bus laughing, happy to be out of school, off into the village for our encounters with the merchants. As always, adults walking by were friendly. "*Guten Tag*," they would say with a smile and a nod, even though few of them knew us. Maybe they felt they needed to show friendliness to anyone speaking English, even school kids. Behind the smiles and greetings, though, I knew many of them resented and disliked the Americans. I heard plenty of those kinds of comments from people who didn't know I understood them.

The butcher had small packages of meat for me, things my mother had ordered, wrapped in brown paper. I dropped them into my mesh shopping bag. As usual, he also had a treat for me. Reaching into a glass-fronted case filled with sausages, salamis, hams, and cheeses, he pulled out a piece of Leberkäse, a square, reddish-brown liver sausage encased in a thin layer of fat. As it melted in my mouth. I wished I had a fresh roll to accompany it.

As I headed for the door, he called after me, "If you like it, tell your mother. I can have some ready for her tomorrow."

Next, I was off to the baker again.

The five of us skipped and jostled our way down the street. The boys teased Maureen, who always reacted with mock outrage. Dean stayed close to me, less sure of himself, being the youngest in the group by three years.

We passed row-houses with their stone stoops and stucco facades. Flower boxes hung from some windowsills, but few flowers grew this time of year. We meandered on and off the uneven sidewalk with its stone curb, careless about watching for traffic on the narrow side streets.

Absorbed in our horseplay, we didn't notice a boy step out from an alcove at the entrance of a house and block the sidewalk. Walking at the front of our group, but looking back, I nearly ran into him. I turned and saw a boy bigger and a little older than me, with close-cropped black hair, dressed in a dark jacket, corduroy knickers, and knee socks.

Breathing heavily and sweating, he yelled in German, "What do you want? Why are you here?"

His tone grew angrier, his face reddened, and he bared his teeth. I pulled back. I didn't know this boy, had done nothing to provoke him.

He grabbed me by my right arm and shoved me into the alcove. At the same time, he reached his own right arm into his jacket and pulled out a homemade knife fashioned like a bayonet. I fixed on the crude blade, at least twelve inches long, set into a cross piece and handle. As he pressed the point against the center of my chest, it felt like the blade had gone through my clothing and was already stabbing me.

My assailant continued to yell right into my face, "I hate you Americans!"

Tom and Mark started into the alcove after us, but stopped when they saw the blade. Maureen screamed, but no one answered. Dean's eyes bulged.

"What are we going to do to?" someone yelled.

I could see no one knew what to do.

They say that nothing concentrates the mind as clearly as a hanging. Not true. Having a twelve-inch blade pressing against you works equally well. Breathing rapidly, my heart pounding, I struggled not to look down at the weapon. Yet, in a moment of intense concentration, one clear thought burst through the fear and screaming and anger.

What would John Wayne do? My mind flashed to westerns at the Saturday matinees. I pictured an outlaw, gun drawn, challenging him to a shootout in the street, and the Duke striding toward the gunman as if daring him to fire.

So I stepped forward, pressing myself even harder against the bayonet point. With that, I felt calmer.

The attacker's mouth dropped open. His eyes looked wild. Sweat dripped from his nose and chin. At last, he yelled at me one more time, "Damn Americans, I hate you!"

The blade drew back from my chest as he cocked his left arm and punched me hard in the side of my face. Then he ducked out of the alcove and disappeared down the street. It took a few moments for me to realize I was in pain.

When our breathing returned to normal, Mark and Tom slapped me on the back, congratulating me for my unexpected performance. Maureen leaned against a wall at the mouth of the alcove, still shaking. Dean stood in front of me, his mouth agape, trying to speak but unable. I shook my head. What had just happened didn't seem real.

The door inside the alcove flew open. A middle-aged German woman in a faded housedress leaned out, saw several unknown children, and asked, "What are you doing? What do you want?"

"Nothing," I assured her, backing out to the sidewalk. The others followed.

We skipped the baker and grocer, and headed straight home. My right cheek ached from the punch, but there was no blood or tears.

The rest of the way home, and from then on, my friends treated me with new respect. I felt like that about myself too. We still bantered and played around but the others, even Tom, let me take the lead in a way they rarely did before. It reminded me of the aftermath of the confrontation with the Roma boys.

When we arrived home, my mother noticed Dean's anxiety and the obvious bruise on my cheek. She asked what was wrong, so we told her the whole story. Upset, she wanted to call the authorities. She tolerated the Germans' attitude, but this really upset her.

When my father got home from work, she related the events to him. As usual, he responded more philosophically.

"Something must have upset that boy to make him so angry," he declared. "I don't think he actually would have hurt Cary."

It didn't feel that way to me, but I didn't argue. I knew my father to be a reliable judge of people.

We lived in the apartment in Bierstadt for several more months. For a couple of weeks, I worried I would again encounter the boy who attacked me, but I never saw him again. I imagined reasons for his anger. Maybe he had a bad experience with some other Americans. Maybe his father lost a job at one of the military bases.

I described the incident to Freddie. He told me to forget it, that there were lots of crazy people in the world, that it meant nothing.

It meant something to me, though. It taught me a lesson about the importance of taking control of a bad situation and perhaps literally saving a life, whether mine or someone else's. Just like in the movies.

CHAPTER 16
COMING TO AMERICA
(BUT NOT QUITE LEAVING EUROPE)

My parents talked from time to time about moving permanently to the United States. In 1961, they made their decision.

The Air Force transferred a colonel with whom my father worked to Hanscom Field, a base near Boston. If it interested my father, a position was available there for him too, but he had to act soon.

The timing was not ideal. It meant moving before the end of the school year. Our parents regretted the disruptive effect on me and Dean, but explained it was a valuable professional opportunity for my father and a perfect way to get us to the United States. So my father accepted the offer and we prepared to move.

We had moved many times during my short life. One more time shouldn't have mattered, but I had conflicting emotions. Old enough now to have serious friendships and connections to the place where we lived, I felt sad about leaving. At the same time, I felt excited at the prospect of moving to the United States, maybe forever. It would be the biggest step I could take toward becoming fully an American.

Our move went pretty seamlessly. The packing and preparation seemed similar to the move to Ramstein, except this time I had to say permanent goodbyes to friends and classmates. The Air Force also packed up and shipped our car so it would be waiting for us.

The trip itself virtual repeated our outbound flight on the 1957 visit to the United States, flying from Frankfurt to Scotland to Newfoundland to New Jersey. Waiting to board at Rhine-Main Air Base, I saw my first Constellation, much larger than the older transports and sporting its distinctive triple tail. We heard airlines were flying them cross-country in the US and that they could fly non-stop across the Atlantic. I hoped that would be our plane, but instead we again flew in an old C-54.

A freak spring hurricane barreling up the East Coast welcomed us to New York, almost causing our flight to divert. By the time we made our way into Manhattan, I could barely walk upright into the wind and rain. Dust and debris flew about like locusts, and mature trees bowed over like twigs. For two days, we huddled with Tom and Magda, waiting for the storm to pass.

We retrieved our car at a warehouse on the East River and headed north to Boston. New England was magically in bloom. Driving up the Connecticut Turnpike, through tiny Rhode Island, and finally into Massachusetts, forests of oak, maple, and elm surrounded us. The storm left everything clean and sparkling. Small towns we passed, each with a towering steeple over a Unitarian church, reminded me of European villages, except for the colonial architecture—houses with clapboard exteriors, multi-pane sash windows, steep roofs, and white wood trim.

As we circled around the west side of Boston on Route 128, my father pointed to the many buildings housing well-known companies—IBM, Polaroid, Raytheon, Intel.

"This is called the 'Science Highway'," he remarked. "The base where I'll be working gives out billions of dollars' worth of technology contracts. Plus, the Boston area has more great universities than any other city. The companies want to be near all that."

We left the freeway and got our first glimpse of Bedford, our new home. The sign at the town line informed us it was incorporated in 1729. We later learned the first settlers arrived there in the early 1600s, less than a generation after the Pilgrims landed. We were in the heart of the American history I had been reading about since the third grade. Bedford sat directly between Lexington and Concord. While Bedford was not as famous as its neighbors, militia minutemen from Bedford fought in the first battles of the Revolutionary War. The flag they carried at the battle of Concord Bridge, the one memorialized in the Emerson poem, now rested in the town library.

Town Cemetery with Revolutionary War Minutemen's graves, Bedford

The two-lane street through the middle of town was named The Great Road and had been for three hundred years. Along its entire length, just a single traffic light near a new shopping center interrupted its flow. In the middle of town, opposite a row of single-story brick shops, lay the Town Common, where residents once grazed cattle. Now a public park, elms lined its edges, towering over any structures in town. Except the white wood Unitarian Church facing the Common, with its steeple reaching up to heaven. Sadly, the majestic trees succumbed to Dutch elm disease a few years later, along with the rest of the elms in the Northeast.

Across The Great Road from the Town Common lay the original town cemetery, the Old Burying Ground. When we visited there soon after settling in Bedford, it impressed me to see graves and crypts of minutemen who had fought and died in Revolutionary War battles. Also, among the other early graves, a few identified as being those of freed former slaves.

Driving through town the first time, we received an unexpected welcome. A local police officer pulled us over and informed us it was illegal to drive without state-issued license plates. Our car still bore its original overseas military plates. It didn't matter that we had just arrived.

For the first few months in Bedford, we rented an apartment in a rowhouse development just off The Great Road. My parents meanwhile contracted with a local builder for a house in a new neighborhood set in the woods at the other end of town.

We moved into our home that fall. I stood in the driveway at the edge of Wildwood Drive and surveyed the two-story house, set back a hundred feet from the street among mature pines and hardwoods, covered in gray clapboards and decorated with white shutters and trim. For the first time in my life, we would live in a home we owned. That meant putting down roots in a way we hadn't done before.

I had a room of my own, with one window looking out at the street and a second facing the forest. The wallpaper I picked surrounded my room with travel scenes from all over the world, places I had been and places I hoped to see.

Behind the house, the forest went on for a least a mile before it encountered another street. Exploring back there for the first time, I discovered stone walls two feet in height dividing the forest into large rectangles. Settlers in colonial times had cleared the original forest and then built the walls from stones they removed to prepare the land for farming. When they later abandoned the farms, the forest reclaimed the land. Now, within the corner stakes that marked the boundaries of our lot, I could run about, fell trees, and pick wild blueberries. On our elevated rear deck, I could sunbathe, listen to birds chirping, and watch deer, squirrels, and skunks glide about the forest. I began to appreciate why having one's own home was called the American dream. No one we knew in Europe had a home like this.

Notwithstanding all that, our home maintained a distinctly European aspect. Paintings and etchings of scenes in Vienna, Paris, and London hung on the walls. The stereo mostly played European classical music, at least until I discovered American rock and roll and later rhythm and blues. By late afternoon, familiar aromas of goulashes, roasts, and dumplings filled the house. We never spoke German at home, but my mother's voice retained a strong accent, reinforced by my parents' tendency to lapse into Czech when they wanted to have a private conversation. And we talked about Europe a lot, not out of regret at leaving, but with many fond memories and our continuing interest in events there.

My mother resurrected the training of her youth, opening a custom dressmaking business in our home. She developed a strong, loyal clientele who appreciated her European training and sense of style. It thrilled me to learn that the women waiting in our foyer included a Mrs. Adams from Concord, married to a direct descendant of President John Adams, and the wife of famed Bauhaus architect Walter Gropius.

Within days of our arrival, Dean and I enrolled in school. The combined junior and senior high school, a long, two-story, brick and glass structure, reminded me of my school in Wiesbaden.

Half my new schoolmates were local kids, mostly of Irish or Italian ancestry, with a small number from families whose roots went back to colonial times. The other half came from the Air Force base or from recently arrived families associated with the technology industries. The latter half seemed similar to the mix of kids who were my classmates in Germany.

The daughter of my father's Air Force colleague was the only classmate I knew when I started, but I found it easy to make new friends. The large number of newcomers wanted to make acquaintances, just as in Europe, and most of the local kids seemed happy to have us.

A new school with only about a hundred fifty students per grade, Bedford High attracted outstanding teachers. I thrived in that environment. The curriculum required studying a foreign language. The school did not offer German, I had no interest in learning French, and I saw no benefit then in learning Spanish. After all, I reasoned, I would never live in Spain. But classical culture fascinated me, so I enrolled in four years of Latin, as well as two years of Russian. My father's influence stimulated my interest in history and politics, so I took every course in those fields.

My father also urged me to take courses in two areas that he correctly observed would have great practical value later, speed reading and typing. In typing class, I met Gary, the only other boy. Our being there amused the teacher, as no boys had ever before enrolled in this class, which most saw as a training ground for secretarial work, in those days meaning girls' work. Gary came from an Air Force family and also had recently arrived there. He enrolled with me in Latin class, where the two of us excelled but drove the teacher crazy by playing dot games whenever she turned her back. He would become a lawyer and then a judge in California, and we would remain friends for decades.

Bedford provided me with an opportunity to complete my Boy Scout experience. We hiked and camped in forests around New England and spent part of the summer at a scout camp on a lake in New Hampshire. In the summer of 1964, a group of us traveled to the historic site of Valley Forge, Pennsylvania, for the Boy Scouts' National Jamboree, where we convened with thousands of scouts from throughout the country and received a personal address from President Lyndon Johnson, The following summer, before my senior year, I joined with a half dozen others in a multi-day hike across a series of peaks in the White Mountains. As we summitted Mounts Lincoln, Liberty, Lafayette, and others, we felt as if we were walking in the paths of giants of American history. That experience spurred me to complete the requirements to become an Eagle Scout. This made my father especially proud, as his own youthful scouting activity in Europe had been curtailed by the need to emigrate, and he viewed my accomplishment as a strong indication of my having become assimilated into American culture.

Soon after, I joined the Explorer Scouts, created to keep older scouts involved by providing more diverse activities. The significant thing about this group for me was its sponsorship by the local Police Department. I got to know many of the local police officers and, for the first time, developed a relationship with a law enforcement agency. That experience was entirely positive, so it took me by surprise the next summer when I had a much more negative experience with the police, being accosted and falsely accused of a crime by an officer at a New Hampshire beach town where we often went for the day. Nothing came of that, but it showed me how easily abuses can occur by people holding any amount of power, even in a democratic society.

***

After we got settled in Bedford, my father went in search of a Jewish temple. Few Jewish families lived in our town, and I knew of only one other Jewish student in my high school class. So we joined a congregation in nearby Lexington. It was a Reform congregation, the most progressive form of Judaism at the time, with a politically liberal rabbi and community. As in Wiesbaden, we attended services only on occasional Sabbaths and on the high holidays of Rosh Hashanah and Yom Kippur. My parents enrolled me and Dean in weekly religious classes and I joined in social events for teenagers, but I never felt as connected there as I did to my high school classmates.

The one big moment in my participation in the temple came soon after we joined, when the time came to celebrate my *bar mitzvah*. Ordinarily, this would have been the culmination of months of study in preparation for standing before the congregation and reading in Hebrew from the Torah. I had no such preparation. Instead, my ceremony consisted of a phonetic reading before a small group at a Sabbath morning service, without any celebration afterward. It was about as cursory an experience as I could imagine, but it made my father happy.

When I moved away to college a few years later, I put involvement with organized religion behind me, except for attending high holiday services occasionally at the invitation of friends. But in no way did I give up my Jewish identity and cultural connections. Those had been bred into me in childhood and would remain important to me the rest of my life.

***

I never viewed myself as a "gun nut," but I grew up around guns and felt comfortable with them. I had fired rifles at military ranges, Boy Scout camps, and National Rifle Association clubs. When Bedford High started a rifle team in my sophomore year, I joined. No one had thought of designing a rifle range into the school, so we created a make-shift range in the cavernous concrete basement with a dirt floor and just enough room to stand up.

Ten of us met for rifle practice and competed in weekly matches. We had basic equipment—very old, single-shot, bolt-action .22 caliber target rifles with sights that kept going out of alignment. We placed discarded mattresses on the dirt floor as cushions for shooting prone. A middle-aged aerospace engineer volunteered to serve as our coach.

On the afternoon of Friday, November 22, 1963, we held our usual practice. I shot in the first group. My friend Mike, the best shot on the team, fired to my right. We finished our initial set of ten bullets and moved up to retrieve our targets.

Walking back to the scoring table behind the shooting positions, I heard the coach call to me, "Cary, go up to the office and ask them how long we can use the range today."

Still clutching my rifle, I exited the basement through a heavy security door and started up the industrial metal stairs leading to the main corridor of the school. I saw no one around as I emerged from the stairwell and crossed the locker-lined corridor to the office.

School had let out for the day and I found just two women still at their desks—the middle-aged office manager sitting at the back of the room and a young clerk sitting near the front counter. Neither of them appeared to notice me enter the office. The office manager listened intently to the radio.

Suddenly, she turned to the other woman and screamed, "Someone shot the President!" The radio had just reported the shooting of President John Kennedy in Dallas.

They both stared at me. I stood before them holding my rifle. A mere high school sophomore, just turned fifteen, I had never thought of myself as a threat to anyone. Yet, looking at me, their mouths gaped, their eyes opened wide, and they became speechless. Struggling for words, I lowered the rifle and hid it in front of the office counter.

As I joined them in listening to the radio, I recalled how, three years earlier in Germany, I had done my small part for Kennedy's election. His letter thanking me for my interest remained among my most cherished mementos, a highlight of my first involvement in American politics. That afternoon in Bedford, amid the anguish of knowing Kennedy might die at any moment, it all seemed so pointless.

CHAPTER 17
REBELLION

In high school, I became particularly known for two things. I wore a four-inch killer whale tooth on a leather cord around my neck. I also showed some talent for writing, dashing off short stories or satirical essays to amuse myself and my friends.

My senior-year English teacher, Mrs. Kahn, and the school librarian, Miss Dowling, became my most important influences. Both encouraged me to read widely and to write often.

The oldest of the faculty, Mrs. Kahn spoke with a distinct New York accent and dressed with flair compared to her dowdier colleagues. She had married into a family that owned a prominent supermarket chain, so she taught out of dedication. Her husband taught at Boston University and the two of them engaged prominently in liberal politics. In addition to critiquing my writing, Mrs. Kahn suggested books to read. And she made me co-editor of the school newspaper.

"Practice your writing," she counseled me, "and keep reading about what's happening in the world. You can become a political commentator."

With that encouragement, I began writing editorials for the school newspaper. The most prominent and most controversial one critiqued a class election that I thought had been conducted unfairly. I appreciated that both teachers and fellow students complimented me on the writing, even if some disagreed with the content.

Ten years later, Mrs. Kahn's vision for me would begin to take shape when I published my first opinion essay in the *Los Angeles Times*. First, though, I had to learn a lot more about American politics.

Mrs. Kahn's closest friend on the faculty was the librarian. At first glance, Miss Dowling couldn't have seemed more different—tall, slender, with long brown hair in a flip hairdo, and facial features of a model. She dressed in simple but impeccably tailored outfits and very high heels. A child of a wealthy Boston family, she too worked for the sheer joy of it, presiding over her library like it was a jewelry store in which she handed out precious gems in the form of books.

We had an impressive library for a small school, filled with both classics and contemporary literature. I eagerly dove into James Michener, Leon Uris, Herman Wouk, Alister McClain, and a score of other contemporary novelists, as well as more traditional books. In a back room, Miss Dowling kept a special store of books she made available to students whom she deemed to be serious readers, but which might have upset some parents, not to mention the school administration. Books like J. D. Salinger's *Catcher in the Rye* and D. H. Lawrence's *Lady Chatterley's Lover*. I filled my school locker with a revolving collection of books that the librarian recommended to me.

What united Mrs. Kahn and Miss Dowling, and what made the most profound impact on me, was their determination to challenge arbitrary authority. Our school administration engaged in plenty of that. When they tightened the already-strict dress code even more to prohibit girls from wearing wrap-around skirts or open-toed sandals, Mrs. Kahn wore those things to school the next day, daring the vice-principal, the rules enforcer, to challenge her. He didn't. When new rules prohibited students from entering the library between classes without a pass from a teacher, Miss Dowling ignored the rule. The short vice-principal confronted her about it one day in front of a group of students. Towering over him in her four-inch heels, she feigned surprise and told him, in her lilting tone, "You'll have to speak upward if you want me to understand. My shoulder can't hear you." He turned crimson and stormed out.

In Latin class, Roman history and culture fascinated me. Reading Julius Caesar's *Commentaries on the Gallic War* in the original Latin catapulted me back to that time. I half believed in reincarnation and imagined myself there as a Roman centurion.

On my desk at home stood a six-inch statue of the Greek goddess Athena that my father brought back from a business trip to Athens. One night, as I lay in bed, I had a vision of Athena speaking to me through the statue, encouraging me to explore my nascent interest in the occult. That interest sprang from my father's mention of our family connection to Rabbi Judah Loew and creation of the Golem. Over the ensuing months, I explored literature on occult beliefs in religions and philosophies worldwide. But I saw I needed to make a choice—whether to delve more deeply into that world or treat it as a mere curiosity. I opted for the latter. Doing otherwise would have distracted me from the path I saw myself traveling academically and culturally. But I never lost my interest in Rabbi Loew, and hoped someday to visit his tomb in Prague.

Meanwhile, my studies drew me into active participation in the Junior Classical League, a national network of high school classical language students. The summer before my senior year, a group of us from Bedford High traveled to Los Angeles for a national convention held on the campus of the University of Southern California. Midway through the convention, on August 11, 1965, the Watts rebellion began. I had seen urban riots in other cities on television, but this was up close. I didn't know then about the Police Department's horrible reputation for abuse of power within the Black community of South Central Los Angeles.

From the top of an eight-story men's dormitory, we saw a constant pattern of fire breaking out, fire trucks racing toward the column of smoke, then more fires starting at other locations. Sirens continued through most of the night. When we wanted a break from the rooftop panoramic view, we switched to the close-up television view of police battling demonstrators and firefighters battling an endless succession of blazes. The smell of smoke, the noise of sirens, and the uncertainty over what would happen next kept us all on edge.

In the morning, conference officials had us pack our bags and prepare for evacuation. Under police escort, our convoy of buses made its way across the city to the airport. Scattered storefronts and cars still smoldered from the fires of the previous night. Thousands of people, nearly all of them Black, milled about as if waiting for the next scene of this drama. National Guard troops with machine guns manned checkpoints at intersections along the way. We rode through all this silently, taking in scenes we previously had experienced only on television during similar events in other cities.

That people would rebel against perceived injustices did not surprise me. What did astonish me was how massively the force of the police and military reacted. I thought of the Boston Massacre in 1770, when British troops shot and killed residents protesting the heavy-handed rule of the colonial authorities. Was there really now that great a schism between large numbers of ordinary Americans and their government?

All the way home, and long afterwards, what I saw in LA got me thinking. We lived in the cradle of the American Revolution. Soon after our arrival in Bedford, my family visited all the notable historical sites. I shivered as I looked up at the granite minuteman standing like a sentry at the Lexington Green, site of the first engagement of the Revolutionary War. At the Concord Bridge, I read the inscription on the memorial: "There the embattled farmers stood and fired the shot heard 'round the world." I closed my eyes and saw the minutemen engaging the British redcoats on a chilly April day almost two hundred years earlier. Concord was home to the Adams family that produced two of the earliest United States Presidents. Also, Walden Pond, where Thoreau proclaimed his unwillingness to support a later American government in wartime. So many of the local heroes and heroines were considered subversive in their time. Would today's subversives, I wondered, someday be seen as heroes in the mold of the colonists fighting off British oppression?

By my junior year, I had already undertaken my own first bit of activism. A small one, to be sure, though a first step toward things to come. The previous summer, while at the Boy Scout National Jamboree in Valley Forge, I traded a scout from the Northwest a kerchief from a previous jamboree for that killer whale tooth. Composed of yellowing ivory, it had a slightly curved shape with a cavity at the base and ended in a blunt point. Some prior owner had drilled holes near the base to allow stringing it as jewelry. I laced a leather cord through the holes and wore it around my neck, where the tooth hung down to the middle of my chest.

The whale tooth became my symbol. I loved the attention it drew and the compliments I received. I didn't realize how much it antagonized the school authorities, who apparently felt frustrated at their inability to classify it as a violation of the dress code. After enduring my amulet for a few months, the administrators brought it up at a faculty meeting.

Miss Dowling later recounted to me with great glee what happened at the meeting. The vice principal was adamant that the tooth was a disruptive element, though none of the faculty could identify an instance where it disrupted class. Mrs. Kahn and a couple of others tried to get him to drop the subject but he persisted.

At the far end of the table sat Mr. Morgan, the head guidance counselor. He and I had developed a wonderful rapport as he helped me with college plans. Mr. Morgan was a bit of a loner but a lot like Mrs. Kahn and Miss Dowling in seeming to be there out of genuine dedication to the students. He stood six foot four, dressed in vested suits, and decorated his office with pictures from places he had visited throughout the world.

One teacher, a prim young woman, perhaps hoping to endear herself to the administration, declared, "Anyone who would wear something stupid like that around their neck doesn't belong here!"

At this, Mr. Morgan cleared his throat for attention. Slowly, for dramatic effect, he undid his tie and unbuttoned his collar. With his eyes ranging around the table, he reached into his shirt and drew out a chain from which hung a silver Navajo thunderbird amulet. Holding the chain up so that the amulet dangled at eye level, he swung it back and forth.

The room went silent. After several seconds, the vice principal drew in a deep breath and wearily said, "Alright, I guess we can live with this. It's just one student." Then he moved on to the next item on the agenda. The issue of my tooth didn't come up again.

Hearing Miss Dowling relate the story thrilled me. It simply amused her, but I felt my simple decision about what to wear had struck a minor blow for students' rights. It wasn't exactly the Battle of Concord but, in a small way, with help from Mr. Morgan, I stood against the tyranny of arbitrary power. And, I thought, isn't that the American way?

I related this story to Uncle Tom on one of our frequent visits with him and Aunt Magda at their weekend home north of New York City. Sitting on their veranda, looking out over a tranquil lake surrounded by forest, Tom chuckled at the story told to me by Miss Dowling.

"Do you think that experience will have a big effect on my future?" I asked him.

He pondered that for a while before responding. Then, he brought up a Zen story I had heard him use before as an instructional device. In the story, a young man's life took many surprising turns, causing those around him to make assumptions about his future but leading the town wise man to comment each time, "We'll see." And that was Tom's response to me: "We'll see." He was right. It would take a while before I would know. When it came, though, the effect would be life-changing.

CHAPTER 18
IT'S MORE THAN ROCK AND ROLL

Western movies at theaters in Europe provided my first significant American cultural influence, but rock and roll music sealed the deal.

My earliest exposure to American music had been to country-western. Hank Williams and Ray Price blared from the loudspeakers in the military base theaters before every movie. On Friday evenings in Ramstein, I sometimes accompanied classmates and their families to square dances at social clubs on the base. Men in embroidered western shirts and cowboy boots twirled women in tight tops and billowing skirts, while a country band played and a caller announced the dance steps. Once I learned the basics, I had fun seeing which older girls I could get to dance with me. I enjoyed the socializing, but the music grated on me.

In Wiesbaden, I discovered the American Youth Organization club near the school. To keep teenagers occupied and out of trouble, it provided an ice cream bar, pool tables, and televisions. Best of all, it contained a jukebox, the first one I'd seen, stocked with dozens of current 45-rpm records of songs then popular back in the states. Kids a little older than me dropped nickels into the slot and danced to Elvis Presley, Bill Haley, Chuck Berry, the Coasters, and Ricky Nelson.

Then the Army drafted Elvis Presley and stationed him in nearby Frankfurt. Shopping with my parents one day at the Army Post Exchange there, we glimpsed Elvis in the checkout line. I wanted to get closer, but my parents restrained me. My mother was dismissive.

"I don't understand why you kids get so excited about him," she shrugged. "What he sings isn't real music."

I knew she was wrong but saw no point in arguing. Adults raised on the *Blue Danube Waltz* would never understand someone like Elvis.

By the time we left Wiesbaden for Bedford, I had fallen hard for every kind of early rock and roll, from doo-wop to rockabilly to R&B. In high school, while doing my homework, I listened to WBZ, the top Boston rock music station. The radio in my room woke me every morning to top 40 hits and resumed playing them when I got home from school.

One evening in October 1963, as I lay on my bed, plowing through a novel for English class, the radio disc jockey announced a record being played on the station for the first time, by an English group called the Beatles. He then played "I Want to Hold Your Hand." I sat up and listened like I'd never listened to any piece of music before. So, apparently, did a lot of other teenagers. Calls must have flooded the station, because the DJ played the song several more times that evening.

The next day in school, everyone seemed to have heard the song, and everyone who heard it loved it. We learned later that Beatles records had been played on a few other radio stations in the United States but, for us, that evening was when the British Invasion landed. In no time, we were listening to the Dave Clark Five, Gerry and the Pacemakers, Chad and Jeremy, and the Rolling Stones.

I didn't see the Beatles perform on their first American tour in August 1964 but, along with my family and half the US population, I did see them on the Ed Sullivan show that year. By the time of their second American tour a year later, I determined to get tickets to their Boston concert at Suffolk Downs racetrack. I bought tickets for myself and Dean from the newsstand in Harvard Square for just $4.50 apiece.

The evening of the concert, full of anticipation, we rode to the site on a subway train packed with teenage fans. By the time we got there, we could only find seats high in the grandstands. We looked down on a stage set up on the home stretch of the track.

Once the Beatles emerged and began playing, pandemonium took hold, as 20,000 fans screamed non-stop, almost drowning out the music. Midway through the show, I led Dean down to the track level, where we made our way through the packed crowd right up to the fence that separated the audience from the track. So close to the Beatles that we saw every guitar string, every drumbeat, every lip movement.

As we stood spellbound by this proximity to our first musical heroes, something struck the back of my head, almost knocking me to my knees. I turned to see a scowling, red-faced Boston cop reaching back with his wood billy club, threatening to hit me again.

"Move!" he screamed at me. "I told you to move!"

Maybe he did, but I hadn't heard him over the music and the screaming fans. As the cop confronted others in the crowd, I grabbed Dean and together we returned to a safer place back in the grandstand for the rest of the concert. Despite the altercation with the cop, my first rock concert turned out to be everything I had hoped for.

A few months later, I attended another memorable concert and had another memorable interaction with the police. The Rolling Stones opened their 1966 US tour on a cool early-summer day at a local sports stadium outside Boston. I went with my friends Gary and Mike.

The small venue had a performance stage set up at one end of the grassy football field. Just a thin line of cops stood between the audience and the band. An hour into the show, the crowd got rowdier and noisier, as Mick Jagger launched into the band's then biggest hit, *Satisfaction*. As if on cue, the crowd surged out of the stands and stormed the stage. While concert organizers hustled the band into limos for a quick escape, the outnumbered and unprepared police retreated toward the stage and fired tear gas grenades into the crowd. In moments, 15,000 fans who had been racing toward the stage reversed course and ran in the opposite direction. The tear gas burned our eyes, but also created a weird kind of excitement.

Years later, the Stones talked about how memorable that scene was, coming so early in their careers. We certainly never forgot it. As with the Beatles, we would never experience a band of that caliber in such a small venue again. When I attended the Stones' concerts in subsequent years, I had to share them with as many as 100,000 other fans in venues like Dodger Stadium and the Rose Bowl.

My parents and my friends' parents all told us this would be a passing fad. They said it was just rock and roll, not what they regarded as genuine music. Only rock and roll? Maybe so but, as the Stones' lyrics years later would declare, we really liked it.

The other music that shaped me in those years came from the folk movement. As much as my friends and I loved the drive and excitement of rock and roll, we also found ourselves drawn to the serious lyrics and calmer melodies of folk, blues, and other traditional music.

By the sixties, the Boston area had become a mecca of folk music. The best place to hear it, and to see musical icons up close, was the Club 47 in Cambridge. A group of us from Bedford became regulars there, packing into the smoky basement room with its tiny stage but excellent sound system. Though Bob Dylan, Joan Baez, and Phil Ochs had graduated to larger venues, a two-dollar ticket still got us into shows by up-and-coming performers like Tom Rush, Judy Collins, and Maria Muldaur. When I first heard Tom Rush, he still played mainly adaptations of traditional American folk and blues songs, but I never forget the evening he first played *Urge for Going* by a then-unknown Canadian songwriter named Joni Mitchell. He and his contemporaries increasingly turned to songs of social and political protest related to the civil rights and anti-war movements, shaping our views in ways we didn't even recognize at the time.

The other major draw at the Club 47 consisted of southern, mostly Black, blues and R&B musicians. We didn't know how famous many of them were—performers like Howlin' Wolf, Sonny Terry, Lightnin' Hopkins, Brownie McGee, and John Lee Hooker. I wondered what they thought of us, a roomful of White teenagers deeply engrossed in their stories from the Mississippi Delta, with rhythms and lyrics that came out of experiences we couldn't imagine.

By the end of high school, I realized how much my musical tastes had evolved. At home, we still played European classical records. When out with my friends, though, nothing could replace the sounds we heard in the clubs and concert halls. Rock and roll, rhythm and blues, or folk, it was all American, and immersing myself in it became part of making myself more of an American.

CHAPTER 19
THE BOYS OF AUTUMN AND WINTER

Although I sensed my political awareness growing, I was not yet an activist in high school, notwithstanding the incident involving my whale tooth amulet. My interests focused more on my studies and sports.

I was a good student, not great. I took a lot of honors classes for the challenge, but sometimes stumbled in the math and science courses. At graduation, I won an award as the best social science student in my class, a reflection of where my real interest lay.

To my surprise, I developed a genuine love for sports. I had shown little aptitude as an athlete in my younger years, being particularly dismal at Little League baseball. Hiking became the one outdoor activity I enjoyed. Then, at the start of my freshman year, I heard an announcement about new students being sought for the cross-country team. A classmate urged me to join him in trying out.

From the first day, I knew I had found a perfect match for my personality. Distance running provided the ideal combination of individual effort within a team setting. At practice, whether I had a good or bad day had no effect on anyone else. In competition, points only went to the first several finishers from each team. I rarely placed but enough others did that my performance didn't hurt the team. I enjoyed the camaraderie and the physical fitness aspect of the sport, even though I wasn't very competitive. This flexibility struck me as a very American approach to amateur sports.

Cross-country running took place in the fall. Later, I joined the track team in the spring. I tried various events until I found my niches in the middle-distance races and the long jump. I also grew a little more competitive over time.

I loved running with the cross-country team on narrow back roads during the fall. Trees along the roadside stretched out to form a canopy of dazzling colors. Sunlight filtered through the red, yellow and orange leaves, playing on a dozen of us striding along almost effortlessly.

We started at the athletic field behind the high school and followed the colonial-era stone wall out to Concord Road, a nice easy run on flat terrain. Other times, we crossed The Great Road and ran five miles out to the bridge over the Concord River.

My favorite route, though, took us out North Road, toward my home. The toughest run, it started with a mile-long incline, past small, neat clapboard cottages behind low stone walls. At the top of the hill, we passed a roadside stand piled high with squashes of every shape and color, from plain yellow and green crook-necks to odd-shaped gourds in burnt orange and bright red, as shiny as if they were coated with shellac. The family of one of our schoolmates operated the stand at the edge of their farm. We turned off on a small country lane, little more than a trail, flanked first by fields, barren by this time of year, and then by forests of oak, birch, and maple.

Once we entered the woods, the magic set in and we hit our stride. In mid-October, when the leaves reached their peak of color, we found the collage dazzling. A light breeze blew in from the north, signaling the approach of winter and knocking the leaves down to form a carpet that thickened each day. Mile after mile passed, our steps so light one would have thought we were barely touching the ground. Other than an occasional word from one runner to another, we heard only the gentle swishing of leaves underfoot.

Eventually, we turned again, circling back to North Road. Sometimes we continued uphill, past my house at the top of Wildwood Drive, looping around to The Great Road back to the high school. Then, into the showers, where torrents of hot water and steam massaged our tired muscles and eased our way back into the world of home and school.

I recall those days as being among the happiest of my youth. We were young and strong, and we felt like we could run forever. And a young man who could run like that felt like he could do anything, be anything.

* * *

I also learned to ski. In Europe, even though we lived near the Tyrolean Alps in Austria and vacationed in the Swiss Alps, we most often journeyed to the mountains in the summer. My father skied in his youth, but didn't take it up again after returning to Europe and never taught me and Dean. Distances in New England were short, as in Europe. I learned at local hills outside Boston, but soon began driving with friends to the mountains of New Hampshire and Vermont.

During the winter holiday break of my senior year, I took a memorable ski trip with three friends—Gary, Mike, and Tom. After skiing the first two days at Stowe and Jay Peak in northern Vermont, we crossed over into Canada in search of a place to spend the night. While a heavy snow fell, we found a hotel in a small town just inside Quebec Province. Early the following morning, we headed back to the border, intending to ski that day at Cannon Mountain in New Hampshire.

We took a small back road. Blinding sun reflected off six-foot-high snow drifts. Fresh snow carpeted the road, but our VW chugged along. Suddenly we heard a siren and saw a car with flashing lights chasing us. With nowhere to pull off the road, we just stopped. A husky fellow in a blue parka with a badge pinned to the front marched up to our car.

"You ran the border!" he exclaimed, as puffs of steam poured from his mouth in the frigid morning air.

Mike, who was driving, turned to me and shrugged, then looked back at the officer.

"We didn't see any border signs," Mike said.

"You better turn around and follow me," the officer ordered.

As we followed him back to the Border Patrol station, we saw a split in the road, with the southbound lane veering off to the right. We should have taken that, but the snowdrifts and the snow on the road made it impossible to tell.

We followed the officer inside, where two of his colleagues were drinking coffee. They joked about our missing the turn, but still told us it was a serious matter. They asked us all for proof of US citizenship. Of course, none of us carried passports, as we didn't need them for visiting Canada in those days. The only identification we could offer was our Massachusetts driver's licenses. Ordinarily, that would have been enough, but they had already declared our offense to be serious and they seemed uninclined to back down.

"Where were you born?" the first officer asked me.

"Austria," I answered. That drew a quizzical look.

The other three guys all came from Air Force families. Two of them were born overseas, in Germany and Libya. The officers looked more concerned at hearing this.

Looking for a way to break this impasse, I asked if we could get someone to vouch for us.

"Call Hanscom Field and ask for one of our fathers," I suggested. "You'd accept the word of an Air Force colonel, wouldn't you?"

They agreed and soon had Gary's father on the phone. He verified our identities and assured the officers we must have made an innocent mistake. That satisfied them and we soon were on our way.

I suspected the whole incident was just a way for the Border Patrol officers to relieve their boredom. Still, we got an interesting lesson in the significance of being American, and being able to prove it.

CHAPTER 20
BECOMING OFFICIALLY AMERICAN

While still in Europe, I loved watching a dramatic series called *Men of Annapolis* on Armed Force Network television. This weekly show depicted US Naval Academy midshipmen experiencing conflicts, adventures, and even romances, all within the historic setting of the academy. The *Victory at Sea* documentaries shown at school fascinated me even more, presenting actual footage of World War II sea battles, backed by powerful narration and Richard Rodgers' dramatic musical score.

The only actual sailors I saw during those years served on naval patrol boats along the Rhine. But those television shows triggered something in me. By my junior year in high school, I decided to pursue a career as a naval officer.

My father knew me better than I did and convinced me not to seek an appointment to Annapolis. I already had shown too much of a rebellious streak, especially in my encounter with the high school administration over my whale tooth amulet. The rigid rules and discipline at the academy would have overwhelmed me. Instead, I applied successfully for a Naval ROTC scholarship, which I could use at any of dozens of universities. I narrowed it down to three—Harvard, Columbia, and the University of Southern California. Harvard rejected me and Columbia delayed in responding. Faced with a deadline from the Navy, I picked USC. Then Columbia accepted me, two weeks too late.

Author's high school graduation, Bedford, 1966

That accident of timing led me to California and set the path for the rest of my life. Before I could start down that path, though, there remained one important thing I had to do. I had to become officially American.

Despite having been born in an American military hospital, because it was overseas and my mother was not yet a US citizen, I did not get automatic American citizenship at birth. I received an Austrian birth certificate. Nonetheless, because my father was already a citizen and employed by the US government, I received an American passport. Meanwhile, Dean received US citizenship at birth, as both our parents were citizens by that time.

When my mother became a citizen shortly after my birth, my parents registered me at the US Consulate in Salzburg in some fashion that allowed me to gain citizenship by simply undergoing a formal ceremony at a future date. Then we forgot all about that. Even when my parents decided to move to the United States, it apparently didn't occur to them to have me complete the citizenship process.

The Navy scholarship brought that issue to life. To claim my scholarship, I had to present proof of US citizenship.

So, at seventeen, I went with my father to the federal courthouse in Boston, a novel experience for me. And my father found himself in a courthouse for the first time since finishing his work on the Nuremberg war crimes trials.

After a brief wait, a clerk ushered us into a judge's chambers. A middle-aged jurist sat at his desk. He motioned us to sit in the dark leather chairs in front of him while he scanned my papers. I underwent no test, no requirement to demonstrate my fitness for citizenship. Just a few questions.

"Do you understand what we're doing here today?" he asked me.

The question puzzled me. Of course I understood. "Yes," I answered in as serious a tone as I could muster.

"Why do you want to become a citizen at this time?"

I explained that I always intended to, and that my desire to become a naval officer triggered this timing. He smiled at that.

"Do you have any hesitation about becoming a United States citizen?"

"No."

"Alight, stand and raise your right hand." I complied.

He recited the oath of citizenship, then asked me to affirm it.

"I do!" I declared.

"Congratulations," said the judge, extending his hand to shake mine.

"Thank you," I replied. I exhaled a deep breath and smiled broadly. I hadn't realized until that moment how tense I felt in the preceding fifteen minutes since entering the judge's chambers.

Three weeks later, I would receive my Certificate of Citizenship in the mail.

Walking out of the courthouse to our car, I thought about the significance of this day. It culminated a long series of events that began early in my childhood, when my parents told me that someday we all would be Americans. It didn't mean much to me then. We lived in the heart of Europe, surrounded by the devastation of the war. America was just a place name. I had few images to attach to it.

By the time I stood before the federal judge to take the oath, much had changed. I had seen and experienced the transformation of Europe as it recovered from years of slaughter and destruction. I also had undergone a personal transformation, from a German-speaking child of post-Holocaust Europe to an adolescent in a surging postwar America.

As I took the oath, I became officially a US citizen, but not exclusively an American. People and places that filled my life long before that day continued to shape who I was, how I thought of myself, and how I looked at the world.

That would remain true the rest of my life. As Paris was to Hemingway, the Europe of my youth was a sort of moveable feast. Even as I became officially an American, surrounded by the wealth and privilege of that time, I still had one foot back in Europe, amid the shattered cities filled with shattered lives I saw and experienced as a child. Europe as a whole had picked up the pieces of its former self and set about reconstruction. Our family did as well. And I would build the rest of my life on that foundation.

CHAPTER 21
BECOMING EDUCATED AND POLITICAL

I left Bedford for Los Angeles in the fall of 1966. With that move, my life took a new trajectory.

LA in the late sixties meant sunny days on uncrowded beaches adorned with girls in skimpy bikinis. The heart of America's pop music scene, it allowed us to hear the Doors and the Beach Boys on the radio by day and see them live in clubs at night. For food, it featured pastrami sandwiches at Langer's by MacArthur Park, giant burritos at El Tepayac in East LA, chiliburgers at the original Tommy's on Rampart Boulevard, French dip sandwiches at Philippe's near Union Station, barbecue at Mr. Jim's in Watts, and mu shu pork at Chinatown's Plum Tree Inn—a collage of culinary cultures.

I lived for the first time among large numbers of Black, Asian, and Hispanic people. The USC campus is south of downtown, in what was then a borderline ghetto neighborhood. The school cautioned new students not to venture too far off campus, especially at night, but I didn't listen. Two weeks after I arrived, while I used a phone booth just off campus, a teenager robbed me at knifepoint. That single confrontation didn't sour me on the city or the neighborhood, though. It just seemed like part of urban life, tame compared to what I had seen during the riots the previous year.

Older parts of the city, especially on the east side, looked and sounded like an annex of Mexico. The food, music, and culture all were new to me. Now I wished someone had provided me back in high school with a reason to learn Spanish.

I also discovered big-time college sports., especially football. Saturday afternoons in the storied Memorial Coliseum with its classical peristyle and Olympic flame, packed with 100,000 screaming fans. A national college championship my second year. Four consecutive trips to the Rose Bowl. Playing pool with O. J. Simpson and other stars. I was hooked. What could be more American?

As soon as I turned eighteen, early in my freshman year, I took great pride in registering to vote. Although I was not yet politically active, I saw this as a key step in becoming fully American. Since my parents were Democrats and my only political experience had been with John Kennedy's presidential campaign in 1960, I registered as a Democrat too. Though I rarely voted a straight Democratic ticket, especially since local races were nonpartisan, that would remain my official identity from then on. I read later that the vast majority of voters never change their affiliation from that first registration.

* * *

On my way to LA, I had flown over vast, undeveloped expanses of the American Southwest, dotted with occasional cities but more often with ranches, small communities, and Indian reservation. Since my childhood days watching western movies, that region intrigued me. Determined to begin exploring it, I used my second-year winter break as an opportunity. With my skis in a rack on the rear, I set out in my tan VW Beetle. I had barely left Greater LA, when I began to experience the fabled wide open spaces—the Mojave Desert stretching to the horizon; rocky escarpments rising from the desert floor; soon, snow-blanketed peaks far taller than anything in New England, more on the scale of the Alps; river gorges carved deep into high plateaus. Best of all, I experienced the national parks of the west for the first time.

Making my way from one ski resort to another, I circled through Arizona, New Mexico, Colorado, Utah, and Nevada, on routes that took me through an eye-popping array of national parks and monuments. Crossing northern Arizona on what had been fabled Route 66, now becoming Interstate 40, I paused to tour Petrified Forest, which exceeded everything I had read about the trees turned to stone in deep shades of brown, red, and orange. The adjacent Painted Desert showed off bright bands of purple, yellow, and sienna spreading across eroded mountainsides and washes. Driving north from Taos on US 64, I passed over the Rio Grande Gorge Bridge, where I could look down hundreds of feet to the river that had etched a channel through the broad plateau on its way to the Gulf of Mexico. West of Durango, close by Four Corners, the sight of Mesa Verde was like stepping back in time, conjuring up images of early Native Americans building rock houses high up a cliff, beneath the cover of a massive stone overhang. By the time I reached Bryce Canyon, I felt sensory overload, scarcely prepared for the intricate, wind-carved towers and arches glowing golden in the afternoon sun. Nearby Zion National Park impressed me too, for the scale of its towering rock faces and jagged ridges.

Then came the stunning finale—the aptly named Grand Canyon. No photographs, films, or written descriptions could have prepared me for this mile-deep, many-miles-wide wonder. Millions of years of volcanic eruptions, floods, and winds, coupled with the non-stop flow of the Colorado River, had produced this mystical panorama of colored layers, sheer valleys, geological faults, and steep spires, all surrounding the central namesake canyon. No wonder explorers had given its features names like Vishnu's Temple and Bright Angel Canyon. As I stood hypnotized at the South Rim, visitors around me spoke in a dozen languages, all with the same intensity and reverence. It exceeded by far anything I had experienced in Europe. That moment impressed on me how special the United States looked and felt, both to its own people and to those from around the world.

The trip became a launching pad for decades of exploring state and national parks, forests, and wilderness. Desert areas, especially in Southern California, would become particular favorites for the subtle beauty of their dunes, arroyos, and oases. And, I would return to the Grand Canyon many times, twice hiking down to the bottom and back, always propelled by the impression made by my first visit.

***

College flew by. After completing a BA in English literature in three years, I convinced the Navy to let me stay a fourth year for graduate school. I switched to international relations and earned an MA with a focus on Middle East studies. My father had done intelligence work relating to the Middle East during his time at USAFE Headquarters in Wiesbaden. He talked with me about his work, to the extent he could, and stimulated great interest on my part in that region.

My graduate school mentor, Dr. Willard Beling, laid out a plan for me, once I completed my naval service. He liked that I was writing my graduate thesis on *Major Legal Issues in the Arab-Israeli Conflict*. Using his extensive commercial and academic connections, he would arrange for me to first study at the Sorbonne in Paris and then at the University of Tunis. With that in-depth grounding in languages and Middle East culture, I would be ready for government service. He didn't specify, but I suspected what he had in mind for me was the CIA. I felt excitement at his plan, which I saw as continuing to advance my American identity. Although I had some hesitations, it all seemed far off in time and didn't require any immediate decisions.

***

Meanwhile, I remained on course to get my officer's commission and go on active duty at the end of the school year. As I neared that day, however, I didn't know that I soon would have my first major political awakening as a full-fledged American.

The Navy ran the NROTC program, but the university treated it as a regular department called naval science. The program occupied a suite of offices in the brick-and-stone physical education building, and the commanding officer had the status of a temporary university professor. As

ROTC midshipmen, my colleagues and I were both students and military reservists. In addition to our regular college courses, we received training from naval officer instructors. Every Thursday, we wore uniforms and practiced close-order drills on an athletic field. During summers, we trained aboard ships and at naval installations.

I enjoyed my final training cruise, on a World War II-era, diesel submarine deployed to Vietnam but returning home soon to be decommissioned. I joined the crew in Japan, participated in exercises with the Japanese Navy, and then experienced a three-week Pacific crossing back to San Diego. Comradery among the officers and crew particularly impressed me.

The one negative experience that summer came during a day trip to Nagasaki, where I visited the memorial to those who died in the American atomic bomb attack. Though dressed in civilian clothes, I stood out as an American, drawing stares as I viewed graphic images of the bomb's impact on the city and its residents.

Back at school, I had felt like a poor fit from the start of my NROTC training. I lacked the discipline and motivation of most of my colleagues, and I sometimes associated with what the Navy viewed as the wrong people on campus. To my instructors, this was a problem of both aptitude and attitude.

Midway through my second year, my instructor, a southerner with a contempt for all things Californian, even suggested I quit the program. He disclosed the Navy had one of my fellow midshipmen keeping watch on me and filing reports on my conduct and associations. I related to him my lifelong association with the military, my interest in a naval career, and my many relatives who had served, including a distant cousin who had been an admiral. None of that changed his view, but I turned down his suggestion. Despite what they thought, I still wanted to be a naval officer, for now.

By contrast, the Navy instructors adored John Kelly, my best friend in the NROTC unit. Tall, lean, clean-cut, and gregarious, he seemed like the classic all-American boy. So much so that the staff picked him to serve on the honor guard, the select group that carried the US and Navy flags at ceremonial events. John came from a blue-collar family in San Diego County, had been a star student and athlete in high school, and then earned a coveted NROTC scholarship to USC. But he decided to take his life and career in a different direction and left the program at the end of our first year. I overheard two of our instructors bemoan losing him, as they regarded him as their model midshipman. For John, however, it turned out to be the right move. He went on to get a graduate degree in education, taught in public schools for many years, and founded a highly regarded, college-sponsored charter high school in the San Joaquin Valley. We remain close friends to this day.

Spring break in 1968 gave me an opportunity to get away for a little while. I traveled to visit my father, who was attending the Air War College at Maxwell Air Force Base outside Montgomery, Alabama. Going to the South felt uncomfortable even though I had many relatives there. The civil rights movement was peaking. George Wallace, who five years earlier had campaigned on a platform of "segregation forever," had finished serving as governor of Alabama, replaced by his wife, Lurlene.

One day, while my father attended class, I drove into town to see the sights, including the white marble statehouse that had been the capitol of the Confederacy. In my Navy dress blue uniform, I climbed the long steps and strode into the rotunda. A capitol guide, an elderly White woman, silver-haired with a touch of purple, immaculately dressed in a skirt, jacket, and heels, approached me and offered a tour. A lapel pin identified her as a member of the Daughters of the Confederacy.

Midway through the tour, she led me into the Governor's office. The Wallaces liked to welcome visiting service members, she told me. Neither of them was available, so I settled for a pair of autographed official photos. I followed her outside to the top of the steps. Bright sunshine fell on the crowds swarming the Capitol.

"This is the spot where Jefferson Davis stood to declare the secession of the Confederate States," my guide declared in a voice bursting with pride, as she pointed at a brass plaque set in the stone. "When the colored people were protesting here, we covered that up, so that none of them could stand where he stood."

"Them" meant Reverend Martin Luther King, Jr., and the thousands who had assembled with him. Before I could reply, a Black girl, perhaps ten years old, bounded up the stairs directly in front of us. Reaching the top, she flung her arms in the air, as a middle-aged Black man snapped her picture from below. Her right foot rested on the brass plaque, though I doubted she realized it. I notice it, though, as did my guide, who scowled. I had no idea that, less than a year later, Dr. King would be assassinated. In that little girl on the capitol steps, I saw the future and believed the clock could never be turned back.

Meanwhile, at school in LA, the Vietnam War increasingly pushed me to think differently about my future with the Navy. Anti-war demonstrators swarmed the Democratic National Convention being held in Chicago in August 1968. After completing my summer NROTC training, I had driven to Las Vegas for a break before school resumed. In my visiting officers' quarters room at Nellis Air Force Base, I joined the rest of the country in watching on television what an investigative commission later called a police riot. Thousands of Chicago cops beat, tear-gassed, and arrested anti-war protesters.

I viewed this spectacle for hours, as news reports flipped back and forth between the chaos in the streets outside the convention and the near-chaos on the convention floor. I sweated at the intensity of what I saw. The odor and burning of tear gas virtually seeped from the television. Mayor Richard Daley made clear his disdain for the demonstrators and his determination to keep control of the streets. Other Democratic Party leaders vilified him and turned the convention into a referendum on the war. Instead of going into town to drink and gamble, I remained glued to the TV screen.

I thought about recent events that set the scene for the confrontation in Chicago. In April, Reverend Martin Luther King, Jr., had been killed in Memphis by a White supremacist. That was what non-violent resistance to segregation and the war got him. Just two months later, as the nation still reeled from the King assassination, Senator Robert Kennedy, in the midst of an insurgent campaign for the Democratic presidential nomination, was shot and killed at a rally in Los Angeles.

A family friend and former Air Force officer, Ira Cooperman, worked as a speechwriter for Kennedy and got me involved as a campaign volunteer. The photograph of Bobby lying bleeding on the floor in the Ambassador Hotel, appearing the next day in every newspaper, haunted me. His death two days later shook me and millions of other young people whom he had inspired to engage in politics for the most altruistic reasons. I felt the classic *déjà vu* all over again, less than five years after we had experienced the national trauma surrounding President John Kennedy's assassination.

Until the events in Chicago, I had maintained low-key support for the war. What I saw on the television screen shocked me into rethinking that. Thousands of people about my age battled with the police, putting their bodies on the line for what they believed. The police response looked to me like something out of a totalitarian dictatorship. Was this the America I was preparing to serve and defend?

Amid the scores of television interviews with spokespeople on both sides of the conflict, one person stood out—an articulate man with tousled hair and an acne-scarred face, Tom Hayden. A federal grand jury later indicted him and seven others on charges of crossing state lines to incite a riot. Judge Julius Hoffman convicted all but one of them and sentenced their lawyers for contempt of court, but a federal appeals courts threw it all out based on judicial misconduct. I followed those events closely, and I remained interested in Hayden in particular.

The events in Chicago remained a hot topic when school resumed two weeks later. Around the NROTC unit, I kept my mouth shut. Talking to friends and family, however, I increasingly questioned the war. And I felt disappointed though not surprised when Richard Nixon defeated Humbert Humphrey in the presidential election that November. Even my father, still doing intelligence work for the Air Force and long a supporter of the war, began to change his views. Previously, when we had talked about the war, the discussion often ended with him telling me I would support it if I knew what he knew, but he couldn't share that classified information. What he knew must have changed.

"I don't know if the war is winnable anymore and, either way, it isn't worth what it's doing to our country," he said with resignation in a late-night phone call soon after Nixon's election. What the war was doing to our country. Not to mention what it was doing to the people of Southeast Asia. But it would go on for years. We would only learn much later that Nixon, through National Security Advisor Henry Kissinger, had induced North Vietnam not to sign a peace treaty prior to the election and then extended the war until 1973.

In May 1970, as opposition surged to expansion of the war, National Guard troops killed protesting students at Kent State University in Ohio and Jackson State University in Mississippi. As students closed colleges across the country in response, USC joined in the protests.

The Navy seemed oblivious. Despite the school being closed, the NROTC leadership proceeded with the annual dress parade scheduled for that week. This formal occasion preceded graduation and commissioning of the senior class of midshipmen, including me that year. As a precaution, the Navy moved the ceremonies off campus to a National Guard armory near Dodger Stadium.

I was aghast to learn it was proceeding, even as the rest of the campus community held teach-ins and debates in the park in front of Doheny Library and on the steps of Von KleinSmid Center, where most of my graduate classes met. I started calling the few other senior midshipmen whom I thought might feel the same way I did. Several were just as upset. This situation brought my feelings about the Vietnam War even more sharply into focus. I felt sorrow for the students who had been killed, kinship with the students on the USC campus, and alienation from the naval officers who seemed so out of touch.

On the day of the ceremonies, as the midshipmen, along with officers and guests, gathered at the cavernous armory, a few of us considered staging a walkout. We huddled in small groups with other midshipmen and talked about it. Some expressed sympathy, while others grew angry. I felt confused about what to do. Ultimately, we gave up on the idea, as we just didn't have enough time or support to organize a meaningful protest.

Word of our discussions got back to the Navy authorities. Our commanding officer left town for the weekend right after the ceremonies. In his absence, his executive officer and the Marine officer instructor took matters into their own hands. They called in me and two others, Jim and Mike. They viewed us as ringleaders. The executive officer, a commander with a shaved head and a permanent scowl, leaned forward across his desk, his face flushed and blood vessels bulging at his temples. The Marine instructor, a tall, lean major with a crewcut, lounged off to one side, looking like a predator about to pounce.

"As midshipmen, you're subject to the Uniform Code of Military Justice," the commander yelled. "You can be court-martialed for attempting to incite a mutiny!"

As the commander confronted us, the major smirked. We stayed silent. Having succeeded in scaring us, they then dismissed us.

"Do you think they're serious?" I asked the others, my voice trembling in a way I hadn't experienced before.

"They can't do anything before Monday," Mike replied, also sounding shaky. "The captain will be back and maybe we'll have a chance to talk about this rationally."

I wasn't so sure. I needed a reality check, so I called home and told my father what had happened.

"You know I still disagree with you about the war," he told me, "but threatening you like that is just wrong. Let me think about this. Maybe I can do something."

Then I talked to Mark, a former neighbor in the dorms, now involved in organizing the campus protest. Long-haired and mustached, he was a visible figure in anti-war activities and a person whose friendship with me the Navy had been monitoring. He saw both our dangerous situation and an opportunity to turn it into something positive.

"Wow! That's outrageous!" he responded to my description of our experience with the commander and the major. "I'll talk to people at the campus strike committee."

I felt a little relieved at the prospect of having allies. Still, I sweated at the prospect of how badly this might turn out.

When word of our predicament spread, the university community reacted with outrage. Some students and faculty had been calling for a long time to have both Navy and Air Force ROTC expelled from the campus, and this provided new fuel for that cause.

Students from the law school offered to organize a legal defense for us. One of them jokingly referred to us as the "USC 3." I remembered the Chicago 7 from the demonstrations at the Democratic Convention in Chicago. Years later, I would become friends with Tom Hayden. Now, we felt scared and uncertain what to do. I had never imagined being in trouble like this. Even if we avoided being court martialed, the Navy could deny us our commissions and activate us as enlisted men. Or they could discharge us and throw us into the draft pool. With my low draft lottery number, I would be gone as soon as my college deferment expired.

I felt a growing sense of outrage. We had done nothing more than talk. Nothing actually happened. And, even if it had, didn't the Navy bear some responsibility for creating this situation? As I vacillated between fear and anger, what impressed me most was those law students. They stood up for us because they believed the law and the Constitution meant something and that those principles should protect us, like anyone else.

I previously had an interest in law only as it applied to my studies in international relations. Now I saw a whole other aspect of it—law as the basis for enforcing our entire American system of values, our sense of right and wrong. The words in my oath of citizenship about defending the US Constitution took on a more concrete meaning. For the first time, I thought about becoming a lawyer.

Not knowing what the immediate future held, I made an impulsive decision to apply for admission to law school. Fortuitously, at the urging of my graduate school advisor, I had taken the Law School Admission Test the previous fall, just to try it out and maybe ease my future entry to law school as a step toward a diplomatic career. It was too late in the year to apply anywhere else, but USC accepted my application. Since I was already a graduate student there with a good academic record, they gave me a quick approval. That opportunity provided me with reassurance, in case things went the wrong way with the Navy.

Throughout the weekend, we talked back and forth among ourselves, with our parents, with other midshipmen, and with our naval science instructor, who was the one officer standing up for us. At one point, we met at his apartment, where we smoked, ate junk food, and tried to make sense of our situation. We felt more confident, but still uncertain.

The following Monday morning, the commanding officer returned to a situation that had spiraled almost out of control. At a faculty meeting, he heard calls for ending his program. When he got to his office, he received a call from my father, who had been stewing about this all weekend and now threatened to fly to Washington and demand a Congressional investigation. A quick poll of other midshipmen showed strong support for us within the ROTC unit, to the captain's surprise.

Making a good, rational decision, he took the matter out of the hands of his crazed subordinates. Then he called the three of us into his office one at a time. I went first. Our instructor had briefed us in advance, so I knew what to expect.

I knocked at the captain's office door. A stern voice ordered me in. I entered, marched to the front of his desk, and stood at attention.

"Sit down," the captain said, gesturing toward a chair behind me. His voice sounded weary as he studied some papers on his desk. I sat upright, waiting for him. I had been in his office before, but this time I felt like the walls were closing in on me. The brief silence seemed endless. He finally looked up, stared at me for a moment, and shook his head.

"I never expected anything like this," he said. "I had no idea any of you felt this way. Maybe I should have seen it coming."

He paused, then went on. "Do you still want your commission?"

"Yes, sir."

"Do you understand, however you felt about the situation, you went about it the wrong way?"

"Yes, sir, I do. We realized that even at the time. That's why we didn't go any further."

He smiled at that last statement. Apparently, it was what he needed to hear.

"All right, let's put this behind us. The Navy still wants you. When you leave here to go on active duty, no record of what happened here will follow you."

With that, he stood up. I did the same, returning to attention. The weight of the past few days lifted from my shoulders. The captain extended his arm and we shook hands. He nodded, dismissing me. As I turned and walked to the door, he instructed me, "Don't say anything to your colleagues when you leave."

Jim and Mike were sitting in the anteroom, waiting their turns. Walking out the door, I heard the captain call Jim in. I said nothing, but gave him a quick smile as we passed.

The three of us got together later and compared notes. Jim felt relieved. He wanted to be a pilot and still looked forward to a possible Navy career. Mike said little, except that he was glad to have this behind us. I was most disappointed. While I respected the way the captain handled resolution of the situation, it all left me with an empty feeling about going on active duty. I had no remaining interest in a naval career.

A few days later, with a friend from the Air Force ROTC unit, I drove to West LA to see Robert Altman's new satirical film *M*A*S*H* about a medical unit during the Korean War. With our military haircuts and preppy attire, we stood out in the ticket line. To our dismay, the show had sold out. While we stood outside the theater, considering our options, a long-haired, bearded, middle-aged man in baggy clothes exited the theater and approached us.

"You look like guys who should see this movie," he declared. "You want to get in?"

We nodded, and he motioned for us to follow him. At the theater door, he pulled out Motion Picture Academy credentials and showed them to the ticket taker, who waved us in.

Our benefactor couldn't have been more correct. I sat through the movie alternating between being spellbound and laughing out loud. It captured in perfect satire every bit of craziness I had already experienced in and around the military and previewed others to come. Because of the timing, on the eve of going on active duty, it became one of my favorite films, which I would see two dozen times in succeeding years.

As the end of the school year approached, the captain convened a meeting of the entire midshipman battalion, about a hundred of us, to discuss our relationship with the rest of the university. Some younger midshipmen, in particular, expressed concern about the future of that relationship. After listening to others for the better part of an hour, I raised my hand.

"I'll be done here at USC soon," I began. "If this unit wants to remain on campus, you have to recognize that you're guests here, that you have to show more respect for the institution and its values. You need to get out of your cloistered environment and interact more with the rest of the students and faculty." I felt pleasantly surprised at the murmurs of approval after I sat back down.

Receiving US Navy commission, Los Angeles 1970

I received my commission a week later at a ceremony in the courtyard outside the NROTC offices. The commanding officer smiled and congratulated me. Neither he nor anyone else mentioned the recent conflict. Afterward, though, I got one unpleasant surprise. The executive officer let me know he had friends at the Bureau of Naval Personnel, which would hand out our initial duty assignments. I had requested what I thought would be service far from the Vietnam War—communications duties aboard a ship in the Mediterranean. I did wind up in the Mediterranean, but first I had to attend virtually every air and surface weapons school the Navy offered. During my first four months on active duty, I attended successive training programs on naval gunnery, conventional bombs, rockets and missiles, and nuclear bombs, all to prepare me for my assignment in the weapons department of the aircraft carrier USS *Saratoga*.

* * *

I completed my graduate studies just in time to receive my MA on the same day as my commission. That meant wearing my dress white uniform to graduation, something that drew stares and a few negative comments as I waited in line for my diploma.

A few days later, I loaded my uniforms, civilian clothes, books, stereo equipment, and personal items into my VW and departed for the East Coast. My orders gave me a week to report in at my first training school in Norfolk, Virginia.

The four-day cross-country drive gave me my first ground-level view of most of the country. On the first day, I crossed deserts in California, Nevada, and Utah before stopping at Hill Air Force Base north of Salt Lake City. The next day took me across desolate Wyoming and then the endless corn and soybean fields of Nebraska. I spent that night at Offutt Air Force Base, headquarters of the Strategic Air Command, where a large sign at the entrance proclaimed "Peace Is Our Profession." I recalled seeing a picture of that sign at another base, with a separate motto below it reading "War Is Just Our Hobby." Then, across the rest of the farm-filled Midwest, up to New York, and a final half-day drive to my parents' home outside Boston. The entire way, I marveled at the size of the country, the variety of the landscape, and the diversity of the people. For those few days, I put aside my reservations about the military and felt great pride at identifying with the country.

I spent the summer in training, first at several bases in the Norfolk, Virginia area and then in Jacksonville, Florida. My unease over this barrage of weapons training simmered, and I grew increasingly uncomfortable about what I soon would be doing with it. One weekend, I drove up to Washington, D.C., where I found a large bookstore in Georgetown and bought a dozen political science and philosophy tomes containing perspectives on war. As I read them, I struggled to reconcile my positive thoughts about the American role in World War II with my negative view of the current Vietnam War. It would take me a while to come to a conclusion, especially since I still felt gratitude to this country for taking in my family and giving us a new start. In the meantime, I kept my head down and completed my training.

CHAPTER 22
ANCHORS AWEIGH

To reach my ship, I first flew to Madrid. I requested leave, hoping to travel back to Austria and Germany. The Navy allowed me only a week off, not enough time, so I instead made an interesting but brief circuit around southeast Spain. Still, I was excited to be back in Europe for the first time since my family emigrated nine years earlier.

In Madrid, the sight of Generalissimo Francisco Franco's Guardia Civil throughout the city, with their submachineguns-and trademark black patent leather hats, shocked me. I wasn't a subject of their attention, but such a blatant reminder of the fascist regime that still ruled forty years after their civil war made my skin crawl. Franco remained Europe's last governing vestige of the Nazi era. I knew our military bases helped keep him in power and I had trouble reconciling the use of a supposed force for good in the service of such evil.

Waiting at a downtown travel office for a city tour to begin, I talked with three American men my age, also recent college graduates, hanging out on the front steps. They liked the culture and people of Spain but found conditions in Madrid oppressive. They planned to go to Ibiza, in the Balearic Islands off Spain's Mediterranean coast. The island had a reputation as a haven for hippies, artists, and anyone else looking for a laid back environment. They didn't know if they ever would return to the United States.

The notion of never returning surprised me, even shocked me a bit. I knew of draft-age Americans who had gone to Canada to avoid being drafted into service in Vietnam, but these guys in Madrid weren't running from anything in particular. They just didn't want to be in America, at least not right now.

On the tour bus, I sat by chance with a tall, gray-haired American man in a Hawaiian shirt. He turned out to be a retired US Air Force colonel who had soured on the political environment at home and now lived most of the year in Sri Lanka. He mused about perhaps never returning to the United States. It startled me that a career military man could feel this way. Like the young men I talked to earlier, he wasn't running away from something as much as gravitating to a place where he felt more comfortable.

I met many more like them over the next week, in cafes and on trains and ferries. Talking with them, I got to understand their feelings, even if I didn't entirely share them.

I took the advice of the men in Madrid and went to check out Ibiza. On the train from Madid to Valencia, I met a Canadian woman also headed there. She introduced me to a friend, a Hispanic US Army veteran from California who had converted from Catholicism to the Baha'i faith and now served as a missionary on Ibiza. Another one who might never go home.

On the ferry back to the mainland two days later, I fell into an hours-long conversation with a couple from Los Angeles, a thirtyish Native American man who had worked as a stuntman in Hollywood and his younger Jewish girlfriend from West LA. They had been touring the rim of the Mediterranean by motorcycle. She described getting in touch with her Jewish side and wanted to hear about my graduate school work on the Middle East. They probably would return to California, but not soon.

As I traveled by train around the Costa del Sol, up through Cordoba, Granada, and Toledo, and back to Torrejon Air Base outside Madrid, I thought a lot about all these expatriates. I had become a full-fledged American just a few years earlier and, as much as I hoped to visit my former homes in Europe again, I couldn't imagine leaving the United States for good. That reluctance wasn't blind patriotism on my part. I had acquired genuine feeling for my adopted country. By contrast, the people I kept meeting, after growing up in the United States, were casting off that connection as easily as I might change apartments. Even my negative experiences with the Navy back at USC only soured me on a military career, not on the country. Rather, they made me think about how I could take what I learned from those experiences and apply it to making America a better place, a place that would make even those expats proud.

After checking in with the Navy liaison at Torrejon, I flew to Rota Naval Station, near Gibraltar, to await a flight to the Souda Bay Naval Base on Crete, the closest US installation to where I would join my ship in the eastern Mediterranean. Sitting in the lounge of the visiting officers' quarters at Rota, I got into a conversation with a fortyish African American man in civilian clothes.

"What brings you to Rota?" I asked.

"I'm part of a Pentagon group looking into racial conflict on ships and bases around the Med," he replied. I knew about a recent series of confrontations between White and Black service members.

Several other men, of varying age but all dressed in civilian clothes, joined us in the lounge. I noticed that all of them addressed the first man as "sir." A tall, athletic African American man, who turned out to be a Marine colonel, suggested going into town for dinner.

"This ensign is headed for his first deployment," said my initial conversation partner, pointing at me. "Let's take him along." Off we went.

Drinking white wine with my new friend at a long wood bar in a dimly lit Rota *bodega*, I resumed the conversation we began at the base.

"You seem to be in charge of this group, so who are you."

"I'm the head of equal opportunity for the Pentagon. I used to be a college professor. I was one of Nixon's few prominent Black supporters, so this was my reward."

"What are you finding? How bad do your think race relations are in the military right now?"

"Worse than they should be, and worse than most people thought. The military was a leader in integration, but there is a lot of bad feeling under the surface. You've probably read about racial fights at several bases."

His assessment saddened me. I recalled the racial animosities I observed years earlier around military bases in Europe—the casual use of racial epithets, the bullying of Black kids, and even disrespect toward senior Black officers.

"I wonder what I'll find when I get to my ship."

"We're not visiting the *Saratoga* on this trip, but we've heard they're having problems. They'll be having meetings to talk about it."

Great, I thought. I'll see soon enough how serious it is.

Early the next morning, I flew to Crete aboard a Navy C-2, a twin-engine cargo plane used to ferry supplies to aircraft carriers at sea. We landed at a mountaintop airstrip, the only place on the island flat enough for a runway. After spending the night there, I boarded a helicopter taking me and another officer to the *Saratoga*. The whomp-whomp-whomp of the chopper's twin rotors filled the air above us, drowning out any conversation. Their sound made me recall almost falling out the open rear door of a similar helicopter during war games at Camp Pendleton during summer training two years earlier.

I got my first glimpse of the *Saratoga* through a porthole-sized window to my right, tiny at first, far off in the distance. Nearing our landing, the ship looked every bit as big as I had imagined, a floating steel airport steaming across the eastern Mediterranean.

Clambering out of the helicopter, I grabbed my nylon flight bag, held onto my hat, and ducked beneath the still-moving rotor blades. The steel flight deck spread in all directions. I had no idea where to go, like they had dropped me in the midst of an alien country. Amid the noise of the chopper, the shouts of flight deck crew, and the roar of aircraft engines, a sailor appeared to guide me down into the bowels of the ship to report in and meet my new colleagues.

Based on my extensive weapons training, I found myself assigned as assistant to the ship's weapons officer, a middle-aged commander who maintained a stern demeanor but turned out to be quite intellectual. My primary job was to manage the weapons department office and its staff of yeomen, like running an office anywhere. Except that the staff were all men who called me "sir," we regularly handled and burned classified documents, and the memos I wrote and received dealt with high explosives and weapons technology.

I had ancillary duties too. When we conducted gunnery exercises, I operated the guns on the ship's starboard side from within an enclosed director—a steel box with a foot-square forward window and a radio connection, perched near the stern. From there, I aimed and fired two pairs of automatic five-inch guns in turrets on both sides of me, shooting at targets bobbing far off across the water. After a few tries, I got the hang of it and started bracketing the targets.

As the Weapons Officer's assistant, I needed to become familiar with the operations of all the divisions of our department. I climbed down steel ladders encased in tubes running through several decks to inspect munitions magazines filled with artillery shells, rockets, guided missiles, and conventional bombs. The only storage magazines I couldn't enter were the ones containing nuclear bombs, secured by armed Marine sentries. That restriction struck me as odd, as I had graduated from two nuclear weapons schools and I managed a nuclear weapons loading team.

Nuclear weapons loading exercises always drew a crowd. We cordoned off a fifty-foot circle around an attack jet on the hangar deck, the cavernous space below the flight deck where airplanes were stored and maintained. Marines carrying loaded M-16s stood around the perimeter. Crewmen brought up an unarmed, but otherwise functional, nuclear bomb from below on a special elevator, rolling it out on a wheeled sled. The bombs' shiny casings and aerodynamic lines made them look much less ominous than their conventional counterparts, camouflaging the thousands of tons of explosive force inside.

Back at the nuclear weapons loading school at Jacksonville Naval Air Station, I stood in awe of my first view of half a dozen different models of these weapons lined up on display. Now, working with them had become routine. That realization bothered me, especially when I thought back to my uncomfortable feelings at the memorial to atomic bomb dead in Nagasaki during my last midshipman training cruise.

On one occasion, as dozens of sailors ringed the loading area and my crew rolled the bomb sled under the airplane, I noticed a man in the crowd taking photos while trying to hide his camera from view. Security rules prohibited photographing nuclear weapons handling. As my training back in Jacksonville kicked in. I walked to the loading zone perimeter and confronted the sailor.

"Give me the camera," I demanded, with as much authority as I could muster.

"I didn't do anything," he whined. "I didn't take any pictures."

"I don't care. Give me the camera, now!" I stared straight at him. Other sailors backed away.

When he continued to resist, I called one of the Marines over.

"Point your weapon at this man," I ordered. The Marine raised his M-16 and pointed it at the sailor's chest. I repeated my demand for the camera.

His eyes got very wide. He thrust the camera toward me, almost dropping it.

"OK, I'm sorry!" he blurted.

I took the sailor's name and rank, then motioned to the Marine to lower his weapon. At that, the sailor melted into the crowd.

After concluding our exercise, I wrote a report on the incident. We heard nothing further about it, and I never saw the man again. My boss guessed that the sailor with the camera was a plant from the Naval Investigative Service testing our security. If so, we must have passed.

Several times a week, I stood bridge watches. I had done this before on a submarine, during a summer training cruise crossing the Pacific, but there the bridge was open to the sky, perched atop the conning tower, a mere twenty feet above the water. On the carrier, the bridge occupied a space twice the size of my last apartment. It sat high on the island, the structure jutting up from the flight deck, ten stories above sea level. Through the slanted windows, we had a panoramic view of the flight deck and the surrounding ocean. The captain sat on a raised chair at one front corner, directly above the flight deck. The navigator and his assistant, the quartermaster of the watch, worked at a map table at the opposite corner. The helmsman, steering the ship with his four-foot-diameter wheel, stood between them, against the rear wall, flanked by a radio operator. The officer of the deck, in charge of managing all this activity, roamed the bridge, consulting with the others and relaying orders from the captain. And I, as an OOD in training, followed him. From time to time, he allowed me to act as OOD, giving orders for course changes and talking to other ships sailing in formation with us.

Flight operations provided the most exciting moments on the bridge. Flight deck crews hooked the front landing gear of F-4 Phantoms and A-6 Intruders to the twin steam catapults at the bow. When the jets had revved their engines to an eardrum-shattering pitch, the catapults flung them forward over the ocean. Movement of aircraft, machinery, and crewmen formed an intricate dance. After each pair of planes launched, the deck crew moved another pair into position. An elevator big enough to carry a house, projecting from the starboard side, brought up more planes from the hangar deck below.

I found recovering aircraft just as exciting. One plane at a time dropped out of the sky, following signals from the flight deck to maintain the necessary angle of descent. When it approached the ship's stern, the plane lowered its tail hook. In a matter of seconds, the plane performed a barely controlled crash onto the flight deck and the tail hook dragged across a series of arresting wires, heavy cables connected to hydraulic cylinders. I always experienced a moment of apprehension, unsure if the hook would snag a wire. When the hook caught, the wire released just enough to bring the plane to a quick halt without snapping. If a pilot missed all the wires, he applied full power, lifted off again from the angled portion of the flight deck, and flew around for another attempt. Landing seemed by far the most difficult and harrowing part of flying from a carrier.

Flight operations rose to a special level of excitement at night, my favorite time to be on the bridge, especially when we launched F-4s. The Phantom's engines roared as twin cones of fire blasted from the afterburners against heat shields that rose from the deck. Then, the catapult fired and the plane shrieked off into the night sky.

A moment of suspense followed each launch, as the plane dipped slightly once clear of the bow, when the force of the catapult had ended and the engines thrust the plane forward. I knew it was illusion but it always seemed as if the plane might not lift off. Then, one time, it didn't. While off the coast of Israel, an F-4 lost power during launch, stuttered its way a few hundred yards, then crashed into the ocean. As I watched from the bridge, the plane hit the water and exploded. The two-man crew had no opportunity to eject. A subsequent search found just a few body parts and fragments of the plane.

I recalled the fighter that crashed back at Ramstein, reminding me again that neither our planes nor our pilots were invincible.

During our several months in the eastern Mediterranean, we led a task force watching the action before and during the short 1970 Middle East war. We jockeyed with the Soviet Navy and prepared to enter the war if the wrong side prevailed. Despite all the ships and troops we had assembled, I knew from my recent training that our commanders were nervous, and with good reason. The Soviets had far more effective ship-to-ship missiles than we did, impossible to detect until they were too close to react. We had no interest in getting into a firefight. So shock and anger followed a report that some pilots flying off the *Saratoga* had buzzed Soviet warships, taunting them. But no one fired a shot, and the war on land soon ended. The Jordanian military pushed the Palestinians into Lebanon and defeated invading Syrian armored units. We, the Israelis, and the Russians all avoided getting directly involved.

Once that crisis passed, other on-board issues resurfaced. Notably racial tension, as the inspection group I met in Spain predicted. The officers all were White. Despite the crew being racially integrated overall, White sailors held most of the "clean" administrative jobs, while most stewards and cooks were Black or Filipino. No open conflict occurred, but I saw little personal interaction between White crew members and others. They all worked together and lived in the same spaces but, once off duty, they had little to do with one another. They sat separately in the mess decks, hung out in different areas after work, and even seemed to speak different languages at times.

When I asked other officers their opinions about that, most expressed surprise, as if they hadn't noticed. I was friendly with many of the officers, especially those in my department, but I found them overall to be pretty oblivious to events outside their immediate surroundings. Or, in some cases, jaw-droppingly conservative. One lieutenant wore a pin reading "Nuke the Chinks" on his uniform lapel—an obvious violation of dress rules. I wondered about the reaction if someone wear a button with an anti-war message. But, after my experience back at college, I knew better than to test that limit.

On orders from the Pentagon, the captain announced a meeting, with voluntary attendance, at which both officers and enlisted men could air racial issues. A couple dozen crew members attended. I was one of just two officers, apart from the senior officer running the meeting.

"I hear White sailors talk about us like we're less than they are," complained one young African American sailor. "They call us colored, instead of Black."

"I've been called a lot worse than that," responded an older Black chief petty officer.

No one voiced any specific grievances. Most made restrained comments, probably, I thought, out of fear of repercussions. No one said they regretted joining the Navy. None expressed the alienation from their country that I had heard from the White expats I met in Spain.

Then a Black sailor pointed at me and asked, "Why are you here? You haven't said anything."

All eyes focused on me. I wasn't prepared for this. I felt very White and very exposed.

"Racism and racial conflict have always bothered me," I began. "I admire the military for breaking down racial barriers, even if a lot of people in the military still have racist feelings. So, I want to understand what people think is wrong on this ship and what should change. Finding that out is important to me personally."

That quieted the room. Before discussion could resume, the officer in charge thanked everyone for attending and adjourned the meeting.

The next morning, I received a message to report to the ship's executive officer, an old-school commander with a personality like a weasel. No one seemed to like him, not even the captain, whom I saw dismiss him abruptly from the bridge on several occasions.

The Marine sentry outside the XO's office door announced me and I entered.

"Who are you to question how this ship is being run?" he demanded in a shrill voice, just as I came to a halt in front of his desk.

"I don't understand what you mean, sir."

"I heard about what you said at the meeting yesterday. You think we're discriminating against the Black sailors, don't you?"

"No, sir, I never said that. I just said I wanted to understand why some of them felt they were being treated unfairly." I tried hard not to roll my eyes or shake my head as I spoke.

He screwed up his face and glared. "It's not up to an ensign to question his superiors' performance. Watch what you say from now on," he admonished me. "All right, you can go!"

As I turned and left, I felt like I was back at the NROTC detachment. The XO's accusations were less scary and less offensive than the ones from the two officers at USC. But this bothered me more. Now, I was an officer, and I shouldn't have had to deal with such disrespectful treatment. This alienated me more than ever from the Navy. They resented rather than appreciated my simple, good-faith attempt to act on the encouragement I had received from the Pentagon group back in Rota. I resolved further to look for an opportunity to get out of there and to keep a low profile in the meantime.

CHAPTER 23
GETTING BACK TO THE WORLD

Soon after that, our tour of duty in the Mediterranean ended and we started back to our home port of Mayport, Florida, near Jacksonville. I regretted leaving the Med, hoping to see a few more ports. But I had developed a nagging and painful condition in my knees and needed more medical attention than the ship's medical staff could provide.

Then came news that President Richard Nixon, several of his Cabinet members, and some of the Joint Chiefs of Staff would detour from a European trip to visit our ship, now that hostilities in the eastern Mediterranean had ended. Most of the officers acted excited. Not me. I had disliked Nixon as long as I could remember, beginning with his failed presidential run in 1960, when I campaigned for John Kennedy among my classmates in Wiesbaden. Still, the visit might bring some entertainment to what I expected would be a long, uneventful voyage home.

To prepare for the presidential visit, I worked in the VIP coordination center, charged with ensuring that our guests had a smooth and pleasant stay. They would be with us for three days, with scheduled events filling their time. To minimize disruptions, the captain assigned officers as personal escorts for each of the dignitaries.

The first evening the entourage was aboard, a frantic call came in to the VIP center. Henry Kissinger, Nixon's National Security Advisor, wanted to see the president, but the lieutenant assigned as his escort was missing. Kissinger had stepped out of his stateroom only to find a maze of unmarked corridors. A sailor who found him wandering about had the presence of mind to call us. We dispatched a more senior officer to help. When he got there, he told us later, he found Kissinger jumping up and down in anger, his face flushed.

"I need to see the President!" Kissinger screamed. "Take me to him right now! And I never want to see that stupid lieutenant again!" Kissinger was known for saying that "power is the ultimate aphrodisiac." In his case, it apparently also was a license to act out. I had long viewed Kissinger as a loose cannon in the Nixon administration, but this incident made me more anxious than ever about the power he wielded there.

The following day, we staged a show for our guests. The senior officers, clad in dress white uniforms, including swords, formally received Nixon and his party, while other officers and crew surrounded the ceremony. Jets launched earlier flew by close-in at low altitude, the powerful exhaust blasts and engine roars shaking the crowd assembled on the flight deck.

The next day, Nixon and his entourage flew out by helicopter. We could relax for the rest of our return voyage. When we stopped for three days in Naples, I took a train to the ruins of Pompeii, with Mount Vesuvius towering in the background. At the Pompei rail station, I had a memorable meal of grilled octopus, veal picata, and local red wine. The next day, I rode a ferry to the Isle of Capri. After visiting the luminous Blue Grotto, I bought several paintings at an outdoor market and savored my first caprese salad.

Our last stop was to be the island of Majorca, next to Ibiza. On our way there, I ate lunch one day with several pilots in the flight squadrons' mess. I did this once in a while, finding the pilots an interesting change from the ship's officers. I preferred sitting with the older ones, all of whom had served at least one tour flying missions in Vietnam. While the new pilots, just out of flight school, gulped coffee and talked eagerly about getting into combat, the veterans, who had done their share of combat flying, and had seen friends die, were more subdued and consequently easier to converse with. That day, though, even the veterans talked excitedly in anticipation of our upcoming port visit.

"Well, I just sent my wife home," said one. Several officers' wives followed the ship from port to port.

"Why now?" asked another. "We're headed for Majorca. It's one of the nicest ports in the Med."

The first pilot grinned. "Majorca is where the Scandinavian secretaries go on vacation," he told his colleague. "Meeting my wife there would be like taking a peanut butter sandwich to a banquet."

The other pilots laughed. I smiled politely, but struggled to hide my disgust.

After an overnight stay in Majorca, we headed home. At dusk, the Spanish coast suddenly soared upward over a thousand feet to the ridge of the Rock of Gibraltar, commanding the exit from the Mediterranean. Watching it fade into the twilight off the stern, I knew the next view of land would be Florida, in about ten days.

* * *

During the Atlantic crossing, a painful condition in my knees worsened. I thought it might have resulted from my years of running, long jumping, and hurdling in high school. A Navy doctor had examined it before I went overseas and didn't consider it serious. It flared up aboard ship, where I walked on steel decks all day and climbed up and down tall ladders.

Shortly after reaching Mayport Naval Station, the *Saratoga's* medical officer sent me to the Jacksonville Naval Hospital for evaluation. I sat on the examining table in a plain, undecorated room, eyes closed, wondering where this would lead. A commander in the orthopedic department came in to examine me and review my medical record. When he pressed down on my kneecaps, I let out a gasp of pain and almost jumped off the table.

The doctor leaned back, looked up at me and shook his head.

"This condition probably won't go away," he told me. "We could operate on it, remove your kneecaps, and replace them with fiberglass, but that might be even worse in the long run."

"Do I have any other options?" I asked apprehensively. Having my kneecaps removed seemed as attractive as having all my teeth pulled.

"If you want to get out of the Navy, I can justify recommending you for discharge. Or we can try surgery. It's up to you."

I hadn't expected this. I saw the opportunity, but I didn't want to appear too eager. I pursed my lips and rocked back and forth on the table, considering how to respond.

"I don't want an operation," I said, keeping a serious expression. "If you recommend a discharge, what happens then?"

"It goes to a review board, but they rarely reverse the doctor's recommendation. Especially right now, with Vietnam winding down and the Navy having more junior officers than we need. But it looks like this condition goes back to before you came on active duty. They won't give you a medical retirement for this, so you'll probably have to deal with it later on your own."

This was a moment of truth. My string of disappointments with the Navy briefly wrestled with the long time I had seriously pursued a naval career. But only briefly.

"O.K.," I said with a sigh, "let's go ahead with the discharge."

"Alright, I'll start the process. You'll get orders transferring you over here to the hospital. I'll prescribe some physical therapy for you, so maybe you'll feel better by the time you get out."

I returned to the *Saratoga* and informed my superiors. My boss, the weapons officer, told me he was sad to see me go and wished me the best with whatever happened. My office staff shrugged it off. Another ensign in the weapons department, who had been seeking a discharge as a conscientious objector, congratulated me. I hoped he would be as lucky.

While I waited for my transfer to the Naval Hospital, Dean drove from Houston to visit and to return the VW which I had lent him during my deployment. He also had received an NROTC scholarship, in his case to Rice University, but had resigned after a year. The Navy didn't meet his expectations either. He just came to that conclusion more quickly than I did.

During my brief remaining time aboard the *Saratoga*, I filled the days with routine tasks and spent evenings socializing with my colleagues. One evening, as I sat in the Mayport Officers' Club bar with several others, an older officer mentioned having just seen *M*A*S*H* at a theater in Jacksonville. The film had thoroughly amused him, especially the scene in which the pompous martinet Major Burns is driven to a nervous breakdown from the ridicule of other doctors. I remembered how much the movie had impressed and amused me when I saw it in LA just before going on active duty. Now I wanted to hear the reactions of others before saying anything myself. Most of them hadn't seen it. But one officer, who had been drinking heavily, took offense.

"That was a disgrace!" he blurted out loudly enough to draw attention from other tables. "Major Burns was the only one in that unit with any idea of how to run a military organization. I can't stand to see people like that made fun of."

So much for lighthearted conversation. The rest of us gave one another surprised looks but let it pass. Not the angry lieutenant. No matter how anyone tried to change the subject, he kept returning to his defense of the movie character. When we left the club, we had to hold him up as we walked him to the car and then onto the ship while he continued his ranting.

I realized why the Navy counseled us against discussing anything political in the officers' wardroom aboard ship, if a satirical movie could stir up such intense emotions. I hoped I would get my discharge, and soon.

Thankfully, my orders to report to the hospital came through a few days later. I moved into a room on an upper floor in the new eight-story, concrete building, sharing it with a Marine helicopter pilot who was the sole survivor of a crash in Vietnam. For a month, I underwent therapy, attended movies at the nearby base theater, and listened to my roommate talk about his Vietnam experiences. Despite my opposition to the war, I felt great sympathy for him. He lost friends in the crash, and doctors told him his paralyzed left arm might need to be amputated.

Then I received good news. The medical review board had approved my discharge. It would take another month or so to process the papers. In the meantime, the hospital released me and I moved into the visiting officers' quarters there at the naval air station. The Navy just required me to call in each day while I waited.

I needed to make plans. Thinking back again to my experience with the Navy just before leaving school, and the law students who had rallied to my defense, I made a firm decision to pursue a legal career. Application deadlines had passed at most law schools, so I felt great relief to learn USC would honor my acceptance from the previous year. I could start in the fall.

One weekend, I drove to the naval base at Pensacola to visit Jim, one of my colleagues in the anti-war controversy that preceded our commissioning. Now midway through flight training, he had put those events behind him and looked forward to getting his pilot wings. We had a friendly reunion, but talked more about our respective career plans than about our brush with the naval authorities. That visit was my last encounter with any of my co-conspirators.

The days dragged by like prison time. I filled them with reading, writing letters, and drinking at the VOQ lounge. Some evenings, I chatted with the young Vietnamese woman who tended bar. Otherwise, I felt isolated, just wanting to get on with my life.

A call finally came from the base personnel office, telling me my discharge orders had arrived. I could pick them up that day. I hurried to the office and signed for the orders.

I floated through the next eighteen hours. After packing a footlocker and a single suitcase, I wandered to the lounge, where the bartender bought me a drink to celebrate. I had made myself a promise that, if I got my discharge, I would quit smoking. So, just before midnight, I had my last cigarette.

The following morning, I awoke before dawn and loaded my car. At the gate to the base, I handed my ID card to the sentry as my last official act in the Navy.

Sailors often referred to the end of a deployment as "getting back to the world." Indeed, driving out the gate and turning onto the highway, I felt like I was stepping back into the world I knew. Starting north, I let out a long, loud yell, proclaiming my liberation, even if no one could hear it but me.

CHAPTER 24
LAW AND DISORDER

Three weeks later, I found myself at the head of half a million anti-war demonstrators marching down Constitution Avenue in Washington, D.C. Energized by my newfound freedom, I seized the opportunity to resume what began in LA the previous year when I tried to start a small anti-war protest within the NROTC.

In the spring of 1971, the anti-war mood throughout the country resembled a pressure cooker about to explode. Another year had passed since the shootings of demonstrators at Kent State and Jackson State, as well as my clash with the Navy, but the war in Southeast Asia continued unabated. The National Peace Action Coalition called for a march on Washington on April 24th. It grew into the largest anti-war demonstration to date and kicked off weeks of demonstrations all over the country.

After my discharge, while staying at my family's home in Bedford before returning to LA to begin law school, I heard about the planned demonstration. A notice in the *Boston Phoenix*, an alternative newspaper, identified a church in Washington hosting demonstrators from Boston. I drove down to Washington in my VW, along the way picking up a hitchhiker also headed for the demonstration.

A friend from the Navy agreed to meet me at the church in D.C. It turned out the church also served as a staging site for monitors who would ensure that the march remained orderly, with no vandalism or violence. We readily volunteered. That night, we slept on a wooden stage in the church, waking in the morning with sore backs but great enthusiasm.

As soon as we downed donuts and coffee, an organizer assembled the monitors. My friend Eric and I stood out, notably straighter than the others with our short hair and plain dress. Two dozen of us walked from the church for several blocks, past the White House to the Ellipse park, the starting point of the march. Cherry trees in bloom lined the boulevards. Under a spreading oak at the edge of the park, we joined a larger group of monitors.

"Give me your attention," boomed a tall, bearded man in a flowered shirt, carrying a clipboard and a stack of armbands. "We need straight-looking people up front. It looks better on TV."

After looking over the group, he pointed at me and Eric and ushered us to one side. After a dozen others joined us, we received identifying armbands. By this time, demonstrators had filled Constitution Avenue as far as I could see. They yelled and jostled, growing increasingly impatient.

"Go up to the front," the fellow in charge instructed us. Up we went to the first line of marchers, where we broke into the row of monitors who had locked arms across the front of the column.

"Let's go!" someone yelled, and the mass of humanity inched forward, like a giant snake uncoiling, gradually picking up speed. Thousands of signs demanded "Out Now!", "End the War," or "Bring the Troops Home." Scores of groups yelled out different slogans and calls to action. Thousands of onlookers lined the route, most of them cheering us on. Looking around, I saw the morning sun glinting off the buildings to either side and off the shiny visors of police officers.

The crowd looked like a microcosm of most of America — young and old, short hair and long hair, nuns and rabbis, veterans sporting parts of their former uniforms. Front and center at the very head of the procession, leading the way toward the Capitol, were me and Eric.

As we walked, I grew more and more excited. I felt a part of something much bigger than me, very different from the isolation and vulnerability in the college incident with the Navy. Back then, I was uncertain, just wanting to express my concern about the disrespect the Navy was showing those opposed to the war. Now, a year later, after much thinking about my values,

I felt secure in what I was doing, certain that it represented the best of American values.

At the end of the march, speakers addressed the crowd, demanding an end to the war and exhorting the demonstrators to return home and keep organizing. Between speakers, musicians entertained. Country Joe and the Fish, doing their *I Feel Like I'm Fixing to Die Rag,* brought the longest, loudest cheers.

While the speeches and singing continued in the afternoon, I slipped away from the crowd and wandered down the National Mall, all the way to the Washington Monument. The granite obelisk, rising up into the blue sky, looked like a compass needle pointing the way to a better future. Or, viewed from the south side, like our first president giving a single-digit salute to the current occupant of the White House. By evening, events at the Capitol came to a close and thousands of demonstrators joined me. Impromptu guitar performances, frisbee games, and loud debates filled the grassy Mall.

After dark, powerful lights shone on the monuments along the Mall. I stood for a long time before the Lincoln Memorial, staring at the marble statue of Abraham Lincoln and reading the inscription honoring him for having saved the union of the nation. Where are leaders like that today, I wondered. All I could see in high places, starting with the president, were people intent on dividing us and undermining our shared values, more than at any time since the Civil War. I drew even greater satisfaction from having taken part in the events of that day, expressing my support for values abandoned by those in power. But I wanted to do more.

* * *

Four months later, in the fall of 1971, I returned to LA to start law school. The early brushfires of political consciousness ignited by my experiences with the NROTC and the Navy, coupled with my increasing opposition to the Vietnam War, now burned like a wildfire. Law school fanned those flames even more. Where I once harbored thoughts of focusing on international law and going to the State Department or an intelligence agency, I veered instead toward an interest in domestic urban issues.

Conditions I observed around me drove this change in direction. Although I had only been gone a little over a year, I returned to a city in which racial and political tensions had heightened. The militant Black Panther Party, with its Ten-Point Program of demands for the Black community, had become increasingly active in LA. A notorious police raid on the group's local headquarters two years earlier had raised their profile and garnered them broader support. The following year, thousands of young Hispanics had marched through East Los Angeles as part of the Chicano Moratorium organized by the Brown Berets organization and its allies. That was a massive demonstration against the Vietnam War and the disproportionate numbers of young men of color conscripted and sent into combat. I couldn't have known then how my path soon would intersect with those activists and others like them.

Meanwhile, as I began my law studies, courses in contracts, torts, and probate filled my days but not my mind. Constitutional law and criminal law did get my attention. So did a course on law and politics taught by a young, new professor, Andy Dolan. Just out of school himself, he dressed like a student, didn't talk down to us, and always made himself available to chat. He expressed interested in my Navy experience and helped me relate it to other things I observed, both in LA and in the rest of the world. Surprisingly, a more conventional course in real property law also drew my interest. I had no idea at the time that it set the stage for what I would wind up doing for most of my legal career.

I liberated myself from the pressures of law school with occasional excursions away from LA. My first visit to Death Valley, the lowest point in North America, rekindled my fascination with the landscapes of the southwestern deserts, which looked barren at a distance but teemed with rich esthetic and sensory features. I returned many times, sometime alone, sometimes with friends, to explore the canyons, dunes, and oases.

It also dawned on me that nearby Baja California held more to experience than just the gaudy nightlife of Tijuana. With friends, I camped on beaches along the Sea of Cortez, drove down the rocky Pacific coast, and explored the heavily forested central mountains. Having such easy access to the pleasures of another country took me back to the days in Europe when my family routinely crossed borders for vacations or even day trips.

If law school itself did not particularly stimulate me, some people I encountered there did. I fell in with a progressive, politically active group at the school, much like the students who had offered their assistance during my conflict with the NROTC the previous year. We got our first legal experience volunteering to work with lawyers representing Black and Chicano militants, community organizers, and anti-war activists. We served as legal observers at anti-war and civil rights demonstrations, counseling the demonstrators and monitoring the police response. And we often met on weekends at one another's homes to talk about political ideology and action.

We also knew how to have a good time. A 1920s-era bungalow in Echo Park became a favorite party house. I and Mario Vazquez, a Mexican immigrant and UCLA law student, acted as bartenders, specializing in very popular piñã coladas.

While we and our friends drank, danced, and socialized inside, officers from the Los Angeles Police Department Public Disorder and Intelligence Division, commonly known as the "red squad," sat in an unmarked but obvious car outside, photographing everyone coming and going. Others shrugged it off, but I felt appalled. Nothing happening there could legitimately interest the police. Their behavior seemed like a throwback to the McCarthy era of the early 1950s. Yet, it would be another decade before the authorities disbanded PDID, after multiple scandals and lawsuits involving unauthorized surveillance and improper handling of information.

At the start of law school, I found myself drawn to another immigrant, a biracial woman from Indonesia via the Netherlands. Joyce Luther (later Kennard) had been interned with her family by Japanese occupiers during World War II and lost a leg to disease. She eventually immigrated to the United States, became a citizen, and worked her way through college. We met at the start of law school, hit it off personally, and became sometime study partners. A more dedicated student than me, she began her legal career as a staff attorney for the appellate courts, but then enjoyed a meteoric rise.

Within just a few years, she received gubernatorial appointments first as a trial court judge, then to the appellate bench, and finally to the California Supreme Court. At the hearing on her Supreme Court appointment, I was as proud of her as if she were a member of my own family. She epitomized the struggle and the transcendence experienced by so many immigrants, even if few rise to the heights she achieved.

***

A common law school saying held that the first year they scare you to death, the second year they work you to death, the third year they bore you to death. Nearing the end of the first year, I looked for any opportunity to inject some levity into the oppressive environment of the law school, where professors delighted in humiliating students and learning consisted mainly of memorizing—very different from the more intellectual experience of my time studying English literature and then international relations. An opportunity presented itself in the form of first-year moot court.

For this mock appellate court hearing, I partnered with Bruce Fishelman. Plump, with long black hair and a handlebar mustache, wildly colored clothes, and a reddish mongrel dog named Lazlo that followed him everywhere, Bruce stood out among our classmates. He and I conspired to turn this event into entertainment, but do so in a way that couldn't be intellectually impeached.

We wrote and submitted a solid legal brief but interspersed our analysis with playful references to non-legal materials. The key issue in the case was the location of the defendant's domicile, that is, his home for legal purposes. We concluded our legal analysis by suggesting the answer lay in his having never stopped thinking about Los Angeles, where he had left his stereo and where his girlfriend lived. In support, we cited as authority Simon and Garfunkel's musical treatise on domicile, *Homeward Bound*, quoting, "Home, where my thought's escaping. Home, where my music's playing. Home, where my love lies waiting silently for me."

Our opponents came dressed in three-piece suits. We didn't. Bruce wore a borrowed tuxedo several sizes too large, as if draped over him, along with lime green sneakers. On his head sat a broad-brimmed, black felt hat with a six-inch silver crucifix dangling from a chain that wrapped around the crown and blocked his right eye. Instead of a briefcase, he carried a brown wood box holding a children's tool kit. I looked marginally more conventional, dressed in my naval officer's blue wool jacket, with a gold and white checked tie but no shirt. My hair was longer than it had been in the Navy, but still shorter than that of most of my male classmates.

Lazlo followed us into the courtroom. So did a curious entourage of fifty students and a few professors. When we took our seats, Lazlo jumped up on a chair next to us.

The judges, all third-year law students, looked perplexed but carried on. Bruce and I, as the appellants, opened the oral arguments.

"Your honors," Bruce began, while reaching into his toolbox, pulling out an oversized wooden screwdriver, and waving it at the court, "what this case comes down to is that our client has been screwed!"

He paused to let the craziness of the moment sink in. Then, pulling out a wooden mallet and holding it above his head, he continued, "We will hammer home our arguments!"

And on he went with his soliloquy, looking and sounding like the John Belushi character in the film *Animal House* until he ran out of tools. At that point, he pulled a harmonica from his sagging pants pocket and began to play the Beatles' *"Rocky Raccoon."* That set off Lazlo, who howled in accompaniment. The judges were speechless, but the audience cheered. Had it happened thirty years later, it would have gone viral on YouTube.

Bruce was a hard act to follow but, keeping as straight a face as I could, I rose and delivered our legal arguments. My performance put the judges at ease and drew a smattering of applause from the audience.

The opponents, who actually were friends of ours, then had their opportunity. They had just begun when Bruce leaped from his chair and interrupted.

"Objection," he bellowed. "Opposing counsel is being oily and unctuous!"

The chief judge admonished him, saying, "That's not a proper objection, counsel. And, besides, you can't object in an appellate hearing."

We grew more excited. The judges apparently felt compelled to participate in our drama. And Bruce had the desired effect on the opposition. They stumbled through the rest of their arguments, unable to quite maintain their composure and casting anxious glances in our direction.

When it was over, the judges took me and Bruce aside and lectured us on the impropriety of our performance. They continued to take it all seriously. I flashed on Jerry Rubin and the Yippies interrupting a congressional hearing a few years earlier, and the chair of the House Un-American Activities Committee looking ridiculous as he pounded his gavel and demanded respect for his proceedings. Our moot court judges had fallen into the same trap, unable to imagine their authority being challenged or to see the humor in the spectacle before them.

By the next day, the school buzzed with news of our performance. It had lasted little more than an hour, a single hour out of thousands we spent in that building, but, for us, it represented an important assertion of our individuality, our personal freedom, in what up to then had been a pretty oppressive law school experience.

The second year of law school passed by in a blur, other than Andy Dolan's class on law and politics, where a dozen of us discussed how the making and application of laws impact different kinds of people in different ways. How laws can suppress or facilitate political participation. How the same laws get enforced differently in urban minority neighborhoods than in largely White suburban communities. How authorities are more likely to arrest some kinds of people than others, then charge them more aggressively, and sentence them more punitively. All of this seemed at odds with the America I had grown up learning about in history and civics classes.

Two more important things happened late in that school year. First, I worked on George McGovern's 1972 US presidential campaign. Many of my friends and classmates surprised me by being agnostic about the election, which pitted McGovern's anti-war stance against incumbent Richard Nixon's law-and-order platform coupled with continuation of the war. I saw a clear choice, and volunteered at the LA headquarters, preparing flyers laying out McGovern's policy positions, to be distributed at campaign rallies.

At one campaign event, I picked up a fold-over flyer bearing a scowling photo of Richard Nixon on the front. Framing his image, large black letters read "SIX MILLION VICTIMS. THE COST OF THE WAR UNDER RICHARD NIXON." Inside, the flier detailed numbers of American dead and wounded, Vietnamese dead, wounded, displaced, imprisoned, and so on, until the count indeed reached six million, a powerful number with its allusion to the victims of the Holocaust. The flier came from the Indochina Peace Campaign, the anti-war coalition led by the same Tom Hayden I had seen on television at the Chicago demonstrations four years earlier. IPC printed and distributed millions of copies of this flier, which became the most effective piece of anti-war literature of its time. I didn't know then that the flier had been created by Fred Branfman, an American investigative journalist who had exposed the secret American air war in Laos, written a book entitled *Voices from the Plain of Jars*, and then teamed with Tom Hayden and others at IPC. And whom I would encounter in person soon.

I met George McGovern once during the campaign. After hearing him speak at the Los Angeles Convention Center, I left before the rally ended. As I walked along the outside of the building toward my car, a half dozen doors flew open all at once and McGovern emerged, flanked by aides and Secret Service agents. The agents, dressed in suits and sporting tell-tale radio earpieces, looked shocked at seeing me standing directly in McGovern's path and reached inside their jackets for their guns. I held out my hand to shake his. He took it and smiled as I told him I worked on the local campaign staff. At that, everyone relaxed and the entourage whisked him away.

McGovern lost in one of the worst landslides in presidential campaign history, but the pressure brought to bear by his campaign and the rest of the anti-war movement forced Nixon to sign peace accords the following year, ending American military involvement in Southeast Asia. Then, a year later, the Watergate scandal brought the Nixon administration crashing down, with the president himself resigning in mid-term and many of his aides going to prison. We felt at least somewhat vindicated and not at all surprised. Nixon and his crew had proven to be just as venal and corrupt as we had made them out to be.

It pained me to see how much the Watergate scandal tore apart the country politically, but I privately smiled about it. Few things are as satisfying as seeing mighty, arrogant people humbled. Even though we lost the presidential campaign, we took satisfaction from how our efforts had changed the course of history in a better direction.

Involvement in the McGovern campaign led to another opportunity. Several of us who had worked in the LA research and policy office formed a campaign firm, Political Campaign Management. Some were veterans of numerous previous California campaigns. Van Vibber led the effort. Lanky with a mop of hair and a perpetual five-o'clock shadow, he didn't seem like a campaign operative, but he possessed a genius for promoting seemingly unelectable candidates. His first notable victory was in electing Pieter van den Steenhoven to the Santa Monica City Council, based on the slogan "Van den Steenhoven. A long name worth remembering." Although some group members soon dropped off and returned to their pre-McGovern lives, Van kept at it, operating from a house in the hills above Malibu. I pitched in when I could, first as a campaign worker and later as a lawyer. Ultimately, we got several candidates elected to state and local offices in the Los Angeles area.

Soon after the McGovern campaign ended, a friend at Loyola Law School introduced me to Dan Leighton, a recent Loyola graduate who, with two classmates, had started a law clinic there to give students an opportunity to gain work experience. In an old, two-story, brown stucco office building in the decaying Westlake neighborhood near downtown LA, the Community Legal Assistance Center functioned as a private legal aid office, representing low-income clients in eviction cases, consumer fraud claims, and filing for public assistance. Especially evictions. Dan noticed early that a huge proportion of those cases involved the same landlords. Rather than studying for the bar exam, he instead began studying the web of real estate ownership in and around downtown, identifying the principals, and examining how they operated their businesses. He assembled a group of collaborators, none of them lawyers, to help with the research. This immediately intrigued me, but I wasn't ready yet to sign on.

In the meantime, I completed my law school course requirements in two years and just needed a few more credits to graduate. I chose to earn those credits through clinical programs, clerking at the Los Angeles Legal Aid Foundation and the Greater Watts Justice Center.

I particularly looked forward to spending time at the Justice Center because it gave me an opportunity to work with Hank di Suvero, a renowned criminal defense and constitutional rights lawyer. A Harvard Law graduate, he had given up corporate law practice in New York to become an activist attorney. Silver-haired, well-spoken, and intellectually sharp, he was the kind of lawyer I thought I wanted to become. His wife, Ramona Ripston, headed the American Civil Liberties Union of Southern California.

Hank gave me as much opportunity as I could handle, reviewing new cases, writing briefs, and even making court appearances under his supervision. The highlight for me occurred while defending a felon charged with illegal possession of firearms. I went to the LAPD evidence room to inspect the several pistols and revolvers. Once I handled them, I knew none were operable. I prepared a declaration describing my knowledge of firearms and asserting that, as none of the guns could be fired, they were not actually firearms within the meaning of the law and therefore not illegal for the defendant to possess. The judge agreed with me and dismissed the firearms charges. Even though our client still wound up being convicted on other charges, I felt ecstatic at making the legal system work as I thought was intended.

As exciting as all that was, I found myself drawn more to Dan Leighton's work. I could defend a thousand evictions cases or hundreds of cases of questionable criminal arrests, yet have no effect on the underlying conditions that brought about those cases. If Dan and his crew could expose the operations of even one major slumlord, they might avoid those thousand eviction cases in the first place. I found that a breakthrough realization.

My brief stint at the Justice Center allowed me one last opportunity to collaborate with my first-year moot court partner Bruce. While assisting Hank with a police brutality case, we decided to find out if the officer involved had a record of misconduct. We had heard prosecutors kept files on officers whose past misdeeds might undermine their credibility in court, and we knew this particular officer had complaints filed against him. Armed only with good intentions and profound naiveté, we entered the District Attorney's offices on the twelfth floor of the downtown courthouse. A dozen attorneys stood around the lobby, talking or perusing files.

Bruce and I strode to the counter and asked for the file on the officer in question. The middle-aged woman behind the counter nodded, turned, and walked back into a maze of file-laden shelves. When she returned, she laid a thick file folder on the counter. Then, as I reached for it, she asked us for our DA identification cards. When we hesitated and looked at each other, she yanked the file back.

"You can't see it unless you work for this office," she admonished us. I notice several deputy DAs staring at us.

"Isn't this public information?" Bruce suggested.

"No, it's not," she insisted.

I felt let down, but not surprised. The file sat on the counter, so tantalizingly close yet so off limits. I tried another approach.

"Is there someone we could talk to about that, someone who could approve us seeing the file?"

She stared at us a long time, then told us, "Wait here. I'll see."

I glanced around the room. An even larger number of lawyers now looked on, as if curious to see how this would play out. After several minutes, the clerk returned.

"The assistant DA will see you now," she said, smiling but shaking her head. "Follow me."

I hadn't expected to get access to someone that high in their organization. She led us to a large corner office at the rear of the suite. An older, husky, balding White man sat behind an oak desk stacked high with papers. He didn't stand or extend his hand, but just motioned us to take the two chairs in front of his desk. And he gave us an even more amused look than the clerk.

"What can I do for you?" he asked.

"We're interested in the record of an officer who's involved in a case we're helping defend," I replied. "We know you have a file on him. The clerk brought it out. But she says she can't let us see it. We're hoping you can help us."

"Those files are private. They're property of the DA's office, not open to the public."

Bruce jumped in, sounding more sincere than I'd ever heard him, and far from his usual bantering style. "Sir, we're just law students," he said. "We really believe the law should be neutral, that it shouldn't be a game between prosecutors and defenders. We understand from our studies that information like this is to be shared. Being denied access to information that we know is there, that could help our case, would be so disappointing."

The prosecutor rocked in his chair, curled up his lower lip and stared hard at us.

"I've been a lawyer for forty years," he finally replied. "In those years, I've been disappointed a lot of times. And you're not going to see that file."

We shrugged, picked up our briefcases and walked out. Lawyers who had watched us being ushered in to see their boss smirked as we left empty-handed. We hadn't expected to convince him, but I still felt frustrated. I knew Bruce's innocent approach to the old prosecutor was for show. Still, it expressed our honest feelings about how the American legal system should work.

What happened that day disappointed me in the same way that I felt about my experience with the Navy over the scuttled anti-war demonstration. I had grown up believing that the military and the legal system represented the bedrock values that made America special, but these experiences challenged that belief.

CHAPTER 25
A DIFFERENT KIND OF LAW

My mentor, Hank di Suvero, had an idea for a new form of legal institution—a law school to train lawyers motivated to serve working class clients, recent immigrants, and political activists. Hank, I, and a handful of our colleagues began meeting over the summer of 1973 to sketch out the plan for what would become People's College of Law. The group grew to include lawyers, law students, and activists interested in becoming lawyers—African-Americans, Hispanics, Asians, and Anglos; men and women; gay and straight; scholars and dock workers. The group looked a lot like our first entering class would look.

For months, Hank convened regular meetings, most often in the living room in the mid-Wilshire apartment of former union official Lee Solomon. We sweltered through that hot summer and fall in Lee's apartment without air conditioning, but the heat only added to the intensity of our discussions.

I couldn't have been more impressed with how the entire group took on this effort like a true mission. All agreed that the institution to which we soon would give birth had to be a bona fide law school with graduates capable of passing the California bar examination and becoming real lawyers. We would keep tuition as low as possible to make the school available to anyone motivated to attend and prepared to take on the required work.

During that same time, I completed my own law studies and took the bar exam in January 1974. Preparing for the three-day exam meant several weeks of intense drilling in all the subject areas being tested and perfecting the skill of writing a thorough analysis of a legal problem in under an hour.

I holed up every day in the USC Philosophy Department library, at the top of one of the oldest campus buildings, designed to resemble a medieval monastery. The shelves of scholarly treatises, the hand-painted ceiling beams, and the hushed voices of the librarians created the perfect study environment, as if I were a monk poring over biblical texts centuries earlier.

As the exam approached, I felt energized, like a runner peaking for a big race. Then, in the midst of these preparations, my girlfriend, a UCLA law student, announced she was breaking up with me. I felt blindsided, momentarily stunned. At any other time, I would have argued or cried, but I knew it would make no difference. Mustering all the self-discipline I could, I struggled to keep a laser-like focus on the upcoming event.

When the exam came, I stayed every night at Hank and Ramona's home in the Hollywood Hills. They fed me, encouraged me, and made sure I got out in time every morning. Thankfully, I passed the exam on the first try and was sworn in as a lawyer in June of that year.

Admission to the State Bar thrilled me almost as much as taking my oath of citizenship in Boston had nine years earlier. Standing in a downtown auditorium, taking the oath to become a lawyer, I thought back on the three years I had worked to reach this moment. All the frustrations and unpleasant moments melted away, and I felt excited at becoming able to use the law to advance my values and goals.

Soon after, that sensation merged into an even greater excitement—the prospect of training others, including immigrants like me, in the law and in its potential for social change. In my budding political circles, I had met many people like that, advocates and organizers who I thought would make outstanding lawyers—lawyers motivated not by wealth or fame, but by the opportunity to serve their communities, unlike most of my law school classmates.

People's College of Law set up shop in a two-story, neo-Spanish building on Park View Street, just off McArthur Park, and prepared to admit its first entering class. The building had a distinguished and appropriate history, having housed dozens of activist organizations over the years. The location was equally good, in the middle of a working class and immigrant neighborhood, and across the street from the LA Women's Building, the heart of feminist activism in LA.

In the fall of 1974, as the start of PCL's first school year approached, we felt as much anticipation as kids on Christmas morning. We had a stellar entering class, including local political and labor leaders, as well as students who could have had their choice of law schools but came to PCL because of what it represented. All knew this would be an unconventional experience in which they would take on major responsibilities to themselves, to the school, and to each other.

I volunteered to set up and maintain the school library. A carpenter friend built a roomful of sturdy, white pine bookshelves, which I then filled with legal research materials. The library became a symbol of the school's academic legitimacy, to be shown to prospective students, potential donors, and visitors from the State Bar.

The faculty, all part-time volunteers, included shining lights of the LA legal community. Hank di Suvero taught criminal law. A noted Supreme Court litigator, Sam Rosenwein, taught constitutional law. He and I jointly taught legal research. I also agreed to teach corporate law, a course I had disdained and suffered through myself. It was a required component of the curriculum and tested on the bar exam, so I had the unenviable task of making corporate law relevant and interesting to a class full of political activists who regarded this as the enemy's playbook.

Unlike my own law school experience, PCL was a high-energy environment filled with excited students who came to class prepared to engage. If I posed a question in class, a half-dozen hands flew up to answer. If I expressed an opinion about a statute or a court decision, students competed to express their own, often different opinions. Outside the classrooms, colorful political posters lined the walls and bulletin boards hung heavy with announcements of meetings and events. As excited as the students, I imagined this must be what it felt like to see one's child mature and excel.

A steering committee elected by the students and faculty governed the school, setting policies, making hiring decisions, and overseeing finances. Other committees managed fundraising, admissions, and curriculum.

Students even performed clerical and maintenance tasks. From a paper-strewn office on the ground floor, Lee Solomon served as administrator, keeping the enterprise moving, even if just a small step short of chaos.

Strong feelings and powerful personalities turned committee meetings into raucous but productive sessions. I chaired a particularly intense steering committee meetings in which an aggressive male student and his ex-wife, also a student, battled over school management issues. Then a woman clad in traditional Muslim attire started a hotly contested debate over admissions policies. Finally, a row erupted between Hispanic students and the Gay Caucus over the correct political position on some hot but obscure issue. It took all my mediation skills to keep this from becoming an unmanageable conflict. In the end, as in most instances, the group came to consensus.

I taught part-time and served on committees at PCL for the school's first four years, until we graduated our first class of twenty. By then, the school had assumed a life of its own, with a steady stream of applicants, graduates, and supporters. For one of our fundraisers, Hank's brother, famed sculptor Mark di Suvero, donated a small sculpture to be auctioned. Many notable people graduated and went on to prominent careers, including Los Angeles Mayor Antonio Villaraigosa and several other elected officials. The school even turned up in a play by the Chicano theater group Culture Clash.

But it ultimately didn't have staying power once the founders and original supporters moved on. Over forty years later, it pains me to see PCL as a shadow of its original self. Still, it continues to offer an opportunity to aspiring lawyers, particularly ones from lower-income and immigrant communities, who have little chance of admission to mainstream law schools.

***

I saw that my future did not lie in doing the kind of work Hank did, though I learned from him, as I had from Professor Andy Dolan, how much law and politics intertwine, how legal institutions support political institutions, to the benefit of some and the detriment of others. So, as soon as I finished the bar exam, I joined Dan Leighton's band of investigative activists at the

Community Information Project. The group operated from a battered Victorian home next door to the Community Legal Assistance Center, now run by a friend of Dan's.

CIP's staff could have come straight out of central casting for a television crime drama like the Mod Squad. Dan was strange enough, with his Jewish Afro, overalls, and machine gun staccato speech, but the rest of the group all contributed to the effect.

Larry Larson had a private investigative business and worked with us on the side. Portly, with a full beard and a softly commanding presence, he reminded me of actor Sebastian Cabot. Larry had a remarkable ability to draw information out of reluctant sources, and to find people who didn't want to be found.

Miriam Cutler began as an intern from UCLA but soon became a skilled investigator. Tall and dark-haired, very Mediterranean-looking, a quintessential nice Jewish girl, her perpetual smile masked a gifted and determined researcher. She also played clarinet and piano in a series of bands, including the iconic Mystic Knights of the Oingo Boingo. Later, after CIP broke up, Miriam became a prolific, award-winning composer of film scores.

Others came and went—students, journalists, activists—most of them unusual characters. I may have been the exception in both appearance and demeanor. Miriam remarked on this one day during a particularly wild office meeting in which I maintained my usual placid exterior.

"Cary," she exclaimed, shaking her head in mock frustration, "You're so … normal!" It wasn't a criticism, but not a compliment either.

After my admission to the State Bar, we could file lawsuits ourselves. We sued two members of the LA City Council over conflicts of interest and joined in a political corruption lawsuit against the mayor of San Francisco. And we submitted testimony in scores of legislative and regulatory proceedings, at the LA City Council, the County Board of Supervisors, and various state and federal agencies.

Challenging authority had a dark side, though. Soon after we sued one City Councilmember, someone torched the garage behind my home. Fire investigators found an empty gas can at the side of the house and asked me to identify possible enemies. I told them about the lawsuit, but they weren't willing to pursue that. The arson case was never solved, and I learned to be more vigilant.

CIP undertook the kinds of investigations and exposés that few others did in California at the time. We produced a groundbreaking report on mortgage "redlining," the practice of banks denying mortgage loans in certain geographic areas, typically racial minority neighborhoods. This offended me greatly, as I saw the opportunity for homeownership as key to building generational wealth in this country, and the wealth gap steadily increasing between homeowners and those denied that opportunity.

The entire lending industry paid attention to us after we invoked the novel tactic of challenging the application by a major lender, Gibraltar Savings & Loan, to open a new branch in LA. We contended they were operating their existing branches in a discriminatory fashion and therefore the state should not allow them to open new ones until those practices ceased.

That work led us to join a network of groups engaged on the same issue in cities around the state and around the country, campaigning successfully for passage of the federal Home Mortgage Disclosure Act and the Community Reinvestment Act as well as similar state laws. After decades of discrimination, banks and government agencies would have to change their ways or be held legally accountable.

I experienced every challenge to authority, every policy or political victory, as an affirmation of my rights as an American. I felt especially proud when CIP's challenge to mortgage lending discrimination landed me on the front page of the *New York Times*. I remembered my mother asking me skeptically the previous year if doing this kind of work would ever put me on the cover of *Time*, her benchmark for political and business success. To me, the *New York Times* was even better.

Sometimes we applied our skills to aid particular communities. We learned that the Bank of America and its business associates had bought most of the Temple-Beaudry neighborhood across the freeway from downtown LA and planned to redevelop it with an office complex for the bank. Most residents were renters and recent immigrants. Neighborhood life revolved around a small Catholic church. Most residents had limited English language skills and knew little about their legal rights, but a few of them contacted us and asked for help.

Our hosts organized a community meeting at the church and acted as interpreters. Most of the residents packed in, along with some property owners. We had done preliminary research and related to the crowd what we had found out about their situation. Not a pretty picture. With support from city government, the bank planned to clear out the residents and demolish the neighborhood in a matter of months. I empathized with the residents, seeing in them something of myself at an earlier age, just learning English, trying to adjust to American culture and rules. Addressing that first meeting, I told the crowd about my background and promised we would fight for them. The audience, respectfully quiet up to that time, burst into applause, echoing off the whitewashed walls of the church. Their excited reaction gave me a boost of confidence for the fight ahead.

We recruited two experienced Hispanic community organizers fluent in Spanish and began holding neighborhood strategy meetings at the church. The residents understood they had little chance of stopping the bulldozers. They could expect only to be enough of an obstacle that the bank would have to deal with them and offer something in return for displacing them. Meanwhile, a large segment of the community disappeared—the undocumented families who feared the glare of publicity.

For two months, we rallied the community, held news conferences to gain public attention to their plight, and got the *Los Angeles Times* to run a feature story about the situation. The bank didn't want that kind of publicity and ultimately made an offer of relocation assistance money for all the remaining families, along with a financial commitment of loans to low-income businesses. It wasn't much, but far more than the law guaranteed them, so the remaining residents agreed. I saw how settling for half a loaf was far better than starving.

The mayor's office scheduled a news conference to announce the settlement. I sat at the dais with community leaders and the Mayor's representatives. In the news conference and in a written statement my colleagues distributed, I expressed our disappointment at how the city had been an enabler of the bank's plan to oust such helpless residents. Immediately afterward, a mayoral assistant confronted me.

"We'll never work with you again," she snarled. That threat launched a contentious relationship that culminated in her losing her job due to controversy over a major community development program. No matter. Others in City Hall remained happy to cooperate with us.

By this time, the press covered us constantly. Our exposé of lurid ties between a shoddy bank and various public officials, our documentation of the web of companies and organizations dominating public decisions affecting downtown LA, as well as our advocacy for reform of federally funded community development programs, made us a hit with reporters at the *Times* and *Herald-Examiner*, as well as all the local television and radio news programs. They attended our news conferences at the LA Press Club and called us for interviews.

What set us apart from most of our contemporaries in the activist community was our ability to package a story effectively and present it in a form immediately usable by the media. That positioned us to take a giant stride in our impact as public interest advocates.

CHAPTER 26
FOUR BIG MOMENTS

On a sunny summer morning in 1977, I stood on the front steps of a mirrored building near Lafayette Park housing a dozen state government offices.

"We are appearing before the California Savings and Loan Commission today to expose the discriminatory lending practices of major mortgage lenders," I announced to a group of eager reporters. "We will demand that the commission deny permits to expand institutions engaged in such practices."

The previous day, we had issued a press release declaring our intention to challenge the Gibraltar Savings expansion application. Just blocks away stood some of the very neighborhoods being starved of mortgage credit. While I spoke, my colleagues distributed copies of testimony I would deliver.

Dan Leighton and I then led a pack of activists, reporters, and curious onlookers inside, where we filled the commission's wood-paneled hearing room. After the commission staff and the applicant made their pitches, I presented our research findings. Dan passed out copies of our written report. I then showed a map illustrating a clear geographical bias in where the applicant was and was not making mortgage loans, and how that geography corresponded with the racial composition of the impacted areas. It looked like classic redlining.

I knew mortgage credit provided by savings and loan institutions and banks was a uniquely American opportunity. In Europe, indeed most of the world, one had to save at least half the cost of a house before qualifying for a loan. I also knew that mortgage lenders had a sordid history of denying credit to certain communities and certain kinds of people, mainly racial minorities. That struck me as a violation of the American social contract.

When I finished my presentation, the commissioners sat eerily silent. I felt confident about my testimony, but I wondered what they were thinking. Did my presentation impress them, or was their silence a sign of frustration, or even irritation, that they didn't want to express publicly? Finally, the chair assured us they would consider our testimony and adjourned.

We then held a formal press conference. Word had gotten out that something momentous was happening in the financial industry. Before a roomful of reporters at the Press Club, we announced our plans.

"Today we began a campaign to change the lending practices of the mortgage lending industry," I declared. "Our petition today to the Savings and Loan Commissioner created the first crack in the industry's armor, the first step in opening their business practices to public scrutiny. They will change, or we will shut them down!" Hyperbole, perhaps, but a great sound bite.

By that evening, the press conference was on all the local radio and tv news broadcasts. The next morning, the story appeared on newspaper front pages, including *The New York Times*.

So it began. Groups in other cities had raised the same issues, but we had upped the stakes a lot. Soon we had executives from major lending institutions calling, wanting to know if they could work things out amicably. They invited me to participate in high-level negotiations over how they should address the charges leveled against them.

The president of Home Savings, the largest savings and loan institution in the country, asked me to meet with him and his top executives. They wanted to assure us they were not engaging in the discrimination we were targeting. They made a convincing initial presentation. To conclude, the president asked his executive vice president to bring in their own map illustrating their loan activity. The president turned ashen and dissembled like crazy when the EVP responded, "You mean the map with all the red lines on it?" It wasn't that kind of map, they assured me. I shook my head and laughed, more amused than shocked.

In the months that followed, state and federal legislation passed, outlawing for the first time the practices we had documented and protested. And industry practices did change. Activists all over the country contributed to achieving these results, but we felt our role had been an important one.

We didn't know at the time how much of a jolt we had delivered. Several years later, when I was teaching real estate law classes at USC, one of my former professors invited me to join him for lunch at the faculty club with a lawyer who represented financial institutions. While we ate and sipped wine, surrounded by academics, I mentioned my work on opening up lending practices and cited the Gibraltar Savings hearing in particular. The other attorney smiled.

"You probably had no idea what a furor you created," he told me. "Within twenty-four hours, every executive and lawyer in the industry was reading a transcript of that hearing. I don't mind admitting it really shook things up and made us take a long look at how we were doing business."

I nodded, sat back, and took a sip of wine. That comment validated our efforts better than any newspaper headline.

* * *

If the fight against mortgage redlining was our biggest win for home buyers, we helped accomplish something pretty spectacular for renters too. I had been a tenant since moving to California ten years earlier, and had learned from experience and in school how few legal rights renters enjoyed, especially as to landlords raising rents. In Europe, most people rented. The Vienna city government owned thousands of rental units and leased them to average households. Laws protected tenants there from arbitrary rent increases and evictions. The military owned or leased the apartments I grew up in, so rent was free and eviction was virtually unheard of. The difference in status between tenants and homeowners in the United States shocked me.

In June 1976, the California Supreme Court upheld the City of Berkeley's rent control ordinance, in a broadly written decision making it clear that such laws passed constitutional muster. Anticipating that outcome, the California Housing Council, representing the largest landlords in the state, crafted a bill to outlaw local rent controls and got it introduced in the State Assembly. Caught by surprise, tenant groups failed in last-ditch efforts to block the bill. AB 3788 eventually landed on Governor Jerry Brown's desk, where tenant advocates launched a last-ditch stand to secure a veto.

Arnold Sternberg, Director of the Department of Housing and Community Development, opposed the bill. He had a graduate student intern from the University of California at Santa Barbara, John Gilderbloom, prepare a scholarly critique. Standing well over six feet tall, with preppie looks and demeanor, Gilderbloom seemed an unlikely candidate for this role, but his paper and the passion with which he argued his case impressed the former-Jesuit governor. In response, the landlords brought in a former college classmate of the governor to argue their case.

Meanwhile, an attorney on Sternberg's staff who knew of CIP's work on mortgage redlining contacted me. I didn't have a strong view about rent control, but I saw the pending legislation as just another attempt by a powerful lobby to eliminate regulation at the expense of powerless consumers. The landlords framed their position in terms of their constitutional rights as property owners to raise rents without limit. I saw it instead as an example of unfettered abuse of those rights, exactly what I expected government to rein in through regulation.

I felt complimented that state officials turned to us for help. In a short time, we organized affordable housing advocates in Southern California, held rallies and press conferences, and sent a surge of opposition letters to the Governor's Office.

On the final day the governor had to act, the bill still sat on his desk. He called in both sides to pitch their best arguments.

Early the next morning, I got a phone call from John Gilderbloom. He had given it his best shot and appeared to impress the governor. The landlord lobbyist wound up yelling in frustration at the governor. As the clock on the wall edged toward the midnight deadline, Brown picked up his pen and signed the veto, ensuring the California rent control wars would continue. After this blow-by-blow description of the events of the previous evening, I felt the combination of excitement and equanimity that I had come to experience after any victory.

John returned to Santa Barbara to complete his graduate studies. We later shared several stages and authored articles together. He became a nationally known professor of urban affairs at the University of Louisville. I never heard about the landlord lobbyist again.

* * *

My work at CIP led me into another unique opportunity. In early 1976, I got a call from Mary Jo Von Mach, who represented a group of politically active young people with inherited wealth. They wanted to establish a foundation in LA to fund social change organizations, similar to foundations in Boston and a few other eastern cities. This was a hopeful sign. One of the biggest challenges of CIP's work was finding financial support, especially since most of our efforts targeted public officials and big business.

I met with Mary Jo at a coffeehouse near my apartment in Silverlake. Sitting outside, our conversation almost drowned out by the Sunset Boulevard traffic, I told her this proposal excited me, that a foundation like that could have a tremendous impact in LA.

I met with her again soon after at CIP's satellite office in the Methodist Church next to USC. She told me the group planned to go forward with setting up what would become the Liberty Hill Foundation, named after a site in San Pedro that had been a rallying point in a famous port strike in the early 1900s.

"Would you be interested in serving on the foundation's funding board?" she asked.

"Absolutely." I had limited experience with foundations, but I saw a great opportunity to bring more of that kind of funding to groups like CIP and the others I worked with.

"Great, but I have to raise one important issue. How do you feel about rich people?"

"I've known some I liked, some I didn't like," I replied with a laugh.

"That'll work. Welcome to the funding board!"

I felt elated and relieved. Especially when she told me about others who had agreed to serve on the board—among the people I most admired and respected in LA activist circles.

I soon met Sarah Pillsbury of the flour and cookies family, the initiator of the Liberty Hill idea. She had moved to LA recently to work in film production and wanted to replicate what her brother and others had done elsewhere.

As I told Mary Jo, I had known rich people before, among my classmates at USC. I recalled feeling intimidated by them, especially those from families with longtime wealth and power. Growing up in a more socially stratified society in Europe, I had no contact with such people. And the hierarchy in the military community was based on rank, not wealth or family connections. I looked forward to the opportunity to transcend that social class barrier, in what seemed to me a uniquely American experience.

For two years, I served on the funding board, interviewing grant applicants from a host of community and social action organizations, and then voting on who should receive funding. In those days, the grants were small, just a few thousand dollars each, but I loved being in on the beginning of such an important effort. Now, almost fifty years later, Liberty Hill raises and distributes hundreds of thousands of dollars a year to support activist causes.

**

CIP's biggest local impact came through an unexpected issue. We focused on political corruption and business misconduct, so we were unsure how to respond when a doctor at LA County-USC Medical Center contacted us with a story about low-income maternity patients being forcibly sterilized. I didn't know the sordid history in this country of forced sterilization of poor people and mental health patients. What he told me over the phone shocked me. It sounded like something out of Nazi Germany, where large numbers of people deemed social undesirables had been sterilized in mental hospitals and special clinics.

Dr. Bernard "Buddy" Rosenfeld had ties to a network of doctors exposing such practices at urban hospitals serving inner-city communities. Exposés already had occurred at some cities back east. He needed the help of local public interest advocates who could blow open this story in LA. Many of the victims were recent immigrants, so I felt a special empathy for them.

Rosenfeld came on like a whirlwind, a bundle of energy with a strong New York accent, topped with a mop of curly black hair. As a resident at County Hospital, he saw the abuses taking place there as staff handed women in labor consent forms, in a language they often didn't understand, agreeing to tubal ligations or hysterectomies. Sometimes, he told us, the medical staff didn't even bother with the paperwork. Appalled, Rosenfeld contacted the Southern Poverty Law Center, an Alabama-based organization spearheading a national campaign against such practices.

And he contacted us. Dan Leighton and I shared Rosenfeld's revulsion. He put us in contact with Joe Levin, SPLC's Legal Director, who assured us of their support. Miriam Cutler of our office led the investigation of Rosenfeld's allegations. She interviewed the mostly Spanish-speaking victims, some identified by Buddy, others by the Center for Law and Justice, an East LA legal clinic. A young attorney there, Antonia Hernandez, took this case on as a major challenge. It wound up launching her career on a trajectory that eventually led to her heading the California Endowment.

The story soon became too big to ignore. Claudia Dreifus, a former *New York Times* reporter working as a freelancer, came to LA to write a feature magazine article for *The Progressive*. Starting from our collaboration on that story, we have remained friends ever since. The *Los Angeles Times* assigned several reporters to the story and published a major exposé, as well. Even *The New York Times* contacted me and ran an article. And a group of victims sued the hospital and key administrators.

Forty years later, a documentary film entitled *No Mas Bebes* chronicled the events and their aftermath. Many of the victims' lives were shattered once they and their husbands discovered they could no longer bear children.

Admittedly, much had changed in the practices of County Hospital. Yet, no one held any of the responsible individuals personally accountable. Buddy Rosenfeld, on the other hand, found himself initially ostracized within his profession, but eventually established a successful ob/gyn practice in Houston specializing in undoing tubal ligations, reversing the kind of damage he had observed being done in LA.

CHAPTER 27
A FRESH START — TOM AND JANE AND CED

As CIP's visibility climbed in LA, a pair of supporters held a fundraiser for us at their home in the Hollywood Hills. Jerry and Betty Decter owned a mannequin business in the industrial district of downtown LA. On the side, they crusaded against local government corruption and had collaborated with us on some exposés.

A surprise guest at the party was Fred Branfman, creator of the anti-war "Six Million Victims" flyer that impressed me so much during the McGovern presidential campaign. He had moved to LA to work as the policy adviser on Tom Hayden's 1976 US Senate campaign against incumbent John Tunney.

Tall and lean, with a wry manner that reminded me of Mort Sahl, he had a penchant for taking voluminous notes while talking. Knowing even a little about his history in the anti-war movement, his experiences in Indochina, and his prolific writing, I recognized him as someone from whom I could learn a lot. Under the towering trees by the Decters' swimming pool, we talked at length about my work and CIP.

"I like what you guys are doing," Fred said after a half hour of intense discussion. Then he surprised me, asking, "Are you happy? Are you interested in doing something different?"

He seemed to be studying me, as if to see my reaction. Talking with Fred gave me a much-needed jolt. I loved my work, but I had grown as much as I could at CIP. I needed some new inspiration.

"I'm happy about what we've accomplished," I replied, trying not to sound too eager. "But yes, I think about doing something different if I see an opportunity."

"Well, we should talk some more. I'll be in touch again," he promised. With that, he shook my hand, turned away, and left. I stood there for several minutes, thinking about where that might lead, before putting aside the exchange with Fred and rejoining the party.

I volunteered as an issues speaker on Hayden's Senate campaign, but I didn't run into Fred again until later in the year, after Tom had lost to Tunney in the primary election. During the campaign, a detailed book of policy proposals entitled *Make the Future Ours,* written by Tom with Fred's research input, impressed me. No one had produced such an ambitious piece of California policy work since Upton Sinclair's gubernatorial campaign in the 1930s under the slogan "End Poverty in California," EPIC for short.

In late summer that year, I got a surprise phone call from my law school friend Ray LeBov. Bearded, with long but thinning black hair and an intense gaze, Ray had been part of the activist circle I associated with at USC. Now he worked in Sacramento as legal counsel to a committee of the State Legislature. He had heard that Hayden and some of his campaign people planned to gather at a supporter's home near Santa Barbara the following week to talk about how to build on the campaign, maybe by launching a new statewide organization. No one explicitly invited us, but it sounded like an open meeting and too interesting an opportunity to pass up, so we decided to join the discussion. Ray flew to LA and we drove to the meeting together.

Soon after arriving, I encountered Fred Branfman. "What a nice surprise," he told me, giving me a vigorous handshake. Recognizing just a few others among the twenty or so in attendance, I smiled and nodded at everyone, determined to appear like part of the group.

I sat on the stone fireplace hearth in our host's sunlit living room, with Ray on one side of me, Fred on the other, and Hayden in a chair opposite me. I hadn't met Tom up close before, only having seen him at a distance at campaign rallies. And, of course, my first view of him, on the television screen, amid demonstrations outside the 1968 Democratic Convention. I caught him staring at me, his mouth locked in a slight smile, a kind of quizzical look like he wondered who I was and why I was there. I just smiled back at him.

Tom called the meeting to order and asked us to introduce ourselves. Fred preceded me.

"Fred Branfman, campaign policy director," he said. No further comment. Everyone knew him.

Then eyes turned to me. "Cary Lowe. I did volunteer work in LA and gave talks at campaign events." People around me nodded. I had passed the screening and fit in.

After thanking us all for our efforts on the campaign, Tom kicked off a discussion by posing the questions on everyone's minds.

"Do we want to convert the senate campaign apparatus into an ongoing statewide political organization? And, if we think that's a good idea, is California ready to support such an organization?"

We talked about that for hours. People wandered in and out to use the restroom or get refreshments from the adjoining dining room as the discussion rolled on. I spoke little, but I could feel the level of enthusiasm building as people addressed and overcame one concern after another. Fred scribbled pages of notes and interjected an occasional comment. No one left the meeting early.

By mid-afternoon, the group expressed unanimous support. The remaining concerns had to do with timing and structure. We agreed to organize a conference in Santa Barbara, and to invite political activists from all over the state, not just those who had worked on the senate campaign. Tom would write an invitation and statement of purpose. The goal of the conference would be to define a set of economic issues on which the group had substantial consensus and around which we could build a new organization.

As Ray and I prepared to leave, Fred told me he wanted to get together again back in LA to discuss a proposition. I grew excited, especially after the discussion we had just concluded. I remembered his question to me the first time we met, whether I was open to doing something different.

We met again a week later for coffee at a Mexican restaurant in Echo Park. Fred didn't need much coffee to get started. He described his and Tom's vision of a "think tank" to provide support for the proposed new organization, and also to generate policy support for other groups with which they hoped to collaborate. They had available the shell of an existing but inactive non-profit organization, the California Public Policy Center, formed several years earlier by Derek Shearer, a friend of Tom's and also of Bill Clinton's. Derek wanted to stay involved, but was agreeable to letting them take it over. Fred planned to work there full time. Hayden, Shearer, and a few other notables would serve as the Board of Directors. Then came the clincher.

"I'd like you to join me," Fred began. "We would be co-directors. We'd complement one another's skills. You know about law, housing, finance, and other issues I don't. I've already talked to Tom about it. We need to talk more, but he likes the idea."

What a compliment, and what an opportunity! As satisfying as my work with CIP had been for a long time, I saw here something I wanted more—a chance to influence policy statewide and do it in tandem with an organization capable of mobilizing public support for those proposals.

"That's a great offer," I replied. "How soon do you need to know?"

"Soon. We need to get started preparing for the conference in Santa Barbara."

"All right, but I want to talk with Tom directly about his vision for this. I want to meet with him as soon as possible. Then, I'll give you my answer."

Fred arranged a lunch meeting for us at a restaurant near the Santa Monica pier. We lounged on a sunny patio, looking out at the ocean. Tom surprised me by launching into a description of his new interest in karate and his attempt to get into good physical shape. Then, over soup and salads, we engaged in a freewheeling political discussion.

"Why did you run for the Senate?" I began. It seemed to me an act far removed from his earlier, more radical organizing days in the civil rights movement, the Newark ghetto, and the campaign to end the Vietnam War.

"In the anti-war movement, we worked with a lot of elected officials., especially at the federal level. I developed respect many of them. That gave me a new perspective on working through the electoral process. Win or lose, the senate campaign let us raise a lot of important issues."

"What do you want to accomplish with a statewide political organization, separate from the political parties?"

He described being inspired by the organizing work of Upton Sinclair and Cesar Chavez. He believed an organization like that could push California politics in a more progressive direction for a generation to come.

Then Tom changed gears. Fred had told him a bit about me and my work, but he asked about my background and how I had gotten politicized. I told him about my campaign experiences, my evolution to opposing the Vietnam War, and my work with CIP. We then got into how my skills and experience fit into his plans. He didn't try to persuade me directly. He painted a vision of California's political future and invited me to put myself into it. I saw in him a natural organizer and politician, and I understand how he had become such an important figure in the anti-war movement.

By the end of lunch, I was sold. But we weren't done.

We went back to the house that Tom occupied with his wife, Jane Fonda, near the beach in the decayed but gentrifying Ocean Park neighborhood. Like the others around it, the two-story house filled its small lot and showed signs of recent painting and repairs. At the top of the front stairs, Fred stepped into the enclosed porch to retrieve some papers. He had been living there, on Tom and Jane's front porch, since moving to California, so he could be close to them at all times. If that seemed eccentric then, I had much more to learn about Fred.

We found Jane waiting for us, sitting on a sofa in the living room, dressed in a casual but elegant pantsuit. Glancing around the room, I noticed the furnishings looked comfortable but a bit worn. Jane greeted me with a big smile and motioned for me to sit in a chair opposite her. That gesture put me at ease, even though I was meeting my first movie star.

I found Jane to be businesslike when it came to politics. She impressed me as informed, politically sophisticated, and unpretentious—different from her Hollywood image. And she asked good questions. What was my perspective on current state politics? Why did I want to work with them? What skills and experience did I bring?

Where Tom came across as high-energy and driven, Jane seemed calmer and more inquisitive. I sensed she was an important stabilizing influence on Tom.

After an hour of discussion, Jane leaned back and looked right at me. "I hope you'll join us," she said, in a tone as friendly as it was sincere. "We're going to do great things. You won't regret it."

Tom and Fred, who had been largely silent during my discussion with Jane, both smiled and nodded in my direction. I felt I had passed a key test and they were inviting me to join in an important venture.

"I'm in," I replied, nodding back at each of them.

Driving home on the Santa Monica Freeway, the day's events seemed surreal. Tom, Jane, and Fred had won me over. I felt like a knight joining a crusade. I knew it was an important step, but I didn't quite realize yet how pivotal that day would turn out to be. My work, my associations, my impacts, soon would lead me in a new direction that would determine the course of the rest of my life.

Within days, I met with Dan and Miriam at CIP to share my plans. We huddled in a small room at the Community Legal Assistance Center. Dan slouched in his chair, tapping one foot. He always hated difficult or personal discussions. Miriam sat upright, smiling, eager to hear me out.

"I have regrets about leaving," I told them. "We've been together a long time and done some great things. But CIP has changed. It's still doing investigations, but it's morphed from doing advocacy to being more of a media organization. I think that's wonderful. It just doesn't interest me as much as what we did before."

They knew what I meant. We had developed close ties to television news staffs at the local ABC affiliate and the Public Broadcasting System station, and we regularly collaborated with them in producing investigative stories. Investigative journalism was hot, and our work attracted young, smart, eager journalism school graduates. Dan built up similar relationships with national television networks and shows like *60 Minutes*. I loved being in front of the camera and being quoted in the press, advocating for a cause, but I had much less interest in doing research and turning it over to someone else to report.

As Dan mulled over what I had said, Miriam jumped in. "Oh, Cary, you just want to work with a movie star," she said, then burst into laughter. Her easy acceptance of my decision seemed to relax Dan.

"I understand," he said. "I had a feeling for a while you were looking for something else. That's ok. You've got to do what makes you happy."

That was it. I told them I would stick around for a couple more weeks and help complete some assignments. We would remain friends. And maybe we would find new opportunities to work together.

Fred already had found office space for us in the classic 1920s-era Bradbury Building at Third and Broadway in downtown LA. The four-story, glass-covered atrium, brown glazed-brick interior, and wrought-iron trim were a throwback to an earlier, more glamourous time. Rent was relatively cheap in the recently restored but still antiquated building. The location suited us well—walking distance to all the state and local government offices, as well as the major newspapers; close to the restaurants in Little Tokyo, Chinatown, and Olvera Street; and just across the street from the Grand Central Market with its scores of grocery stalls and food vendors.

We operated on a shoestring budget at first, filling the office with thrift store furnishings and taking minimal pay, but Fred had secured enough funding to get us through our start-up phase. We immediately began work on the planned Santa Barbara conference. While Hayden drafted a vision statement to be mailed out to activists statewide, as an invitation to attend the conference, Fred and I set to work drafting a two-volume set of *Working Papers on Economic Democracy*.

For three months, we labored over this, often late into the night, examining each sector of the California economy and theorizing how to make it more responsive to public needs and regulation. Unlike graduate school, this dissertation would be put to immediate use—and hopefully have an immediate impact.

In February 1977, hundreds of activists gathered at Santa Barbara City College. They came from every part of the state, from the North Coast, the Bay Area, and the Central Valley, to LA, Orange County, San Diego, and the inland counties. They covered the liberal-to left-political spectrum.

Earnest-looking college professors and students. Energetic Hispanic community organizers. Black activists sporting dashikis and huge Afros. Sunburned farmworkers in jeans and flannel shirts. Aging radicals looking for one more cause to champion and young activists engaged in their first campaigns. Even a sprinkling of elected officials. All had received our *Working Papers* before coming.

Tom Hayden and Cesar Chavez led off the event with speeches that energized the crowd. US Representative Ron Dellums, Berkeley City Councilmember Loni Hancock, and other political luminaries followed. The audience then broke up into workshops focused on housing, energy, agriculture, education, environment, natural resources, affirmative action, and a dozen other topics. Each group, meeting in a separate classroom, debated, argued, and sometimes agreed. By late afternoon, they adopted dozens of policy positions to be presented to the entire conference.

I stayed up all night supervising a roomful of transcribers, typists, and copiers, converting notes from the workshops into draft resolutions to be debated and voted on by the entire assembly in the morning. The clicking of manual typewriters and the whirring of copying machines drowned out conversation. Most smiled as they worked, excited at what had emerged from the workshops. Some grew upset over what they read and wanted to revise the text, but I had to veto that. We didn't finish until after sunrise, by which time we all had gotten a bit testy from fatigue and too much coffee.

As the conferees drifted into the main meeting hall for the early morning plenary session, we handed them each the printed, stapled product of their work the day before and our work through the night. How different, I thought, from how issues platforms get developed at the major political party conventions.

Hayden chaired the plenary. Guiding several hundred passionate activists through a discussion of a couple hundred resolutions took every ounce of his organizing experience. Some topics, like establishing a renewable energy sector and promoting residential rent control, went through smoothly. Others, like public ownership of certain industries versus greater corporate shareholder rights, became mired in controversy. From a seat near the front of the hall, I swiveled in all directions to see the speakers and hear their comments. With adoption of each plank of the emerging platform, my level of excitement rose, like watching returns come in on election night.

By late morning, we got bogged down in political minutia. As the clock closed in on a noon deadline to adjourn, Tom pulled a trick from his back pocket. Going off script, he announced we would take a break from the debate and hear a speech by John Maher, head of the San Francisco-based Delancey Street Foundation.

A squat Irishman with a boxer's rumpled face, a New York accent, and a major attitude, Maher worked with ex-convicts, drug addicts, former hookers, and other street people, helping them straighten out their lives and get conventional jobs. He sounded as tough as he looked. A seasoned organizer, like Tom, he would soon help his brother Bill get elected to the San Francisco Board of Supervisors. The moment Hayden announced him, Maher made his way up to the stage and launched into a stemwinder of a speech that held the attention of the entire room.

"The people I work with," he told the crowd, "they don't understand all the fine points of the subjects you're debating. And sometimes they don't appreciate the etiquette that's expected of people in political circles. But we'll work on your causes and we'll walk your picket lines, because we know we're all in this together."

Maher talked for half an hour, but it flew by like mere minutes. Scattered voices punctuated his statements, like intermittent call and response. The air in the room felt heavier and the crowd murmured more and more loudly. I pictured Abraham Lincoln or Huey Long energizing a campaign rally. Reaching the finale, Maher's voice rose to an angry pitch.

"Remember!" he thundered. "Man for man, we're a better gang than the other side. We're going to take them, we'll take them hard!" I had been leaning forward, listening closely. Now I sat upright as if hit by an electric shock.

Maher looked down and his shoulders dropped. After a momentary pause, the crowd broke into wild applause. The building seemed to shake. Waiting for that moment, Hayden leaped back to the podium.

"I move to adopt the remaining resolutions by acclamation," Fred Branfman yelled from the front row. Someone else seconded that and, before anyone could object, yet another person called the question. In moments, a voice vote overwhelmingly approved the motion. A few people protested, demanding a chance to debate further. Too late. We were done. I looked up at Tom still standing at the podium, wearing a wide smile. Our eyes met for a moment, and we nodded in unison. That moment felt almost as momentous as the signing of the Declaration of Independence. Looking back, I know that was a burst of youthful overenthusiasm, but I had just witnessed the birth of the first progressive statewide movement in California in over half a century.

We had a mandate and a program. Days later, back in LA, Tom publicly announced the launching of the Campaign for Economic Democracy, based on the principles he had laid out in the conference invitation and the resolutions adopted at the meeting. Chapters came together in a dozen cities, rising out of the ashes of the Hayden for Senate campaign. Separate chapters of Students for Economic Democracy formed on half a dozen college campuses. And a network of other activist groups connected to the newly formed CED—Black and Chicano community activists, tenant organizations, environmentalists, and more.

Soon after, Jane Fonda bought Laurel Springs Ranch, a former religious camp in the mountains overlooking Santa Barbara. With bunkhouses, a dining hall, meeting rooms, and recreational facilities, it provided a perfect retreat location for statewide CED meetings and all kinds of other political gatherings. We loved the irony of being just down the road from Ronald Reagan's Rancho Cielo. Jane and Tom had a separate small house on the property, as did a caretaker couple. After a long day of meetings, we played baseball, soaked in a huge hot tub, or drove down to San Marcos Pass for a beer at Cold Spring Tavern, a historic one-time stagecoach stop.

I wasn't sure yet where this would lead, but I knew I had hitched my wagon to something that had great potential. Now, I just needed to make the most of it and hang on for the ride.

CHAPTER 28
MAKING A BIGGER IMPACT

After the conference, Fred and I felt like our heads were spinning with energy and excitement. We set to work providing research and policy proposals for CED and for many other groups that had convened in Santa Barbara.

I loved coming to work, starting with walking through the eight-foot oak doors of the Bradbury Building, into the sunlit atrium, and up the broad staircases lined with wrought-iron railings. Once in the office, I began a daily round of non-stop meetings, phone calls, research, and writing that I found thrilling, even as it exhausted me. Elected officials, community organizers, reporters, and political activists passed through, often keeping us busy late into the evening.

We occupied an oak-paneled suite on the second floor, overlooking Broadway, two floors down from the CED offices. Leonard Weinglass, who had been one Tom's defense attorneys on the Chicago 7 trial, shared the space. Pat Hilliard, the wife of former Black Panther Party Chief of Staff David Hilliard, joined us as office manager.

Moving into the office revealed more about Fred. Wanting to remain close to work at all times, he rented a small room in the same building to serve as his home. After living in rural Southeast Asia for several years, he was satisfied with having just enough space for a bed, hotplate, and small refrigerator. When his Vietnamese wife, Thoa, moved back from Washington, D.C. a few months later, she joined him there.

Fred first concentrated on renewable energy policy. He and Peggy Curran, who later served as a manager in several California cities, produced a report entitled *Jobs from the Sun* that laid the foundation for what was to become a burgeoning solar industry. I focused on housing and investment policies, and soon put out a report entitled *Saving Neighborhoods*, analyzing actions nationwide to preserve and restore urban communities. Those issues were a natural extension of my earlier work at CIP fighting discriminatory lending practices.

Every three months, we drove up to Laurel Springs Ranch to sit in on statewide meetings of the CED governing committee, composed of representatives from local chapters, university chapters, and allied organizations. We met in the combination dining hall and conference space of the main building, perched near the edge of the mountaintop ranch, with a view of Santa Barbara and the Channel Islands.

Tom Hayden chaired the two-day meetings with a firm but flexible hand. Two dozen activists representing different regions and constituencies were bound to have intense disagreements from time to time. As an experienced meeting facilitator, Tom insisted that all comments be succinct, respectful, and on point. Fred and I attended as resources, ready to provide information and policy advice, but also to weigh in ourselves on controversial issues. The group took food breaks and adjourned for needed recreation time before people burned out from exhaustion. As a result, they completed even the lengthiest agendas, with consensus reached on almost everything.

For me, the most impressive aspect of the meetings was the ability of such diverse, even disparate individuals to find common ground. Nothing showed that more dramatically than the simultaneous presence of David Hilliard and Ken Msemaji. Where David had been a leader of the Black Panther Party, Ken had been active in the US organization, a rival group that engaged in an infamous shootout with the Panthers in Los Angeles a few years earlier. Now, here they were, onetime violent rivals, working collaboratively to build a new political organization.

Other vivid characters dotted the room: Bob Mulholland, a tall, lean ex-paratrooper, now Northern California Coordinator for CED and later to become Political Director of the California Democratic Party. Bonnie Laidin, physically imposing but with a ready smile, a regional organizer for the Service Employees International Union. Sam Hurst, a blonde surfer and former USC student body president, turned anti-war activist and initial staff director for CED. Robin Schneider, a diminutive UCLA student activist who later became a leader in abortion rights and environmental protection organizations. David Sanchez, co-founder of the Brown Berets and later a college professor in LA. Fahari Jeffers, an intense long-time activist in the San Diego African-American community and now a founder and leader of the United Domestic Workers Union. Michael Picker, the mustached organizer of CED's Cancer Project, later to become Chair of the California Public Utilities Commission. And many more.

***

Tom Hayden used Laurel Springs as a refuge from the intensity of Los Angeles and Sacramento, so I sometimes drove up to meet with him there. One Saturday, with our business concluded, he poured us glasses of bourbon and invited me to stay over. He had recently returned from a trip exploring his family roots in Ireland and was thinking about the identify of Americans who retained only a superficial connection to the country of their family origins. With my background, he wanted to explore that issue with me. As we worked our way through the rest of the whiskey, he grew more intense, expressing his sorrow over assimilation that resulted in a loss of cultural identity.

"Irish Americans celebrate St. Patrick's Day and maybe belong to an Irish social club," he observed, "but most have no real sense of Irish history and culture beyond that. It seems like that happens to most immigrants after even one generation here."

"I see that too," I responded. "My family came here so recently that we still have a lot of connections to Europe. But people we know, whose parents or grandparents came over, don't relate much to the old country. Most don't even seem to know the stories behind their families' immigration, even if it was right before the Holocaust."

"I'm going back again soon. This is something I want to think and write about. It's just as important to me as the issues we're working on."

Tom alluded to that more and more, both in private and in public. He eventually would write a book entitled *Irish on the Inside*, exploring the cross-section of dual identity among Irish Americans, in particular. When I read it, I sensed how well it applied to any ethnic communities here. Even among my own relatives, I saw how little connection remained to their roots. As much as I wanted to be and remain American, I also resolved to keep those ties alive to my family's past. Later, writing this book became a key part of that.

***

Fred and I spent much of our time in the office, but we always welcomed opportunities to attend meetings with CED chapters and other organizations. We traveled the length of the state to wherever we could be useful in advancing our issues. Those travels, as well as events we attended locally, gave me access to many of the political notables of that time. I met Cesar Chavez at the home of a friend, where he stayed when visiting LA. Tom Hayden introduced me to fellow members of the Chicago 7 and other national leaders of the political left. At City Hall and the State Capitol, I met elected officials interested in the same issues that motivated my work. Far from being star-struck, I found those connections and the accompanying conversations inspiring and motivating.

State Senator John Dunlap and his aide John Harrington pushed for reconsideration of how the state managed and invested its massive pension fund and surplus fund accounts. Working with them, we proposed creation of a state bank, patterned after one in North Dakota, that would stimulate the state economy by investing those funds in job-rich sectors like housing construction, renewable energy facilities, and agriculture.

In September 1977, Dunlap's Senate Select Committee on Investment Priorities and Objectives convened in San Francisco for a hearing on the feasibility of creating a state bank. From the raised dais in the State Office Building auditorium, the stocky, bearded Dunlap called the hearing to order. Tom Hayden and I sat with the other invited speakers at the front of the brightly lit, low-ceilinged room. I had only been working with Tom a short time and still held him in some awe, so I was thrilled to appear with him at such a prominent event. Scores of activists, lobbyists, financial industry executives, and reporters filled the rows behind us. Though smoking was prohibited, a stale tobacco aroma lingered from bygone days.

Harrington delivered an opening presentation, followed by Herbert Thorndal, President of the Bank of North Dakota. Hayden came next. The room grew quiet as he stepped up to the witness table. He was the celebrity speaker of the day, though he looked a bit disheveled, as usual, with his hair askew and his tie too loose. Based on research I had done for him, Tom drew attention to the billions in state funds deposited in private banks for use as they saw fit or invested in companies without regard to their business practices.

"We propose that investment of public funds be redirected," he urged, "toward areas of particular social and economic priority that meet essential human needs while simultaneously generating job opportunities."

Current investment practices, he pointed out, had resulted in a $3 billion loss in value over the previous decade. Creation of a state bank would put a stop to that, he declared. I gave him a thumbs up sign as he returned to his seat, while light applause broke out around the room. I turned in time to see a banking lobbyist behind us frown and vigorously shake his head.

I spoke next, on behalf of a coalition of housing advocacy groups. I had appeared many times before the Los Angeles City Council and other government bodies, but this was my first state legislative hearing addressing a proposal that I had helped develop. Looking up at the row of senators, I appreciated Dunlap's smile and welcome, but I still felt a bit uneasy.

"Our goal is equal access to decent housing at an affordable price for all Californians," I began. Most of the senators nodded in agreement. So far, so good. I described the insufficient development of new housing, the high cost of housing that was being produced, and the lack of funding to build or rehabilitate affordable housing. By that time, I had overcome my nervousness and was on a roll. Knowing from my previous work how unfairly many financial institutions operated their lending business, and how they ignored the needs of lower-income communities, I relished this opportunity to press for taking public money out of their hands. Sadly, as I later looked back on that day, my speeches and writings would continue describing largely the same set of problems for decades to come

Wrapping up, I suggested several reforms needed to aid the struggling housing sector, concluding with support for Hayden's call to put public funds to work generating jobs and economic development, especially in housing. And I endorsed the concept of a state economic development bank, again drawing scattered applause from the audience. Dunlap thanked me for my testimony. Barbara Bry, a business reporter from the Sacramento newspaper who had been covering our work, approached me and Tom and whispered questions as the hearing continued. Many years later, after she had pivoted from journalism to become a technology entrepreneur, I would help her get elected to the San Diego City Council and then run for mayor.

Dunlap subsequently introduced legislation authorizing creation of such a state bank, along with other financial reforms. It became a rallying point for CED and other activist groups and the subject of much media attention. While the state bank proposal didn't fly, it nudged the state to realign its investment priorities. I couldn't have guessed that the idea would resurface over forty years later through legislation empowering California cities to establish public banks.

Meanwhile, a national campaign developed for divestment from South Africa, as part of an international movement pressing for an end to racial apartheid in that country. Students and other activists demanded that universities and public agencies withdraw investments from companies doing business there.

The Policy Center in 1978 issued a report entitled *South African Roulette* that detailed investments by California state funds in American businesses involved in South Africa, and proposed strategies for achieving disinvestment. We also worked with groups campaigning for similar reforms in several cities. I saw South Africa's treatment of its Black citizens as being similar to the demeaning treatment of Jews in Germany and Austria leading up to the Holocaust. California became a leader in the ultimately successful divestment campaign.

Lieutenant Governor Mervyn Dymally, an Afro-Indian who had immigrated to California from Trinidad, assumed leadership of the pro-divestment forces at the state level. It would be several more years before that movement succeeded, with the State Legislature eventually ordering the multi-billion-dollar state pension funds to divest. Soon after, the University of California Regents voted to do the same. By that time, Los Angeles, San Francisco, and other localities had already taken action, along with several private universities.

In 1978, however, the issue had not yet taken on the necessary levels of visibility and importance. Financial institutions and corporations that benefitted from their ties to South Africa stymied a series of reform proposals. After the UC Regents rejected his divestment proposal, Dymally set out to raise public consciousness. After meeting in Sacramento with Tom Hayden and me, Dymally scheduled a high-profile public hearing at the State Office Building in downtown LA. Tom and I took part as speakers, reprising our roles at Senator Dunlap's state bank hearing a few months earlier.

Dymally sat at the center of a raised dais, nattily dressed as always, his graying hair and mustache giving him an elder statesman look. Aides and other state officials sat on either side of him. The audience resembled the one at the state bank hearing, except this time anti-apartheid activists outnumbered the bankers and lobbyists. When it came my turn to speak, Dymally warmly introduced me in a deep voice still tinged with a Caribbean accent.

"I want to welcome Dr. Cary Lowe of the California Public Policy Center," he said, giving me a big smile and motioning for me to come up to the microphone. "He has produced a wonderful report on the importance of divestment and has been working with student groups and others to support this cause."

I paused for a moment, basking in the lieutenant governor's praise. I then talked about the role American companies played in supporting the South African regime and the vast sums of public funds invested in those companies. Withdrawing the investments, I urged, would force those companies to cut their ties and would weaken the South African government and undermine its racist practices.

When I finished, Dymally thanked me and gave me another smile. He promised to use our research in carrying on his campaign for divestment. I felt far greater pride and sense of accomplishment at this presentation than I had at the state bank hearing. The optics of the event demanded that. A public official originally from the Caribbean thanking a lawyer originally from Europe for helping reform California laws to help people in South Africa. It doesn't get more American than this, I thought, smiling back at Dymally.

***

Political events during this period provided me with one more opportunity to appreciate the extent of my Americanization. Soon after President Jimmy Carter's election in 1976, his administration relaxed travel restrictions to Cuba. I hadn't previously thought of traveling there but was intrigued when I learned of an invitation by a Cuban lawyers' organization for groups of American lawyers to visit. Two attorneys from Hank di Suvero's office had already signed on with a group of Southern California lawyers planning to go and encouraged me to join them. So, in late 1978, I assembled with the rest of the group in Mexico City for a flight to Havana from there, as even Carter's loosened travel policy did not allow direct flights from the US.

Although a lawyers' association hosted us, the government travel bureau loosely managed our travel within Cuba. They housed us first at the classic Hotel Nacional, once the premier visitor accommodation in Havana but now showing the effects of years of under-maintenance. We saw that everywhere in Havana—crumbling facia, peeling paint, cracked pavement. And mostly 1950s era cars on the streets, other than a few newer Russian models.

I didn't know what to expect in terms of public reaction to visitors from the US. Although it had been nearly twenty years since the Cuban revolution and the subsequent crisis over Soviet missiles being stationed there, relations between the two countries remained tense. Consequently, our interactions with the Cuban people delighted us. As we wandered about Havana, and later in other cities we visited on our week-long bus tour, average people approached us on the street, eager to practice their English and to ask if we possibly knew relatives of theirs living in the US.

On the other hand, the people we encountered, including the lawyers we met with in Havana, showed reluctance to talk or answer questions about social and political conditions in their country. While they boasted about the improved quality of life of most citizens since their revolution, with greater access to health care, housing, and education, they had yet to achieve a meaningful level of democracy. Some acknowledged that, but compared their situation favorably to conditions under the previous Batista dictatorship overthrown by Fidel Castro. And they blamed lack of change on the need for vigilance in the face of continuing threats from our own country.

I enjoyed the visit, with the opportunity to experience a place and people so different from anywhere I had lived in either Europe or the US. I left with a measure of hope that relations between our two countries would continue to improve. That relationship would have its ups and downs in succeeding decades, depending on the leadership in both countries. In the meantime, I felt fortunate to be living where I was. Notwithstanding continuing racism and a certain level of political repression at home, I appreciated living in a society where I sensed continuing movement toward greater social and economic justice. My traveling companions, even the ones with more radical political views, seemed to feel the same way.

On my return to LA, Tom Hayden asked me to make a presentation about my trip to CED activists and friends. Before a social gathering of fifty people, I showed slides and talked about my experiences there. Tom had visited Cuba years earlier. He showed great sympathy for the Cuban revolution but felt much the same as I did in comparing conditions here and there. We could respect the positive changes in another country and culture, and engage in mutually respectful ways with the people there, but still prefer being American.

CHAPTER 29
BACK TO THE FUTURE

Soon after I began work at the Policy Center, I received a call from Carl Werthman, an urban planning professor at USC, about a research project he had in mind. He had read my *Saving Neighborhoods* report and wanted to expand that into a more in-depth analysis of how urban neighborhoods were coping with economic and demographic changes. I knew him to be a long-time friend of Governor Jerry Brown and that he had taught urban planning for years at the University of California. He had worked in the governor's administration for a while until suffering a heart attack and returning to academia.

I met with Carl at Von KleinSmid Center (later renamed after Native American tribal leader and USC alumnus Joseph Medicine Crow), the same red-brick, multi-columned building where I had studied international relations a few years earlier. We sat in his office, surrounded by groaning shelves of books and journals, looking out through the tall, narrow windows into the building's courtyard. A little chubby, clad in polo shirt and slacks, Carl leaned back in his chair, smiling. He had a proposition for me.

"You've already done basic research on urban renewal programs," Carl began. "How about joining with me in studying what these programs are doing to neighborhoods and their residents?"

"I appreciate the suggestion," I replied, "but this seems like it would divert me from my work at the Policy Center. What would be my incentive to devote time to your study?"

"I thought about that. You know, we're starting a new doctoral program in urban planning here, and beginning to accept applications. What if you took courses here on the side and turned your work with me into your doctoral dissertation?"

That caught my attention, but I still demurred. "I have a law degree. I hadn't planned to ever return to school again. Why would I need a Ph.D.?"

In a moment of candor that somehow didn't seem at all staged, he replied, "Everyone like you should have a Ph.D."

I promised to think about it and asked him to set up a meeting for me with the program director. Jack Dyckman, who held the Irvine Foundation Chair in Urban and Regional Planning, became the closer. USC had lured away this urban planning heavyweight academic from Johns Hopkins University to anchor the expanding graduate planning program and develop the Ph.D. curriculum. From the moment I entered his office, Jack struck an imposing, Falstaffian figure, standing six feet four, weighing almost 300 pounds, with wiry gray hair and a tangled beard. Smiling broadly, welcoming me in a booming voice, he extended a hand that enveloped mine like a baseball glove. Motioning for me to take a seat, he began his pitch.

"Carl tells me our new program may interest you. I love the idea of having a land use lawyer in our first entering class, and I like what I've seen of your writing."

"Tell me about the program requirements," I replied. "I need to understand better what I'd be taking on."

"This will be brand new, so there's lots of room for flexibility and experimentation. You've already been to law school. We can give you credit for some of those studies. We expect a lot of our students to be employed, so we plan to schedule most classes in the late afternoon or evening. Carl already talked to you about collaborating with him on his study, and I agree that could be the basis for a dissertation."

That sold me. I talked to Tom and Fred about it, assuring them I wouldn't let either my studies or my work with Carl interfere with my obligations at the Policy Center. With a little reluctance, they agreed to my proposal.

For the next two years I juggled work and school. I enjoyed school more than I expected. My classmates were an impressive bunch, many from outside the United States. Most of the curriculum tied in with issues I knew about through work. After class, I sometimes accompanied Jack and Carl to a bar near campus to drink beer and talk politics. During the second year, I had a pleasant surprise when a childhood friend, Andy Isserman, showed up. My father and his had worked together in Austria, and our families stayed in touch. Now teaching at the University of Illinois, he came to USC for a year as a visiting professor, allowing me to take a course with him.

Carl Werthman's study that triggered my reconnection with USC soon received funding and we began research. For several months, as my schedule permitted, I jetted off to interview local planning and development officials, community activists, and residents of impacted communities. I visited Seattle, San Francisco, Minneapolis, Laredo, Atlanta, and half a dozen others, exposing me to people and places in parts of the country I hadn't visited before. We also did intensive surveying in a few cities, with Carl and another graduate student accompanying me on those trips. After being in LA for many years, these travels gave me a new, much wider sense of America—both the differences and similarities among regions.

The highlight of that research was our visit to Baltimore. Jack Dyckman had arranged for us to meet with the City Council president. In his City Hall office, we talked about the redevelopment programs that were gaining Baltimore national attention. Yet, he seemed weary, not excited about all the positive change. I asked how he felt about his role in it. His response took us all aback.

"When I first got elected, it was exciting," he said. "Now, it's gotten to where every day, when I walk in here and sit down, it's as if my assistant brings me a steaming bowl of shit and a big spoon, and tells me to eat. And I know that, as soon as I finish that bowl, he'll just bring me another one."

That stunned me. I had never heard a public official sound so cynical. It didn't surprise to hear a couple of years later that he had been convicted of taking bribes and sent to prison. That added to my certainty about never wanting to run for elected office.

With my coursework and the research completed, I began work on my dissertation. It evolved into a series of case studies, heavily anecdotal but with a core of survey data and a methodology for evaluating the effectiveness of various community responses to changes in their urban neighborhoods. The manuscript satisfied my doctoral committee, chaired by Jack and consisting of Carl, another member of the USC Planning faculty, a professor from the School of Architecture, and one from the UCLA Planning Department. That allowed me to go on to the final challenge, my oral exam.

When Jack announced he would host the exam at the condominium he occupied with his wife in West Hollywood, rather than on campus, I was surprised but happy. I liked the idea of having it in an informal setting. So, we gathered at Jack's home on a Friday afternoon, seating ourselves on plush sofas in a living room with a cathedral ceiling and walls covered with abstract artwork. Rather than facing the committee members, I sat among them. Jack set the rules for the exam.

"This should be an experience like the exams in the great European universities," he declared. "We'll have a conversation, asking Cary questions, letting him respond, and then responding ourselves to that."

Committee members exchanged glances, but all nodded. Then, before we could begin, Jack disappeared into the kitchen. Moments later, he emerged with plates of snack foods—nuts, crackers, fruit—and a variety of soft drinks. Lowering his huge frame onto a sofa again, Jack then kicked off the discussion. For two hours, the group posed questions, I answered, and we discussed it, just as Jack had instructed. It felt like a colloquium among peers, far from the inquisition that I had heard other graduate students describe from their experience.

At a momentary lull in the discussion, Jack loudly cleared his throat for attention and announced, "Well, I think Cary has demonstrated his mastery of the subject matter. Don't you all agree?" Again, the others looked around, seemingly unsure how to respond, but no one had the temerity or intellectual weight to challenge him. I had passed.

"Now," he went on, "we can just relax and continue our conversation. And we can celebrate." With that, he walked into the kitchen again, this time returning with several bottles of excellent red wine. His wife followed, bringing platters of cold cuts, cheeses, bread, and condiments. Refueled, we resumed talking, pausing just long enough to down a sip of wine or swallow a bite of food. We went on that way for another two hours until we had exhausted ourselves intellectually. We concluded with Jack giving me a bear hug and the others shaking my hand, all offering congratulations. With that, I became the program's first graduate.

That credential provided an opportunity that had long interested me, to teach at the university level. My father had often urged me to think about that. When the UCLA professor who had been on my oral exam committee took a leave of absence later that year, I filled in for him on a law-related course and continued to teach in their master's program for three years. The University of California, Irvine invited me to teach for a year too.

Meanwhile, one of my former professors at the USC Law Center had arranged three years of grant funding for a course on legislation, something not in the regular curriculum, and asked me to teach it. That felt like a high honor, since the only previous teacher of such a course there had been former California Assembly Speaker Jesse Unruh. When that funding ran out, I began teaching graduate courses on law, planning, and policy at USC's School of Urban and Regional Planning, and then the law component of a new graduate program in real estate development. At that point, I had been teaching part-time for ten years, in addition to my regular professional work, and needed a break. With the demands of family and work, I didn't teach university classes again for twenty years, when I resumed at the University of California, San Diego.

Sadly, my closest mentors at USC couldn't see me make good use of my doctorate. Within just a few years after my graduation, first Jack and then Carl died of heart attacks. Among my classmates, and among all the Ph.Ds. I met later in my career, I never heard of another experience like the one I had that afternoon at Jack Dyckman's home. If his intention was to recreate an element of the older European universities he admired, something largely lost in their American counterparts, he succeeded. For me, the experience felt like going back to the future.

CHAPTER 30
UN-AMERICAN?

Just as CED and its allies sensed progress in reshaping state financial policies, an even more significant issue gained momentum. Failure by Governor Jerry Brown and the State Legislature to respond to a brewing taxpayer revolt led to passage of Proposition 13 in June of 1978. With their future property taxes sharply reduced, landlords correctly anticipated a push for rent control in urban areas and rushed to raise rents to a higher base level.

Tenant groups had beaten back the real estate industry's attempts at barring local rent control through AB 3788. But the landlords had succeeded, so far, in blocking it's spread from Berkeley to other communities, by spending vast sums on lobbyists and campaign contributions and by convincing local elected officials that rent control was unfair, confiscatory, and downright un-American. However, in the aftermath of Proposition 13, the dam of opposition prepared to burst.

Author with California Governor Jerry Brown at press conference, Los Angeles 1978

Three months later, tenant organizers from all over the state responded to the wave of rent increases by gathering at the home of Berkeley City Auditor Florence McDonald. I attended at the urging of John Gilderbloom, who was now back in Santa Barbara after helping derail AB 3788 during his stint in Sacramento.

Twenty of us packed into Florence's living room, filling the sofa, a dozen unmatched chairs, and every bit of floor space. I knew half the people and recognized others from the Santa Barbara conference the previous year. By the time the meeting began, the midday sun, combined with the heat of so many bodies, made the room almost stifling.

Despite that, we debated for three hours the next best steps—the merits of local versus state-level action, rent control versus other tenant protections, working through established groups versus creating a new organization. Richard Blumberg from the National Housing Law Project in Oakland, tall and mustached, sat in a corner and dispensed information about tenant organizations in other parts of the country. All the while, grandmotherly Florence kept a lid on the passions in the room, passing around snacks and inserting calming comments when arguments got heated. We reached consensus on the need for a statewide tenant rights coalition, something California hadn't previously seen.

Whether driven by heat, hunger, or fatigue, we also soon agreed on the composition of a steering committee representing all the urban areas of the state. But who would do the day-to-day organizational work? One of the CED representatives made a suggestion.

"Cary has an office and some resources at the Policy Center. How about having him serve as initial statewide coordinator?"

No one had a better idea. I nodded acceptance, though reluctantly, unsure where this was leading.

The new California Housing Action & Information Network (CHAIN) took off like an avalanche down a Sierras peak. CED chapters in Santa Monica, Los Angeles, San Diego, Davis, Orange County, and Santa Barbara began working with tenant and housing rights groups, launching half a dozen local rent control campaigns. For the next two years, in between my other work at the Policy Center, I traveled around the state, meeting with local activists, speaking at rallies, and testifying at hearings.

Local politics could be challenging. Tenant groups organized a public forum at Long Beach City College to spotlight their demand for rent control in that town. I agreed to participate when I learned Howard Jarvis himself would represent the other side. With Jarvis as a draw, local landlords packed the amphitheater-like auditorium, outnumbering the less organized renters. These landlords were not the corporate ones we faced in LA or Sacramento. More individual owners, squeezing their retirement out of a handful of rentals. For them, this was personal as much as business. They came to see a show and Jarvis didn't disappoint. He sauntered up to the stage, his thrift store suit shining under the auditorium lights, as his supporters cheered.

The moderator asked me to explain our support for rent control in Long Beach. I had just begun when a cascade of boos and jeers rained down from the landlords in the audience. Jarvis then got his turn to argue the anti-rent control position, but he had no interest in engaging in a debate. He belittled renters as weaklings who couldn't earn enough to become homeowners, and his supporters cheered. He accused anyone who supported rent control of being stupid, unaware of basic economics, and downright un-American. His supporters cheered some more. All the while, Jarvis grinned, waived his arms, and basked in the adulation.

"The world would be better off if all these tenant activists' mothers had had abortions!" he roared. At that, his supporters went wild, making me recall a tent revival meeting I once witnessed in South LA.

I debated Jarvis again a few months later on television in LA. He toned down his act a little in that setting, but his breath reeked of alcohol and he resumed his favored approach of lobbing insults as soon as the cameras shut off. He even launched racist jibes at a Black minister who was on the show with us. Years later, I would think of Howard Jarvis every time I watched Donald Trump give one of his signature speeches, flinging insults and deflecting serious questions.

The biggest potential prize was the City of Los Angeles, with over three million residents, half of them tenants. And the greatest concentration of tenants lived in the mid-city district of City Council President John Ferraro.

A moderate Democrat, the former USC football lineman and insurance executive struggled with this issue. His friends in the business and real estate communities opposed rent control, but his constituents overwhelmingly demanded it. CIP had done an exposé on Ferraro's ties to a predatory bank and I had challenged him on housing and redevelopment issues at Council meetings, so it surprised me when his chief of staff called and asked me to organize a meeting for her boss with a group of tenant representatives.

"I'm a little shocked," I told her, "considering how John and I have locked horns."

"I know," she replied. "But he really respects you. He wanted me to call you, in particular, to arrange this."

Based on that surprising endorsement, I brought half a dozen activists, including Tom Hayden and CED staffer Mark Siegel. The council president welcomed us to his spacious office on the main floor of City Hall, but I sensed a nervousness I hadn't seen in him before. We sat in a semi-circle facing Ferraro, with me in the middle of the arc and Hayden to my right. From the start, the tension in the room stifled discussion. Ferraro stood and paced, his six-foot-five frame sweeping the room like a caged giant wanting to escape. But he persevered. Like any experienced politician, he could make small talk.

After taking his seat again, Ferraro turned to Tom and said, "I just saw *Julia*," referring to Jane Fonda's most recent film. "I really liked it."

I saw a mischievous look appear on Tom's face.

"Yeah, it's pretty good," he replied, "but the best film I saw recently was *Animal House*. It reminded me of some of the fraternities at Michigan."

The reference to John Belushi's zany college satire seemed to stun Ferraro. I jumped in, seizing the moment.

"I bet it reminded you of your days at USC," I said to the councilman.

"Yes!" he practically shouted. "I was a Kappa Alpha at SC. It took me right back to those days."

That broke the ice. For several minutes, Ferraro and Hayden bantered about their college experiences while the rest of us listened. Soon, we were talking politics and business, agreeing that the city had to respond in some meaningful way to the tenants' demands. Ferraro's chief of staff gave me a big smile.

Within days, Ferraro announced a plan. He appointed a task force comprised of three city council members, me as a tenant representative, and another local attorney as a landlord representative. Recognizing that the tide was surging against him, the landlord attorney settled for inclusion of one special provision in any rent control ordinance, allowing landlords to raise rents beyond the usual limit when someone vacated a unit and a new tenant moved in. The task force then recommended that the City Council adopt a citywide rent control ordinance. The Council did so, and Mayor Tom Bradley signed it into law.

Author and Tom Hayden before Los Angeles City Council

Tenants throughout the city celebrated, but it took us a little while to recognize the magnitude of what we had won. A few weeks later, Mark Siegel and I calculated how much money would stay in tenants' pockets that otherwise would have gone to landlords in increased rent over the next year alone. It appeared to be the largest transfer of wealth from a single legislative action we could identify in the history of the United States!

With LA done, other cities fell like dominoes. The sleepy Republican-dominated City of Santa Monica came next. I helped CED and others form Santa Monicans for Renters Rights, which circulated an initiative petition to establish rent control in the city. Capitalizing on a large-majority tenant population, SMRR not only won that election, but took control of the City Council with a slate led by CED activist Dennis Zane. He later became mayor and, to the surprise of many, led the city into an economic and cultural renaissance. On election night, I roamed the victory party in a hotel ballroom, wearing a non-stop smile and hugging my colleagues.

Our successes in California propelled us to connect with similar organizations, many of them much better established, in other parts of the country. All of us experienced the impacts of high housing costs and lack of legal protections on low and middle-income households. The US General Accounting Office had just released a report entitled *Rental Housing: A National Problem That Needs Immediate Attention*. Sensing the need for a new nationwide push for tenants' rights and affordable housing, leaders of tenant organizations from fourteen states gathered in Newark, New Jersey in late 1979 to discuss issues and strategies. I attended on behalf of CED and was elected to the initial Steering Committee.

That meeting gave birth to a national coalition of tenant groups aiming to inject their constituents' concerns into the upcoming elections and push for legislative action on housing affordability. Coast to coast, from the *New York Times* to the *Los Angeles Times*, the press reported this as an important development. The coalition held conventions over the following four years, pursuing ambitious programs of housing law reforms and supporting tenant organizing efforts. It faded after that, mainly for lack of resources, but it stimulated tenant activism in scores of new places and elevated national attention over tenants' concerns.

In California, the landlords and their allies were not done, though. Angry at having local officials, especially in some of the largest cities, adopt rent control ordinances and other tenant protections, the real estate interests took another shot at a statewide solution. Proposition 10, an initiative that they qualified for the June 1980 ballot, proposed to repeal all those pesky local rent control laws, require a voter election on any future such proposals, and limit what even the voters could approve. In as brazen an act of campaign deception as California had seen in a long time, the measure's proponents entitled it the California Fair Rent Initiative. That was the heart of the proponents' message, that this proposal was fair and balanced, long before Fox News took up that line.

Once again, tenant groups scrambled to respond, though this time the statewide CHAIN network was already in place to offer immediate opposition. And the landlords had overreached. Newspapers and other media editorialized against the proposal, and civic organizations criticized it, all noting the deceptive campaign being waged by its supporters. John Gilderbloom and I wrote an op-ed column for the *Los Angeles Times* entitled "'Fair Rent Initiative' is Unfair to Tenants."

Polls showed the measure likely to narrowly pass, until Ralph Nader struck what turned out to be the decisive blow against it in a widely broadcast television commercial. Nader then was still a household name. At that pre-internet time, with no one able to troll him, his opinions carried considerable weight. In the ad, he first appeared studying a sheet of paper bearing the text of Proposition 10. He displayed his usual serious, slightly rumpled appearance. A narrator's voice introduced him as America's leading consumer rights advocate. Looking up, Nader spoke straight to the audience in a calm, professorial, tone.

"The big landlords behind Proposition 10 tell you this proposal is fair," he began. "They tell you to look at it yourself and decide."

"Well, I've looked at it and I'll tell you what I think," he declared, his voice rising. Then came the clincher.

"It's a consumer fraud!" he practically yelled from the television screen.

That judgment from such a respected figure turned the tide. On election day, Proposition 10 failed by almost a two-to-one margin.

This rapid change in their fortunes mystified the landlord organizations. For so long, they had dominated by financing their supporters to run for public office, hiring powerful lobbyists, and operating high-powered campaigns. Now, a pack of underfinanced activists was beating them at their own game. I knew some of the real estate leaders from meetings in LA and Sacramento, and saw they were successful at their businesses but not as sharp at politics. Eventually, their superior resources allowed them to regain a lot of the initiative, but it took time and a steep learning curve.

Even so, the landlords' power had limits. They contained the tenant movement for the next several decades, even beating back a renter initiative to expand opportunities for local rent control. Over time, however, the economy changed the rules of the game. Faced with a severe housing shortage and soaring costs, the California Legislature in 2019 would adopt a statewide cap on rent increases, marking a major shift in landlord-tenant politics.

Years later, when I was no longer working on tenants' rights, I became friendly with Steve Carlson, director of the California Housing Council. That was the group of major landlords that had promoted both AB 3788, the bill that first drew me into the rent control wars, and the later Proposition 10. We reminisced about past battles like old soldiers who were no longer enemies.

"It was an exciting time," I told him as we chatted over lunch in a downtown Sacramento café. "We often couldn't believe how much success we were having. A lot of our strength was illusory, smoke-and-mirrors. But we wore the white hats."

"My guys were pretty frustrated," he told me. "They spent millions and weren't getting much return for it.

He shook his head and gave a wry smile. "Now that it's behind us," he continued, "I'll tell you a secret. The CHC leaders were looking to up their game. Their previous staff weren't getting the job done, like in the debacle around AB 3788. When they interviewed me for this job, they asked me one last question that they said was most important: Was I ready to go out and do battle with Cary Lowe?"

I gasped, then laughed loudly. Carlson quickly joined in. Our smoke-and-mirrors had been even more effective than we realized.

Around the state, CED chapters, in alliance with other local activists, elected their members and supporters to city councils, county boards of supervisors, utility boards, and state legislative seats, in the greatest shift of political power California had seen in decades. They made local election rules more democratic and energized previously excluded constituencies.

That show of strength forced state authorities to take notice. When the governor appointed a Housing Task Force but left off any tenant or affordable housing advocates, Senate President David Roberti raised hell and got me appointed to fill the void somewhat. Despite the continuing imbalance on the Task Force, I raised issues about low-income housing and tenants' rights that would have been ignored otherwise and won surprising support from some of the major developers. Assembling our recommendations while cloistered in a meeting room in the governor's office, we found consensus on many issues. However, I got substantial pushback when I proposed strengthening eviction protections for tenants.

"I move we recommend supporting legislation requiring landlords to have just cause for eviction," I urged in our final meeting. Major landlords scoffed and the room fell silent.

Then, Bob Levenstein, President of Kaufman and Broad, the largest homebuilding company in the state, chimed in. He and I had become friendly over the course of the task force's meetings, and I had found him to be a very decent, honorable person. "I agree," he announced. "I'll second the motion." Few would argue with him, and my proposal received a grudging positive vote.

But the tenant movement wasn't strong enough to win that fight in the Legislature, or much else. It would be almost forty years before such a law would pass. For now, the victories remained mainly local. And CHAIN suffered from internal divisions, some personal, some ideological. It limped along for a couple more years and then faded when the Policy Center and CED withdrew.

Our relationship with the governor became stronger. Jerry Brown supported CED's campaign for solar energy, and his office invited me to give input on the Urban Strategy that he was developing to guide state land use policy. When he created a Public Investment Task Force to advise him on state investment policy, Hayden got him to appoint me chair of the Housing Investment Committee. For six months, I met with bankers, builders, and financial reformers to produce recommendations on how state pension funds and other pools of public money could stimulate more affordable housing production.

This work elevated my stature considerably. Legislative and agency staff, even elected officials, would return my calls. Heads of financial and real estate companies would meet with me. The press reported on my work and often quoted me.

Walking through the State Capitol one day, I ran into the governor.

"What are you doing up here?" he asked. I described the legislative hearing at which I would testify that day, an outgrowth of the task force to which he had appointed me. That didn't seem to register. Without another word, he turned and disappeared through the oak-and-marble entrance to his office suite.

Brown came across as an enigmatic figure to many. I found him to be intellectually curious and nonmaterialistic, a product of his early Jesuit training. He eschewed the governor's mansion for an apartment across the street from the Capitol, drove an older car from the state motor pool fleet, and had a romance with singer Linda Ronstadt.

The nonmaterialistic part stood out. The next time I encountered him, we both were headed into Los Angeles City Hall. Midway across the lawn, a homeless man stretched out on a blanket sat up and asked for spare change. I had already passed him, but he stared straight at the governor, though not recognizing him. Brown looked perplexed.

"I don't carry money," he sputtered, shaking his head and darting into the building.

**

Spending time around elected officials makes many political activists think of running for office themselves. I briefly experienced that. The councilwoman who represented the part of LA where I lived had succeeded to the seat when her husband died in office. Insiders considered her a weak candidate for reelection in 1981, so I explored running against her. This seemed an opportunity to fulfill the ultimate dream of acceptance as an American.

I researched district voter registration and voting patterns, met with political consultants, and discussed the merits of running with those closest to me. The politics and demographics of the district looked favorable, but I saw one obstacle I didn't believe I could overcome: the need to raise enough money for a credible campaign. By today's standards, campaign budgets then were minimal, but still more than I could manage.

Even before that, I felt conflicted. The prospect of getting elected excited me, but living in a political fishbowl gave me great pause. I saw how, even before the age of the internet and cell phone cameras, elected officials had every detail of their lives scrutinized and every waking moment away from the job occupied with courting voters and donors.

Meanwhile, I discovered that my friend, Michael Woo, then an aide to Senator Roberti, was exploring running for the same seat. Mike's family were immigrants like mine, though he was born in LA. Through his family's business ties and his political connections, Mike had far greater fundraising ability than I could hope to muster. Recognizing that, and not wanting to undercut his chances, I abandoned my exploration and instead supported Mike. He lost that race, but came back to beat the incumbent four years later.

That brief flirtation with running for office was my first and last. The attractions and benefits of being an elected official, in my mind, never outweighed the burdens. Years later, when I again became involved in politics in the community where I lived, local officials asked me to run for the City Council there but I declined without hesitation.

***

By 1982, the political landscape around CED was in transition. The name changed to Campaign California, in search of a broader constituency. Many of the original stalwarts had moved on to pursue conventional careers. Hayden was elected to the State Legislature, where he remained for eighteen years. Fred Branfman took a job as a policy advisor to Jerry Brown, at which point we closed the Policy Center.

I worked for a few months as a consultant to the Governor's Office of Planning and Research, preparing policy papers on housing and investment. The governor passed through once while I was there and we talked awhile, but his mind was more on national politics.

After that, I didn't see Brown again up close for thirty-five years. In the meantime, he had run for president, briefly left politics, became mayor of Oakland, then state attorney general, and then governor again. We ran into each other at a memorial for Stephen Rivers, who had been CED's public affairs director and later became a publicist for notable figures in politics and the entertainment industry. Standing in the lobby of the Creative Artists Agency in Century City, surrounded by Stephen's multitude of clients and friends, I shook hands with Brown and reminded him of when I had served on commissions in his first administration. He nodded, but didn't appear to actually remember me. Or maybe, I thought, he was engrossed again in the possibility of running for president.

CHAPTER 31
MEDIA STARDOM CALLS

My work at the Policy Center greatly increased my involvement with the news media. At CIP, our work received regular coverage in both print and broadcast media, but working with Tom Hayden and Fred Branfman led to much greater opportunities.

Soon after opening of the Policy Center, Tom asked me to accompany him to a meeting with editorial staff at the *Los Angeles Times*. The discussion eventually got around to the rising renter movement and the controversies over rent control.

"We want to run a pair of pro and con op-eds on rent control in the Sunday Opinion Section," one editor said, looking at me. "Would you like to write the pro side?"

"Sure, but I need a couple of weeks," I replied, thinking about all my other commitments.

He paused, then said, "OK, as soon as you can."

As soon as we left the *Times* offices, walking back to the Bradbury Building two blocks away, Tom blurted out, "I can't believe you told them you wanted two weeks. When you get an offer like that, you jump on it!"

He was right, but this would be my first essay for a major newspaper, and I wanted to do it well. Taking his advice to heart, though, I stayed up late to write it and submitted it early. It ran the following weekend, opposite a column by a prominent real estate lobbyist. The *Times* editorial staff liked my style and invited me to keep writing for them on housing, land use, and other policy issues. I became the *Times*' most frequent op-ed writer in my areas of interest. I also began writing for the *Sacramento Bee, San Francisco Chronicle, San Diego Union-Tribune,* and other California newspapers.

As California's tenant movement drew national attention, the press took notice. Columnist Jack Germond of *The Washington Post* flew out and interviewed me and some of the CED staff about the phenomenon we called "tenant consciousness," the growing awareness of the power of the tenant movement. Soon after that, a staffer at PBS's *McNeil-Lehrer Report* called, inviting me to appear on a show they planned on rent control. That had long been an issue in the Northeast, but now was taking on nationwide significance. Appearing with me would be a city councilman from the San Francisco Bay Area who was a staunch rent control opponent and a rising star in the conservative political world. Not only was this an opportunity to appear on national television, but it allowed me to visit my journalist friend Claudia Dreifus from the LA hospital sterilization exposé.

The show couldn't have gone better. Rob McNeil, Jim Lehrer, and Charlene Hunter-Gault asked good questions and I felt comfortable answering them. The councilman, meanwhile, stumbled right out of the blocks and never recovered. He looked uncomfortable and seemed ill prepared. When I watched the show later with Claudia, her only criticism was, "You should smile more on TV. It makes people believe you more easily." I took that advice to heart in future television appearances.

Back in LA, my friend and former colleague, Bob Gottlieb, who had recently published a book entitled *Thinking Big* about the *Los Angeles Times* and LA politics, introduced me to Jay Levin, publisher of the newly established *LA Weekly* alternative newspaper. Levin had come out from New York and wanted to learn the local political scene. He asked me to lunch at a restaurant near his East Hollywood office.

"We want to run more stories about local politics," he began as soon as we sat down. "I've read your op-eds in the *Times*. I want you to write political analysis for us, maybe editorials, starting with the upcoming city election."

As we talked about what editorial positions the paper was likely to take on various proposals, I got a quick introduction to Levin's perspective. The upcoming ballot would feature a controversial measure banning smoking in restaurants, at a time when few cities had yet adopted such restrictions.

"I assume you'll support the smoking ban," I offered.

"No!" he blurted defiantly. "The trouble with regulations like that is, if you want to meet with someone who smokes, you can't take them anywhere for lunch. If you really want to do something about smoking, line up the heads of the tobacco companies and shoot them."

His comment was in jest, but I got the message. On most issues, though, we agreed. I wrote the *Weekly's* analysis and recommendations for the next several elections. More interestingly, he had me write brief profiles of the fifteen members of the LA City Council, which he published collectively under the headline "The Gang of 15." The article ran with no byline, resulting in much speculation around City Hall about the identity of the author.

I also had become friendly with Jim Berland, public affairs director at KPFK, the local Pacifica radio station. The station often received criticism for dwelling on national and international events to the exclusion of those happening in their own backyard. Like Jay Levin, Berland wanted to focus more on local politics and asked me to come up with a radio program format that could build on my work. That invitation led to *Cary Lowe's Newsweek*, a weekly show which combined local political news highlights with an interview of a political notable, followed by taking calls from listeners. During its brief life, I had on the LA City Council President, the head of a public employees' union, the leader of a prominent tenants' rights group, and others of similar stature.

The highlight, though, came when I had as my guest a former investment banker now serving as a top official in the Brown administration. Seated in the sound booth, we talked about state investment policy. Then I opened the phone lines. No one screened the calls, so the first call that day took us by surprise.

"I'm a communist," a booming voice announced through the speaker. "I want to know why the state can't take all its money out of corporations and invest it in things like worker cooperatives and low-income housing."

The official looked at me and held up his hands, uncertain how to respond. I jumped in, made reference to current debates in Sacramento about public investment policy, but noted that the state held that money in trust, which limited how it could be invested. To my surprise, the caller didn't argue. We had not yet entered the age of constantly angry talk radio.

Despite my continuing media involvement, I soon got a lesson in how quickly one can fade from political view. While visiting Ray LeBov, who still worked for the Legislature, I strolled the halls of the Capitol with him, reminiscing about past skirmishes in that arena. Another legislative staffer, someone I vaguely remembered, approached Ray and struck up a conversation. Then he turned to me, stared for a few moments, and said, "I know you. Didn't you used to be Cary Lowe?"

***

When the Policy Center closed in 1982, I felt conflicted. For eight years, I had immersed myself in politics and social change. I saw my work have more impact on my adopted country and culture than most immigrants can imagine, and I felt more American than I ever expected.

Yet, for the first time in my adult life, I had no professional or political focus. Consulting work sustained me for a little while, and I could continue writing articles and doing my radio show. I even had one last shot at media stardom. An editor at the *Sacramento Bee* for whom I had written several op-eds asked if I would be interested in becoming an editorial writer. Tempting as that was, with the prospect of someday becoming a columnist, I wasn't interested in relocating to Sacramento. About the same time, a political consultant friend offered me a chance to manage a gubernatorial campaign in another state. I turned that down, too. Instead, I saw the handwriting on the wall: the time had come to be a lawyer.

CHAPTER 32
THE AMERICAN DREAM

I fell in love in a big way for the first time when I met Joan Lyda. She walked into the room at a party I almost didn't attend at the home of a former girlfriend, and I was instantly smitten. Just five feet tall in heels, slender, with long blond hair, and a smile as broad as Texas. She had come to California from Austin to work on a political campaign and stayed, getting a job on the staff of the LA City Council. She had a young son, Brett. And she had a boyfriend, but she mentioned that was not a lasting relationship.

We talked and talked, and found we made each other laugh easily. I told her I wanted to see her again, soon.

"I'll be at Playa del Rey beach by 10 tomorrow morning," she said. "If you want to meet me, look for me by the lifeguard stand closest to the end of Culver Boulevard."

Sure enough, there she was, stretched out on the sand in a black and pink bikini. She told me later that she didn't recognize me at first. She had been a bit buzzed at the party and wasn't sure what she had told me. No matter. I sat down next to her on the blanket and we picked up where we had left off.

We proved the adage that opposites attract. Joan came from Galveston—BOI, or born on the island, as they say there—and grew up in a blue-collar family in the nearby small town of La Marque. Her father was an auto mechanic, her mother a housewife who hadn't finished high school, and her brother a motorcycle-riding electrician working at the refineries in next-door Texas City. But Joan proved to be smart at an early age, studied hard, and went off to Southwest Texas State College. A young marriage interrupted that path. It produced Brett but ended in divorce. She returned to school at the University of Texas, worked at a saddlery across from the State Capitol, raised Brett, and thrived in the marijuana-laced, Willie Nelson-accented culture of Austin. In that town, an anomaly for Texas, she discovered politics, both the student and the electoral kinds. Before she graduated and left Austin for California, her colleagues elected her university student body vice president and honored her as Texas Young Republican Woman of the Year.

My previous relationships had been with women more like me, with big-city roots. Joan's small-town Texas origins took me back to the first Americans I had known, the military families in Austria and Germany. Getting involved with her felt more like immersing myself in the American heartland.

Sooner than I expected, Joan evicted her boyfriend. Within six months, we were talking about living together. We found a hillside house we could afford in the gentrifying neighborhood of Highland Park, north of downtown LA, and turned it into a place where we could throw parties and hold barbecues. A few months later, we married in our living room, the ceremony presided over by Ramona Ripston's new husband, a local judge. Our reception drew what might have been the most diverse crowd ever to share an event in LA—politicians, activists, lawyers, journalists, and co-workers, from all over the political spectrum. Also, our respective families, meeting for the first time.

That was a great start to a 20-year marriage. Through Joan, I discovered the pleasures of the world in which she had grown up. On visits to Galveston and east Texas, I met her extended family, and I became familiar with Cajun, barbecue, and Tex-Mex cuisine. We traveled to New Orleans several times, including twice attending Mardi Gras. We drove the hill country around Austin in bluebonnet flower season, and we wandered around the Alamo and Riverwalk in San Antonio.

Together, we discovered the California desert community of Borrego Springs. After reading about it in the *Los Angeles Times* travel section on a summer Sunday in 1980, we trekked out there and checked in to La Casa del Zorro, with its cluster of casitas set among a palm grove. It was love at first sight.

On our second visit, as we descended the winding Montezuma Grade into the valley, the setting sun turned the Santa Rosa Mountains a deep violet. Turning to me with a look of childlike wonder, Joan declared, "I didn't really understand what that line meant about purple mountains' majesty, until now." I never forgot that view and that moment.

After many leisurely weekends at La Casa or other Borrego hotels, we bought a weekend home there. A compact, one-bedroom house with a small guesthouse and a swimming pool, it sat close by the runway of the Borrego Air Ranch, a private airstrip community up the road from La Casa. We purchased it from the original developer of the Air Ranch, Ed Fletcher, Jr. He was the eldest son of famous Col. Ed Fletcher, early developer of several San Diego communities and builder of the first road across the desert from San Diego to Arizona. It seemed like dropping into history.

I later earned a pilot's license, so then we could fly to Borrego whenever we didn't need a car there. Lying by our pool, beer or margarita in hand, we watched planes land and take off. Once in a while, we got the thrill of a special visitor, like the B-24 bomber owned by a friend of one of our neighbors, who would buzz the field on his way to some air show, streaking down the runway twenty feet off the ground, the 5,000 horsepower of its engines shaking the whole community.

I had seen vast deserts of the Southwest on a week-long driving trip during college, and I recalled being awed by the open spaces and big skies, unlike anything I had seen in Europe or New England. But the jagged mountains, sandy arroyos, winding canyons, palm oases, and sculptured badlands of the Anza-Borrego Desert transcended those other places. This struck me as a uniquely American place.

***

By the time we returned from our Lake Tahoe honeymoon in late 1980, I knew serious questions awaited on other fronts. When the Policy Center closed, I talked with Joan at length about my future. She respected the work I had been doing, even if she found some of my associates strange, but she urged me to start practicing law in a more conventional way. I agreed, and joined a downtown LA firm that represented both public agencies and real estate developers. The work environment was stifling after the freedom and excitement I had enjoyed the previous eight years, but the experience proved useful. I got to understand better how both government agency staff and developers think and how to interact with them effectively. Both groups respected my dual credentials as a lawyer and urban planner.

Two years after our wedding, we moved to the nearby smaller city of South Pasadena, mainly to get Brett into a better school. We bought a 1920s, neo-Spanish, hillside home with white stucco walls, a twenty-foot-high, timbered living room ceiling, and lots of wrought iron embellishments. The backyard, with a hot tub and a broad paved patio, allowed us to continue our tradition of barbecues.

About the time of that move, I decided to concentrate on real estate development, and housing in particular. The firm had given me an opportunity to work for major builders and to cultivate clients of my own, including developers of lower-income housing. My eyes lit up when I saw a notice in the *Los Angeles Daily Journal* that Lewis Homes, a well-regarded, major homebuilding firm, was looking for a land use counsel. They say homeownership is the American dream. I loved the idea of helping more Americans achieve that dream.

I submitted my resume and soon received an invitation for an interview with the general counsel. That meeting went well. I also took an aptitude test, which the personnel director told me they gave to every applicant, whether to be a mailroom clerk or a top executive. They made me an attractive job offer, but I wasn't ready to say yes. I first wanted to meet the head of the company, the legendary Ralph Lewis. Unfortunately, he was away for a month for a weight loss program at the Pritikin Institute on the beach in Santa Monica. I insisted, so they set up a meeting for me there.

Ralph and his wife Goldy had built a successful homebuilding company from scratch. They began as accountants with builder clients and decided they wanted to be builders, too. Their four sons — Richard, Randall, Robert, and Roger—followed them into the business.

Ralph invited me for lunch. Stocky, balding, and cheerful, he came out to greet me dressed in a loose-fitting shirt and slacks, looking like a blue-collar guy at home on the weekend.

"We need someone with your land use legal experience," he told me. "We've got good lawyers, but they mainly handle transactions. I like that you have a Ph.D. in urban planning. I want you to get really involved with our land buying and our project planning. Stick your nose into everything. If anyone questions you, just tell them to see me."

Ralph's comment about my Ph.D. turned out to be prescient. In the ensuing years, dealing with a multitude of planning and regulatory agencies, the planning degree formed a bond with agency staff that proved invaluable. Rather than seeing me as a lawyer out to manipulate them, or maybe sue them, they treated me as a colleague. When I later was admitted to the American Institute of Certified Planners, the profession's recognition of planning experience, that bond became even closer.

I couldn't have been happier with the opportunity presented to me at Lewis Homes. Two weeks later, I started my new job.

The company had just begun developing Terra Vista, a thousand-acre project that was one of the first planned communities in the Inland Empire region east of LA. I joined the project team, along with engineers, planners, architects, and contractors. Project after project followed, from the coast in Los Angeles to the desert in the Coachella and Imperial Valleys, from our headquarters in Upland to Las Vegas and Sacramento. Following Ralph's dictum about getting involved in all aspects of the company, I gained more practical experience there every month than I could in years at a law firm.

Ralph also got me involved with the building industry, encouraging me to participate in local and statewide organizations. That association took me to Sacramento again, for frequent lobbying trips on land use, education, and environmental bills. It also began twenty-five years of serving on boards and committees of the Building Industry Association, the primary group representing homebuilders and land developers. They knew little of my political past and respected my efforts to temper their sometimes extreme advocacy positions.

The Lewises didn't flaunt their wealth. Around the office, they both dressed as simply as any employee and kept an air of informality with the staff. Their sons joked about the parents' thrifty image. Richard, with whom I worked on land acquisitions, chortled as he related at a staff meeting what had occurred when Ralph and Goldy passed through US Customs on their return from a Pacific cruise. According to Goldy, an officer questioned why Ralph hadn't declared the $25,000 gold Rolex on his wrist.

After explaining repeatedly that he acquired the watch before leaving on the cruise, but still being asked to provide documentation, Ralph blew up.

"Why is it so hard for you to believe I got this watch here in the US before our trip?" he demanded of the customs officer.

"Frankly, mister," the officer replied skeptically, sizing up Ralph's attire, "you don't look like the kind of guy who could afford a watch like that."

**

Throughout law school, the years working with Dan Leighton at CIP, and then the years with Fred Branfman at the Policy Center, Europe was far from my mind. I stayed so focused on work, politics, and personal relationships that I barely thought about my roots or of going back to them.

That changed as my exposure to Joan's roots made me think more about my own. Joan had never been to Europe. So, in 1985, we took a two-week driving trip through Austria, Germany, Switzerland, and Italy. As we prepared for the trip, I received a rude shock when a clerk in a travel store informed me they had no maps of Austria as they only carried maps of "the important countries."

Much had changed from my memories of Vienna, but I was virtually on auto-pilot driving to Linz. After entering the city on an *autobahn* that didn't exist when I last was there, I found my way to my old neighborhood of Bindermichl, to my old apartment house, as if by instinct. The building still looked as I remembered it, except it seemed smaller. Where the refugee encampment had been in an open field across the street, there now stood a park filled with mature trees.

I had the same experience driving from Salzburg to Braunau, I barely needed to look at a map, even though it had been decades and I had never before driven there myself. Herma and her family welcomed us effusively. She cooked some of my favorite dishes, and we drank and reminisced into the early hours.

Author with Karin Zinecker and her father Loisel, Braunau, 2005

Vienna, Venice, and the Swiss Alps all stirred up clear childhood memories. And in Wiesbaden, I found my way by memory to all the places we had lived, to my old school, and to my favorite downtown café.

This was my territory, not Joan's. Seeing something of my roots was interesting for her, but not significant in the way it was to me. And we kept moving, with too little time to immerse ourselves into any one place. By the time we reached Wiesbaden, our last stop, Joan was homesick and longing for more familiar food.

"I don't think I can eat another *schnitzel*," she told a cabbie. "Is there someplace I can get a regular American hamburger?"

The driver looked puzzled. "Of course," he replied. "We have McDonald's, Burger King, Jack in the Box. What do you like?" If I had become Americanized, so had Europe.

It had been twenty-five years since my last visit to those people and places. It was a wonderful trip, but I almost wished I had come alone, to interact with it all on my own terms. I resolved to come back again soon.

In the meantime, we travelled extensively to other foreign destinations. In 1988, we took the first of several trips to the Yucatan region of Mexico, where we drove through jungles to Mayan ruins and sacred sites, climbed pyramids, and discovered an entirely new cuisine of intense flavors unlike any Mexican food back in California. Even more importantly, during our stay on the island of Cozumel, I took an introductory scuba diving class. I found myself bowled over by the colorful underwater sights along Cozumel's world-famous reefs. Within weeks of returning home, I enrolled in a certification course at the local YWCA and began diving regularly amid the kelp forests and undersea pinnacles along the California coast.

That new interest launched us on what became annual tropical vacations to places where I could dive and Joan could sunbathe and read. Though we returned to Yucatan and also visited Tahiti and Hawaii, our primary destination was the Caribbean, where we could experience a different island every year. I immersed myself in the distinctive music, food, and culture of the region. Most of that emanated from the African slaves brought to work sugar plantations and rum distilleries. Most islands also evoked elements of European culture from their colonial past, when many changed hands through successive conquests. That cultural mélange, reminiscent of what I experienced in LA, opened my eyes further to the fluidity of borders and history, demonstrating once again how many different roots contribute to a nation's or a people's identity.

***

By 1988, after four enjoyable and productive years at Lewis Homes, I hit a glass ceiling. The general counsel wasn't going to retire and no opportunity existed to gain equity in the company. I could stay as long as I liked, but I couldn't move up.

A developer friend of the Lewises, Nick Coussoulis, planned to expand his business and wanted an in-house attorney. He made me an offer, one that gave me even more opportunity to grow professionally and perhaps acquire an interest in his company's projects. But he feared offending the Lewises, so he asked me to first go back to law practice for a while before joining his firm. I did that for a year and then, in 1988, began a six-year stint at Coussoulis Development.

A few months earlier, my daughter, Coralea, was born. That event rocked my world more than I imagined possible. I was in the delivery room for the birth and stuck close to Coralea as the hospital staff cleaned, weighed, and measured her. Her arrival gave me a whole new motivation to succeed, both as a parent and in my work.

Joan had just turned forty when she gave birth and had a difficult recovery. As happy as she seemed at being a mother again, the stresses which it unleashed started a gradual mental and physical decline from which she never recovered. It took me a while to recognize this. I was caught up in my new job, including an hour-long commute, and in engaging with Coralea. I thought Joan's fatigue and distraction would pass. Instead, she found it harder to go to work and to deal with me being gone so many hours. We decided she should leave her job with the Los Angeles County Board of Supervisors and we should move closer to my work, hoping that would reduce everyone's stress.

We bought a house in Redlands, a one-time citrus orchard community east of San Bernardino. With me working close to home, and with the help of a housekeeper, the situation improved for a while. Joan's mood lightened, and we both expected her to resume her career soon.

Meanwhile, I immersed myself in my work with Nick and in getting to know him better. Though ten years older than me, his background and mine were somewhat similar. Born in Greece, he immigrated to the United States with his family as a child, landing with them in San Bernardino. With a very competitive streak, he became a star golfer in high school and college, almost turning pro. Instead, he began building custom homes and prospered in real estate. By the time I met him, he no longer was building but had become the most astute land investor I ever saw. Even Richard Lewis marveled at some deals Nick negotiated.

Nick had surrounded himself with a staff recruited from the Greek community in the San Bernardino area. I was the anomaly. Nick often remarked on my Jewish background, not in a bad way, more from curiosity. But sometimes he put his foot in his mouth.

At an office holiday lunch, Nick was in a particularly good mood, as we had just closed a lucrative deal. He stood at the counter in the office conference room, serving carnitas, tortillas, rice, and beans to the staff. Complimenting me on my work on the recent deal, he announced, "I should have hired someone like you a long time ago. I always wanted to have a Jewish lawyer."

A long, heavy silence followed. The company administrator looked at me, his mouth agape. But I knew the best way to respond was with humor.

"That's great Nick," I answered. "So we both got what we wanted." Pointing at the platters of food behind him, I continued, "I always wanted to have a Greek cook."

Nick blushed, at last recognizing his *faux pas*. We all laughed it off and resumed our lunch conversation.

Besides being the company lawyer, I became vice president for land development. That status gave me the opportunity to learn to manage projects and their technical teams. We became the most prolific land buyers and sellers in the region, regularly making deals for hundreds and even thousands of acres, adding value to the properties by designing projects and getting them approved, then turning around and selling them to builders. Or, just as often, we bought land so well that we could resell it in short order at a big profit without doing anything more to enhance the value.

When the economy slowed in California in the early nineties, we made land deals in Arizona instead. A business associate had introduced Nick to

Brian O'Connor, a real estate broker in Phoenix and the son of US Supreme Court Justice Sandra O'Connor. Through Brian, we bought, sold, and planned properties around the Phoenix and Flagstaff areas.

Meanwhile, in California, Nick had me act as his surrogate in political circles. Although moderate politically, he had been county chair of the Republican Party and continue to be a major campaign donor. But he had tired of attending political events and began sending me in his place. At Republican fundraising dinners, policy discussions, and personal meetings, I found myself immersed in a new and different political environment, in which no one knew my background but where everyone accepted my presence on account of my position at the company. I even accompanied Nick to meetings with groups of other major campaign contributors, where they laid out plans for whose campaigns they would support. I saw several successful local and state-level political careers launched at those meetings. This felt like a throwback to the era of political bosses plotting in smoke-filled rooms, something that struck me as an antiquated but very American process.

Like Ralph Lewis, Nick supported my involvement with the Building Industry Association. During my time with him, I served on boards of directors for two local chapters and formed a regular meeting group of real estate lawyers. That led to being asked to organize what became the semi-annual Select Conference on Industry Litigation, bringing together scores of land use lawyers from around the state to discuss and debate recent development in the real estate legal field.

The highlight of that time, though, was meeting and working with another immigrant, a developer from the Netherlands who had become executive director of the Riverside County BIA chapter. Borre Winckel and I hit it off at once based on our similar cultural backgrounds, but it delighted me even more to learn of his family involvement in anti-Nazi resistance during World War II. I not only served on his board of directors, but also represented the chapter in lengthy negotiations over a groundbreaking county general plan that also spawned relationships for me with leading environmental advocates. Borre presented himself as a modern European liberal—supportive of civil liberties while moderate on matters of economic regulation. He agreed with me that we should be able to work across a broad political spectrum and supported me in developing collaborative relationships with environmentalists and other interest groups with whom the building industry was not often in alignment. Thus began a friendship that would continue well past my eventual retirement.

Exciting as that all was, I missed the satisfaction of seeing projects actually getting developed, and especially seeing housing being built, as I had at Lewis Homes. And, while I continued to get valuable experience, many of Nick's promises of financial opportunities didn't pan out. The low point came when two investors he had taken on turned out to be swindling a financial institution and were jailed. Federal regulators foreclosed on several major properties in which I had a profit interest. I watched the foreclosure sales conclude on the courthouse steps in San Bernardino and Riverside. In that one day, I lost at least a million dollars that would have been my reward for my hard work on those projects.

Disillusioned, and with the economy picking up again in California, I returned to private law practice at a firm in Irvine specializing in real estate. Over the next four years, I built up a set of developer and builder clients, whom I took with me when I moved to the Los Angeles office of a Dallas-based national firm, Jenkens & Gilchrist. We followed the adage about buying a home in the best school district one can afford to live in and returned to South Pasadena. I liked the people and work at the firm, but it meant I again had a long daily commute, this time to Brentwood on the other side of LA.

**

Several of my lawyer friends and colleagues were of Japanese ancestry. I knew about the persecution their communities endured for generations since immigrating here, culminating in the round-up and incarceration of large numbers of them following the Japanese attack on Pear Harbor at the outset of World War II. But I hadn't heard firsthand stories of actual family experiences.

One of my colleagues at the firm in Irvine, Susan Hori, sometimes hiked with me. As we walked near the coast one sunny afternoon, we fell into a political discussion. She surprised me by being more conservative than I expected when it came to granting power to governments.

It came straight from her family experience, she explained. Her parents, and their friends and relatives lost everything when they were swept up and put in detention camps during the war. That action by presidential executive order, carried out with little public outcry, was justified on the baseless premise that Japanese Americans might be disloyal. I knew that, and also that not a single case of such disloyalty was found. So, she continued, if the government could do something so heinous to thousands of innocent people to cover up for the debacle at Pearl Harbor, how could she ever fully trust them with such power again?

I understood. Over 120,000 people, most of them US citizens, had been imprisoned for years during the war. They lost their homes, businesses, educational opportunities, and more. Even while many of their young men volunteered to fight and served with great distinction, their families remained incarcerated, jammed into makeshift facilities behind barbed wire at remote locations. They received no apology or compensation for decades.

I understood her perspective and that of others who came from the same experience. My own family lost everything to the Nazis in Europe. The irony is that we wound up trusting the US government more because it led the campaign that defeated the Nazis. I wondered if my parents felt the same lasting distrust of the German and Austrian governments during the years we lived over there. They never said so, but it seemed likely.

Another friend, Susan Kamei, had a similar experience. She used her family's pain and loss as motivation to work in the "redress movement"—the forty-year-long campaign for acknowledgement from the federal government that the executive order mandating the incarceration had no legitimate basis. Instead, it had been motivated by racism and anti-immigrant fervor, as well as economic opportunism by agricultural and fishing interests seeking to eliminate competition. Her book *When Can We Go Back to America?* detailed that history and presented the personal stories of many survivors of those injustices.

After hearing my friends' stories, I thought hard about the similarities between their family experiences and mine. They weren't identical. As bad as the treatment of Japanese Americans was, it didn't rise to the level of mass murder by the Nazis of Jews and other minorities. Yet, in some ways it seemed worse, coming at the hands of a government professing to stand for equal protection of all under the law.

By this time, I already had other reasons to be skeptical of governmental power and opportunities for its abuse. I had seen firsthand racist treatment of Blacks and Hispanics, the falsehoods behind the Vietnam War, the Watergate scandal that forced a president out of office, abuses by law enforcement agencies, and discrimination in government programs. Despite all those things, I still valued my identity as an American. But I tempered it with a realization that we should understand the words in the Declaration of Independence and the Constitution proclaiming equality for all as expressions of goals, not statements of current conditions.

* * *

Soon after moving back to LA, Joan and I traveled to Memphis, Tennessee, for the wedding of Ivan Binder's daughter. Ivan's grandmother, Sophie Frank, had sponsored by father's family in immigrating to the US. I hadn't seen Ivan since our childhood, so I felt excited at reuniting with him and other relatives who would be attending.

On arriving in Memphis, we went for dinner at a restaurant known for its local-style barbecue. Different from the Texas-style barbecue we were familiar with, it consisted mainly of pulled pork rather than pork or beef ribs, and was served with a sauce that was vinegary and less sweet. We loved every bite. The next day, we attended a luncheon at another well-known local barbecue establishment. Again, the fare consisted mainly of pulled pork.

Chatting with Ivan, I commented, "It's surprising to have an event like this for a Jewish wedding at a pork barbecue restaurant. I guess, when in Rome...."

After a laugh, he replied, "Not so surprising. The guy that owns this place is a member of our temple."

That surprised me even more, but I continued, telling him about the place we had eaten the previous day, which I liked a little better.

He laughed even harder, then said, "The owner of that place? He's a member of the temple, too."

The wedding and dinner the next day were a continuation of that experience, especially the rabbi speaking Hebrew with a southern accent. Only in America, I thought.

***

Los Angeles continued to be torn by racial conflicts. Shifting demographics and political representation became sources of tension as new Hispanic residents moved into long-time Black neighborhoods and White gentrifiers displaced residents of historically Hispanic areas. Police brutalizing of a Black motorist a few years earlier had spawned days of violent rioting reminiscent of the Watts rebellion during my first visit to California almost thirty years earlier. Shock over how little seemed to have changed in local law enforcement practices led to long-overdue reforms in the Polic Department, but those events continued to cast a pall over community relations. I heard people talk about the riots as if they had just occurred.

Meanwhile, immigration and the status of immigrants took center stage in California politics. Around the time I returned to private practice, Republican state legislators, with support from a few Democrats, had authored a ballot measure aimed at barring illegal immigrants from utilizing public services, including schooling for their children. It also required public employees, including police, to turn in illegal immigrants to federal authorities. Governor Pete Wilson, regarded as a political moderate but running in a difficult re-election campaign, became the leading spokesperson for this proposal. Although it focused on those immigrants here illegally, especially from Mexico, the rhetoric around the campaign vilified immigrants in general. Despite having been a US citizen for nearly thirty years, I felt targeted too. I also felt a sense of betrayal by public officials and civic leaders making cheap political capital out of this issue.

The measure's backers failed to realize how many families, especially in the Hispanic community, included both American citizens and illegal immigrants. And nearly everyone knew somebody who was law-abiding, economically productive, and civically engaged, but who was undocumented, or had a spouse or parent who was. The proposal inspired a massive backlash, with hundreds of thousands demonstrating against it around the state. Although voters approved it in November 1994, the courts later invalidated most of its provisions. More importantly, it generated a political shift away from the Republican Party in California by Hispanics and younger voters generally, one from which the party would never recover. For me, that eventual outcome removed much of the sting associated with the issue and the vote. Little did I realize at the time how much it presaged national political developments to come twenty years later.

My career prospered at Jenkens & Gilchrist, where I was the sole land use lawyer in their California outpost. Between the clients I had brought with me from my previous firm and those that the firm already represented, I remained busy and productive. It became my best law firm experience. The firm also supported my reentry into local politics, authorizing me to make substantial campaign contributions to candidates in local elections. One of those was Tom Hayden, who waged a nearly successful campaign for mayor of Los Angeles.

The time at Jenkens produced one notable personal development. In cooperation with a former law school classmate now working as a legal recruiter, I engineered bringing several groups of additional lawyers to our office. One group included a woman named Margaret Rosenthal. One day, she approached me with an interesting story. A cousin in Atlanta had asked her if she knew a Los Angeles attorney named Cary Lowe. Of course, she did. It turned out that her cousin, related on her father's side, was also my cousin, related on her mother's side. Further, in chatting about our respective personal backgrounds with another attorney in the same group with Margaret, we discovered our fathers were the same age, both had their *bar mitzvahs* at the Old-New Synagogue in Prague, and therefore must have been acquaintances or even friends.

Author with California Supreme Court Chief Justice Ronald George, Newport Beach, 1999

* * *

During those years, as my career progressed, Joan's collapsed. After leaving her job at LA County, she never worked full time again. Despite promises of assistance from local officials I knew through Nick, no job offers materialized. And her health steadily declined, as a congenital back condition grew increasingly painful and resulted in her becoming dependent on opioids. Doctors, emergency rooms, and home care helpers became regular parts of our lives. By the time we returned to South Pasadena, I despaired over her condition but needed to give as much attention as I could to Coralea. Joan's health was too fragile for her to consider joining us on the long-planned trip to Europe in 1997.

Then, after I had been at Jenkens & Gilchrist two years, Joan suddenly died of a heart attack. A hospital emergency room doctor who treated her the previous evening had sent her home, telling her to just rest. Coralea was with her when it happened, watched the paramedics take Joan to the hospital, and then learned, before I could get there, that her mother had died.

We didn't say much that night, just drove home and went to sleep, hugging each other. In the morning, we talked about where we would go from here.

"Now it's just the two of us," I began. "But don't worry, we'll be alright."

Coralea stunned me, saying, "I know we should be sad, but I've been expecting something like this to happen. It's kind of a relief that it's over." That from a twelve-year-old.

"I know," I replied. "It's been a long time coming."

Even so, I worried about how Coralea would process all this. I took her to see a child psychologist recommended by a therapist friend.

"What do you think?" I asked the psychologist after several visits.

"She's doing great," the woman told me. "She'll be dealing with this for a long time but, emotionally, she's handing it as well as anyone I've ever seen."

Relieved, I focused on how to reorganize our lives. Coralea by now was in middle school. I needed to be closer to home and couldn't continue to commute daily across LA. Then, just as I prepared to search for a position at a firm on our side of town, Jenkens & Gilchrist announced it would open a second LA-area office, in Pasadena. I juggled my schedule for a few weeks, working from home a lot, and then exhaled as my life changed again with the move to my new office.

I remained with the Jenkens firm two more years. Working in the Pasadena office went well, but I grew uneasy over the firm's reluctance to invest in expanding our land use practice. I felt like a sole practitioner inside a 600-lawyer firm, and I received back too small a share of the revenue I brought in. With the real estate development cycle picking up speed in the early 2000s, I decided the time had come to strike out on my own.

In the meantime, I had developed a new romance, with Patricia Butler, an environmental planner from San Diego whom I met at a conference.

Auburn-haired, tall, and vivacious, Trish was as different as I could imagine from Joan. She had grown up in the San Fernando Valley, part of a very Irish Catholic family originally from Detroit. On her own, she migrated southward, eventually landing in San Diego, where she built a successful consulting firm.

Our relationship blossomed, but a hundred twenty miles separated us. I would not force Coralea to move again before she completed high school, and Trish could not abandon her company in San Diego. So, for the next four years, we enjoyed what we called an Amtrak romance, with one of us riding the train to see the other on frequent weekends. On one of those trips, I ran into Tom Hayden, heading for the horse races at the fairgrounds in Del Mar with a group of friends. He grinned as I told him about my Irish American girlfriend. Tom had recently published his book about Irish American identity. He figured our discussion at Laurel Springs a few years earlier must have had an influence on me. And I confirmed to him how much Trish's family conformed to his image of Irish immigrants who rapidly gave up their cultural ties beyond parades and social clubs.

Our different backgrounds notwithstanding, Trish and I shared a love of travel. In fall 2004, we embarked on our first international trip together—a two-week journey to Prague, Budapest, and Vienna, with a final stop in Braunau. This took us to some of the same places I had visited with Coralea a few years earlier.

By this time, Trish had begun to exhibit symptoms of multiple sclerosis, a condition that would worsen over the ensuing years. That slowed us down a little, but didn't keep us from having a memorable adventure: strolling through Old Town Square and visiting Rabbi Judah Loew's grave in Prague; finding my way back to the Strakonice cemetery; cruising on the Danube in Budapest; and feasting on Wienerschnitzel and luscious pastries in Vienna. I especially enjoyed showing Trish my hometown of Braunau—my childhood residence, the historic town square, and the monumental church spire. Karin and Loisel welcomed her like part of the family. All of that gave her insight to my roots and how far I had come in my Americanization. I looked forward to exploring her family roots too, though that would not occur until years later.

On our way to Braunau, we made a memorable stop at the Mauthausen concentration camp. I had trepidation about this, my family having avoided the site during my childhood years in that vicinity. Still, I knew we would be passing close by and had an urge to see it. Wandering through the gate into the stone fortress-like compound, I felt shivers at what I knew had transpired here. Seeing the quarry where the Nazis had worked so many to death and the gas chamber where they murdered so many more left me silent and somber. I knew that relatives on my father's side were among the victims.

As emotionally difficult at that was, we didn't let it undermine what had otherwise been an exhilarating travel experience. In the following years, we would travel far and wide, from the Arctic Ocean to Caribbean islands, from Death Valley to alpine glaciers, from modern cities to medieval villages. But this first trip together would remain a standout in our travel memories.

The weekend shuttling situation would end once Coralea graduated and began college. And I would miss South Pasadena, where I had lived longer than anywhere else in my life. Our hillside home there had a splendid view of the San Gabriel Mountains to the north and a sunset view across the LA basin to the west, plus a kidney-shaped swimming pool that I used regularly. Midway through my stay there, the mayor appointed me to head a new redevelopment commission that formulated a plan for upgrading the city's dowdy downtown. Notwithstanding all that, San Diego offered a greater attraction.

As soon as Coralea left for college, I moved south to join Trish in her Point Loma home overlooking San Diego Bay. We married a year later at the historic original Jewish temple in San Diego's Old Town neighborhood. My high school friend, Gary Bounds, now a judge in Los Angeles, officiated.

We honeymooned in New England, timing it to coincide with the turning of leaves in the fall, something Trish hadn't seen before. Her feelings about seeing historical sites she had studied for years in school were similar to mine on moving to Bedford forty years earlier. But she was unprepared for the small scale of many places, which struck her as looking like models.

Standing at the Concord Bridge, site of one of the opening skirmishes of the Revolutionary War and situated at a narrow point along the Concord River, she exclaimed, "It's so tiny compared to what I expected. I can't believe they fought a battle over this."

In the spring of 2003, with Trish's encouragement, I had left the Jenkens firm and opened my own office in the lower level of my home. Again, my real estate clients stuck with me, including ones I acquired while at the firm. My timing couldn't have been better, as the real estate economy surged for the next few years. My homebuilder, land developer, and investor clients kept me busier than I even wanted to be, working on transactions and projects all over Southern California and occasionally further north. But it paid off. Over the next decade, even after joining Trish in San Diego, I did well enough to think about retirement.

At that point, I took stock of the course of my career in the real estate world—the people I had helped gain access to mortgage financing through my work at CIP, the new funding for housing development I had successfully advocated for at the Policy Center, the hundreds of planning students I had taught at several universities, the communities I had helped develop at Lewis Homes, the projects I had planned at Coussoulis Development, and the many developments I had assisted for other clients in private practice. Collectively, I estimated I had helped develop at least 25,000 homes and innumerable offices, shopping centers, schools, and parks, in some cases entire new communities. A veritable city, more than twice the size of either Braunau or Bedford. I noted with great satisfaction that I had indeed helped fulfill the American dream, my own and others'!

Sadly, none of my immediate family were there to see the outcome of my career. My father died of lung cancer while I worked at Lewis Homes and my mother died of breast cancer during my time practicing law in Orange County. I had both their names inscribed on a plaque at Ellis Island. In between, Dean died of a gunshot wound, ruled to be suicide, after disappointments in both his business and his marriage. Still, had they been around, I thought they would have been proud, like a typical immigrant family.

CHAPTER 33
THE FIRST AMERICANS

In the last years of my professional career, as I saw myself nearing the finish line of the process of Americanization, I had an important realization. People around me, whether they descended from families that immigrated generations ago or they came here as immigrants themselves, all were late arrivals. The real Americans were here before the European explorers who claimed the land in the name of their sovereigns, before the even-earlier Viking adventurers. The real Americans were the original inhabitants, descendants of people who crossed over from Asia to Alaska on a land bridge 15,000 years ago during the last Ice Age—the Native Americans.

I had been interested in Native American cultures for many years. That may have originated with the Indians I saw in western movies as a child, but it matured as I read books by and about Native American leaders, their tribal cultures, and their interactions with the European invasion. I came to understand the vast cultural differences between tribes of the Northeast, the Great Plans, the Southwest and the Pacific Coast. Like the nations of Europe, they had remote common ancestors, but had developed independently to suit the climactic, topographic, and biological conditions of their respective regions.

During my years of political activism, books like *Bury My Heart at Wounded Knee*, as well as encounters with Native American activists, taught me more about the tragedies that befell Native American tribes, especially in the West. European settlers and the military battled them for land, forced them onto barely habitable reservations, suppressed their cultures., and hunted them down.

Those issues first came to my attention in 1969, when members of the American Indian Movement (AIM) occupied Alcatraz Island in San Francisco Bay for nineteen months as a protest against continuing mistreatment of Native Americans. Alcatraz had been a high-security prison for decades and once served as a holding place for captive Native Americans, so the symbolism was strong.

Four years later, AIM led a takeover of the Wounded Knee community on the Oglala Sioux Pine Ridge Reservation in South Dakota. That drew even greater national attention. I heard South Dakota referred to as the "Mississippi of Indian Country," comparing it to the racist treatment of Black residents in that Southern state. And Wounded Knee was the site of a massacre by federal troops in 1890 of hundreds of tribal members. This seizure led to a violent confrontation with federal police agencies resulting in the killing of two FBI agents and the arrest and prosecution of several AIM leaders.

During that siege, an anti-war activist, Bill Zimmerman, flew relief supplies into Wounded Knee, an event he chronicled in his book *Airlift to Wounded Knee*. I met and became friends with Zimmerman a few years later, during the time I worked with Tom Hayden.

Many Americans considered these events overly violent stunts. However, they elevated public consciousness of the injustices and maltreatment faced by Native Americans, much the same way that violent demonstrations twenty years earlier forced Americans to confront similar treatment of Black citizens.

I became far more sensitized to that history when I began working with various Southern California tribes. During my time at Coussoulis Development, I had frequent contact with the Morongo Band of Mission Indians, as our company owned land around and within their reservation. Many native nations lost their original identity during the age of Spanish conquest, when they were compelled to live as part of communities around Catholic missions and became identified as Mission Indians. Although many of those tribes have prospered in recent years from having casinos and resorts on their reservations, their elders still speak ruefully of years of being abused by residents of surrounding communities.

Joining Trish Butler in San Diego expanded those contacts, as her consulting firm provided services to several prominent tribes. San Diego County contains the largest number of reservations of any county in the nation. I worked closely with the Rincon Band of Luiseño Indians, preparing a succession of master plans for their thriving reservation. And I provided legal services to the Viejas Band of Kumeyaay Indians and their partners in connection with a proposed business and casino development.

But my relationships with Native American tribes culminated in my appointment as a trustee of California Indian Legal Services. CILS is a quasi-governmental entity that provides legal assistance to tribes and individual in California. Serving on the Board of Trustees for six years, I gained great insight into the legal and cultural issues affecting our constituents, and had opportunities to interact with tribal representatives from throughout the state.

In 2016, I accompanied Trish to a celebration at the Cameron Trading Post on the Navajo Reservation in Arizona. A former neighbor of Trish who was born on the reservation operated the trading post and was celebrating its centennial anniversary. For two days, we experienced blessings by trial medicine men, watched Navajo and Hopi dancers, observed cultural presentations, and joined the two hundred guests in feasts. I felt like I had been inducted into the tribe.

By the time I retired from the CILS Board and concluded my work with the Rincon Band, I had come to appreciate Native American history and culture in its many dimensions. Tribes are considered sovereign nations with which the US Government entered into treaties, as it would with foreign governments. Based on that relationship, tribes and their reservations are subject to federal laws but typically not state or local laws. These tribes are federally recognized and overseen by the Bureau of Indian Affairs. Other groups, often vestiges of tribes, are not recognized officially in the same way.

Despite the ways in which they have been mistreated and marginalized, Native Americans have long prided themselves on their high level of patriotism. Disproportionate numbers of tribal members have served in the US military, with great distinction. On a lighter note, a poster often seen in

Native American organization offices showed a group of tough-looking, rifle-carrying warriors over the inscription "Fighting Terrorism Since 1492."

Looking back over my experiences with Native American communities, I see cultures that predate any others in this country and people who are as American as anyone can imagine. To me, these are the first and the most real of all Americans.

CHAPTER 34
END OF THE SEARCH

Six months after my mother's death, and eight thousand miles after embarking on the search for my great-grandparents' graves, I stood before the gates of what I hoped was the cemetery holding their remains. Getting inside, over the high walls or through the locked gates, remained a challenge. Determined not to be stopped after our adventurous search for this place, I declared to Coralea and our Czech guide, Ivo, that I would climb over the wall.

"Help me," I told Ivo, making a basket with my hands, showing him what I wanted. Before he could boost me up, two tall, muscular men appeared from the behind the farmhouse to the left. From the military base, I guessed, judging by their crewcuts. The older of the two began talking to Ivo.

"They are working on that house," he told me. "They saw us drive up and want to know what we are doing."

I gestured for him to tell them and to keep translating. Now more eager than ever, Ivo explained our plight. The inquisitive man laughed.

"All the way from California?" he mused. "No, there is no easy way to get in. Sometimes a caretaker comes here, but we don't know how to find him."

He agreed with my plan to scale the wall and offered a homemade wooden ladder that he and his partner used in their construction work. Ivo held the rickety ladder as I clambered up. I balanced myself on the uneven bricks on top of the wall and then leaped down on the other side, landing on soft earth just a few paces from the front row of gravestones. I trembled, torn between a feeling of intruding and a determination to succeed in our search.

Interior of Strakonice Jewish Cemetery, 2005

I looked around in awe. Rough, stuccoed walls surrounded the place on all sides. Towering oaks lined the inside. Gravestones stood in twenty or so even rows, each containing perhaps two dozen graves. To my relief, I saw no signs of vandalism.

I glanced back toward the gate, at Coralea and Ivo. With a deep breath, I stepped forward and surveyed rows of markers, a mix of stones, obelisks, and upright slabs. Somewhere out there, I hoped, I would find the connection to my past that had inspired our search.

This small place, I realized, held the history of the Jewish community of that region for centuries back. These people had farmed the land, sold goods, raised families, and left their mark, amid often-hostile circumstances. Maybe that accounted for the cemetery's location, far from the daily sight of those who might desecrate it. The Nazis virtually erased the area's Jewish community, but missed this place.

The late afternoon sun faded behind hills and trees in front of me. Soon it would disappear below the top of the far wall. Shadows already covered the faces of the gravestones. I had to work fast before it grew too difficult to read the markers. Stones in the front rows looked like they dated from biblical times and could not include those of my great-grandparents. I moved on to the slabs and obelisks of the middle rows.

In some rows, the names all varied. Other rows contained family groups. A pathway separated the cemetery into two parts and led to a simple stone building against the rear wall, perhaps once a mortuary. I made rapid progress on the south side, as someone had tended those graves recently enough that the headstones were visible. On the north side, however, weeds and nettles, some as high as the cemetery walls, had overgrown the graves. I dared not miss one, so I pushed aside the weeds, scratched my arms on the nettles, and twisted my ankles and scraped my legs on metal frames marking the borders of graves. I found no Lowys or Loewys.

Every few minutes, I looked back toward the gates, where Coralea and Ivo watched my tortuous progress while keeping an eye out for the approach of any authorities. I had, after all, entered surreptitiously by climbing over the wall. I had no idea what the consequences might be if they caught me inside, regardless of the purity of my motive.

The dates on the gravestones were still a bit too early. With half the cemetery yet to search, I saw the shadows lengthening further. On an impulse, I ran up the pathway to the rearmost rows to see what dates the stones there bore, then turned left into the more accessible markers on the south side. They dated from the early 1900s, close to what I was seeking.

As I moved further to the left, scanning names on the markers in the last row, I stepped in front of the third stone and stopped. Before me stood a simple, upright plate of black granite, five feet tall, inscribed in gold, partly Hebrew and partly old-style European lettering. An oak tree standing behind it provided it with a slight canopy, and ivy vines framed it on both sides. I gasped as I read:

Julie Lowyova
Wolenic
14. 9. 1854 — 28. 7. 1925
Samuel Lowy
21. 3. 1851 — 24. 12. 1932

I stepped up beside the stone, reached out my right hand and caressed it. Feeling lightheaded, I took a few deep breaths to steady myself, then stood before the stone, experiencing the exhilaration of the moment.

"I've found you, I've come home," I whispered.

Then, turning back toward the cemetery entrance, I screamed, "I found them!"

Bounding back down the path toward the gates, I called to Ivo to help Coralea up the ladder. The two of them, along with the construction workers, cheered my discovery. I reached up to my eager daughter sitting on top of the wall. She leaped into my arms, as excited as I was. Ivo stayed behind and let us have this moment to ourselves.

I led Coralea to the stone, lifting her up and allowing her to feel it, connect with it. We looked at each other and beamed.

"I knew you'd find it," Coralea declared, with a confidence that I could share only now that our search was successful. Just minutes earlier, I hadn't been so sure.

We took pictures of the marker and pictures of each other beside it. Then we just stood there, enjoying the fruit of our search.

After some time, I picked up Coralea again and hugged her. By now, the shadows had engulfed us, signaling an end to our visit.

"The search is over," I said. "It's time to go."

She nodded, and I carried her back toward the gates. Ivo lowered the ladder on the inside of the wall for us to climb back over. I thanked the construction workers. They smiled too, pleased for us, happy to have been able to help.

As we walked to Ivo's car, I looked back a last time, catching sight of the marker through the cemetery gate. As we got back into the car, I joined Coralea in the back seat.

The two-hour ride back to Prague felt eerie, as if we had crossed a time warp and stepped back again. I thanked Ivo for all his efforts. He acted almost as triumphant as we did, turning and smiling at us as he drove. The search had become important to him too, and we never could have completed it without him.

"Dad," Coralea said, giving me a quizzical look, "why are you smiling like that?"

I hadn't realized it, but I was. A sense of contentment, of satisfaction, overwhelmed me, reminiscent of what I felt at reaching the top of a mountain or completing a difficult assignment.

"I'm so happy we found it," I replied. "I wasn't sure we would. I can't wait to tell Aunt Mimi and the rest of the family."

"I'm happy too," said Coralea. "And I'm proud of my daddy."

I smiled and put my arm around her. Then we both grew silent, immersing ourselves in our memories of the day's adventures.

Except once, when Coralea asked, in an echo of her question at Rabbi Loewe's crypt in the Prague cemetery earlier that week, "Dad, do you think they knew we were there?"

"I'm sure of it, Doll," I replied, my voice cracking and my eyes brimming with joyful tears. "I'm sure of it."

CHAPTER 35
AMERICAN AS ...

Speeding down the highway in the dark toward the lights of Prague, I felt connected to my family's past in a way I hadn't previously known. I meant our trip to reconnect to the past that still lived in me and that I wanted Coralea to feel too. This trip differed from the one with Joan twelve years earlier. Coralea was far more open to new experiences. She didn't have a lifetime of other memories blocking what she was experiencing now. And we were just beginning.

We flew from Prague to Bratislava. Cousins of a friend back in California met us at the airport. With their help, we spent the next few days exploring the significant places in my mother's early life.

First, Zilina, where my mother was born and where she lived until going into hiding during the war. She had so suppressed memories of that time, she could not tell us her former address or even describe her old neighborhood. We found an industrial town, filled with small stucco homes, and notable now mainly as a railroad junction, but I was happy to see it at last, to attach a place to a name.

Then Poprad, where my mother hid during the war. She described her hiding place as a bakery on the town square. We found no real square, more a commercial street lined with old, two-story buildings, many of them shuttered. None contained a bakery, at least not anymore, but we thought we must have found the place she remembered only vaguely.

Finally, Banska Bystrica, where she and Magda joined the partisans in the Slovak Uprising, fighting the Nazis near the end of the War. The curving road we took over the mountains traversed the forests the two young women must have hiked through on their escape.

I wished we could have located the places we sought more precisely. I had my own mental images of them based on my mother's brief descriptions. I had expected Zilina to be a welcoming place, somehow fitting my mother's personality. And I had felt sure I would recognize the square with the bakery in Poprad, perhaps even finding the same family still operating the bakery.

Coralea didn't care. She remained excited at just being in the places in her grandmother's stories.

Once our hosts drove us across the border to Vienna, I was on more familiar ground. We stayed at a fancy hotel on the Ring, the wide, tree-lined boulevard circling the old center of the city. Names and places flooded back from my childhood and from my one later visit. Here, I wanted Coralea to connect with my own experiences from the time I was her age.

We visited landmarks of my early years. Demel pastry shop, my father's favorite and mine too, still serving rich pastries in a two hundred-year-old, wood-paneled dining room. The Stephansdom cathedral, with its signature multi-colored tile roof. The Stadtpark, the leafy central park just outside the Ring, adorned with a golden statue of Johann Strauss. And the Riesenrad, the towering Ferris wheel in the Prater park, providing a soaring view over the entire city and recognizable to any fans of the Orson Welles film *The Third Man*.

Coralea reacted most strongly, though, at seeing my father's family home in what was still a middle-class residential neighborhood near our hotel. He died before she was born, but she often told me she wished she could have known him.

Looking up at the two-story row house, she said to me, "You told me he lived here when he was my age. I like thinking about him being a kid, like me. I like this even better than the house in Volenice."

We traveled by train across Austria from Vienna to Braunau. Loisel and Karin met us at the station and brought us home. Herma was overcome with emotion, more over Coralea than me, as if getting me back in a new child.

With the three of them, we visited yet another set of my childhood landmarks. The house in Ranshofen, where I pointed out to Coralea the window of what had been my room. The Braunau town square with its medieval buildings and parapets overlooking the Inn River. And the "Silent Night" chapel in nearby Oberndorf.

Author in front of childhood home, Ranshofen, Braunau, 2005

Herma remembered my favorite dishes. She cooked us plum dumplings, chicken soup with liver dumplings, pot roast with red cabbage and a huge bread dumpling. Dumplings still ruled.

Coralea basked in Herma's attention, but also soaked up the experiences of the people and places she was visiting for the first time.

"Dad, I want to come back here by myself," she told me, as we packed to return home. Exactly what I hoped to hear. This trip had already strengthened my connection with my daughter. I knew her return, which would happen a few years later, would burnish that connection further and connect her even more strongly to our family's roots.

Karin drove us to the Munich airport. We knew each other only as children, but we heard about one another our whole lives, through the letters and photographs that passed back and forth between our families. Herma served as the common element that bound us together, almost like siblings.

Flying home to Los Angeles, Coralea and I had plenty of time to talk about our trip. But I also took time to reflect myself on all we had seen and experienced. So much had changed, yet so much was virtually as I remembered it. I came as a visitor, but my sense of self and my emotions remained deeply rooted there.

Europe had reassembled itself. It valued its cultural past but looked to the future socially and politically. I had done the same. In picking up the pieces of my family's experience, I held those pieces within me but emerged as an American.

In that experience, I arrived at being the kind of American I had been developing into since the days in Braunau, Linz, and Wiesbaden, the kind of American my parents hoped I would become. As American as apple strudel.

THE END

ABOUT THE AUTHOR

Cary D. Lowe is a California lawyer, writer, and political activist. Born in post-war Europe, he immigrated to the United States and became a citizen in his teens. After serving in the U.S. Navy, he earned a law degree and a Ph.D. from the University of Southern California. He has been in the leadership of numerous political and environmental organizations, served as an advisor to state and local governments, published over eighty essays on current affairs, and taught at USC and other major universities.

NOTE FROM THE AUTHOR

Word-of-mouth endorsement is crucial for any author to succeed. If you enjoyed *Becoming American,* please leave a review online—anywhere you are able. Even if it's just a sentence or two. It would make all the difference and would be very much appreciated.

Thanks!
Cary

We hope you enjoyed reading this title from:

www.blackrosewriting.com

Subscribe to our mailing list – *The Rosevine* – and receive **FREE** books, daily deals, and stay current with news about upcoming releases and our hottest authors.
Scan the QR code below to sign up.

Already a subscriber? Please accept a sincere thank you for being a fan of Black Rose Writing authors.

View other Black Rose Writing titles at www.blackrosewriting.com/books and use promo code **PRINT** to receive a **20% discount** when purchasing.